English as a Local Language

PEFC/16-33-111
CATG-PEFC-052
www.pefc.org

CRITICAL LANGUAGE AND LITERACY STUDIES
Series Editors: Professor Vaidehi Ramanathan, *University of California, USA*
Professor Bonny Norton, *University of British Columbia, Canada*
Professor Alastair Pennycook, *University of Technology, Sydney, Australia*

Critical Language and Literacy Studies is an international series that encourages monographs directly addressing issues of power (its flows, inequities, distributions, trajectories) in a variety of language- and literacy-related realms. The aim with this series is twofold: (1) to cultivate scholarship that openly engages with social, political, and historical dimensions in language and literacy studies, and (2) to widen disciplinary horizons by encouraging new work on topics that have received little focus (see below for partial list of subject areas) and that use innovative theoretical frameworks.

Full details of all the books in this series and of all our other publications can be found on http://www.multilingual-matters.com, or by writing to Multilingual Matters, St Nicholas House, 31–34 High Street, Bristol BS1 2AW, UK.

CRITICAL LANGUAGE AND LITERACY STUDIES
Series Editors: Vaidehi Ramanathan, Bonny Norton, Alastair Pennycook

English as a Local Language
Post-colonial Identities and Multilingual Practices

Christina Higgins

MULTILINGUAL MATTERS
Bristol • Buffalo • Toronto

Library of Congress Cataloging in Publication Data
A catalog record for this book is available from the Library of Congress.
Higgins, Christina.
English as a Local Language: Post-colonial Identities and Multilingual Practices/
Christina Higgins.
Critical Language and Literacy Studies: 2
Includes bibliographical references and index.
1. English language--Africa, East. 2.   English language--Variation--Africa,
East. 3.   Sociolinguistics--Africa, East. 4.   Africa, East--Languages. 5.   English
language--Globalization.
I. Title.
PE3431.E545 2009
427'.676 2 22 2009017378

British Library Cataloguing in Publication Data
A catalogue entry for this book is available from the British Library.

ISBN-13: 978-1-84769-181-1 (hbk)
ISBN-13: 978-1-84769-180-4 (pbk)

Multilingual Matters
UK: St Nicholas House, 31–34 High Street, Bristol BS1 2AW, UK.
USA: UTP, 2250 Military Road, Tonawanda, NY 14150, USA.
Canada: UTP, 5201 Dufferin Street, North York, Ontario M3H 5T8, Canada.

Copyright © 2009 Christina Higgins.

All rights reserved. No part of this work may be reproduced in any form or by any means without permission in writing from the publisher.

The policy of Multilingual Matters/Channel View Publications is to use papers that are natural, renewable and recyclable products, made from wood grown in sustainable forests. In the manufacturing process of our books, and to further support our policy, preference is given to printers that have FSC and PEFC Chain of Custody certification. The FSC and/or PEFC logos will appear on those books where full certification has been granted to the printer concerned.

Typeset by Techset Composition Ltd., Salisbury, UK.
Printed and bound in Great Britain by the MPG Books Group.

Contents

Acknowledgements vii
Preface ix
1   Multivoiced Multilingualism 1
2   From Pre-colonial Beginnings to Multivocality 21
3   Double-Voices in the Workplace 37
4   Miss World or Miss Bantu? Competing Dialogues
    on Female Beauty 65
5   The Polyphony of East African Hip Hop 92
6   Selling *Fasta Fasta* in the East African Marketplace 116
7   New Wor(l)d Order 148
Appendix 157
References 159
Index 169

Acknowledgements

The research in this book is the culmination of fieldwork in East Africa that I have done over a seven year period, beginning with my doctoral dissertation in 2001. I am forever grateful to the warmth, acceptance and guidance of the many Tanzanians and Kenyans whom I have met over the years who made it possible for me to study their language practices. I would like to thank the entire staff of the Tanzanian Gazette (pseudonym) in Dar es Salaam for their generosity and understanding while I followed them throughout their daily activities and recorded their work conversations in 2001. They not only made it possible to study their multilingual practices, but they also welcomed me into their lives with a kind of hospitality I had never before witnessed. *Asanteni sana!* I would also like to thank the many hip hop artists who graciously allowed me to study and reproduce their lyrics, especially those who entertained my questions about transnational identification with American forms of music. I am particularly grateful to Ngwair, Dola Soul and Crazy GK. In addition, I would like to thank James Gayo, the talented cartoonist and producer of *Kingo*, for allowing me to reproduce some of his fine work, and also for helping to spark my interest in the tensions, double meanings and double entendres found across so much East African popular culture. I would also like to thank the many Tanzanians who helped me to gain a sense of how they interpreted the hybrid literacies in hip hop and advertising, and who always had suggestions for where to look next.

I would also like to recognize the tremendous contribution of the research assistants who helped me to transcribe, translate and make sense of the new forms of language that I never encountered in my Swahili courses in university classrooms in the United States. Most of all, James Nindi Brown has been essential to my appreciation of the linguistic diversity in Tanzania, and his knowledge, good nature and friendship is truly appreciated. I would also like to thank Neema Yohana, Davis Kasongoyo, Gilbert Ndeoruo and Max Rugenge for their helpful assistance.

My gratitude also goes to the Tanzania Commission for Science and Technology (COSTECH) for granting me permission to carry out research. I am also grateful for funding from the Department of English at the University of Wisconsin-Madison and for summer grants from the College of Languages, Linguistics and Literature and the University Research Council of the University of Hawai'i at Manoa.

The quality of this book is much improved thanks to suggestions, comments and guidance from the editors of this series, Alastair Pennycook, Bonny Norton and Vaidehi Ramanathan, three scholars in the field whose work I have long admired. I am also grateful to Tope Omoniyi for his careful reading of the manuscript, and for his ongoing dialogues with me about language, pop culture and identity in Africa and the African diaspora. I would also like to thank Alex Perullo for helping me to connect with the Bongo Flava community, and for sharing his insights on cultural hybridity in East African hip hop. I would also like to express my appreciation for the long-lasting support and friendship of F.E.M.K. Senkoro, my former professor and an esteemed scholar of Swahili who has always retained an interest in my work.

Finally, I would like to thank Patrick Kennedy for his encouragement and understanding while I spent months at a time away from home, and for the many hours of involuntary seclusion he put up with while I sat typing.

Preface

As English continues to spin ever outwards from its assumed former centers, used in more and more contexts and in more and more diverse ways, there is a growing sense that we need new ways to investigate these new conditions of language. We have operated for so long with the standard tropes of (socio)linguistics in the hope that the idea of a language spreading and diversifying into regional varieties will continue to account for this linguistic expansion. The Kachruvian concentric circles of World Englishes have long held sway, with English moving out like ripples across a pond before taking on various national identities (Indian, Singaporean, Nigerian, Philippine Englishes). Conventional concepts such as diglossia and codeswitching have long been employed to explain the relations between languages and the ways in which multilingual speakers make use of them. Notions of bi- and multilingualism continue to be used as ways of accounting for multiple language use. More recently, the focus has shifted to look at English as a lingua franca, engendering new debates about the extent to which this presents a static or dynamic account of English as it is used across different regions.

Increasingly, however, scholars interested in the global spread of English have started to wonder whether these old categorizations of language use really work any more (Bruthiaux, 2003). Developed in contexts very different to those in which English now finds itself, many of these concepts simply do not seem to address the forms of hybrid urban multilingualism in which English now participates. Indeed, there are strong reasons to question the very notion of English, or any language, as discrete entities that are describable in terms of core and variation (Makoni & Pennycook, 2007). On the one hand, language studies need to confront the changing realities of urban life, with enhanced mobility, shifting populations, social upheaval, health and climate crises, increased access to diverse media, particularly forms of popular culture, and new technologies. On the other hand, language studies are confronted by the growing concern that we need to rethink the ways in which language has been conceptualized.

While a great deal of concern has been expressed about language death, about the move from one language to another by different groups of people, there has been less focus on the shifting identifications and new language creations in contexts such as urban Africa. Bosire (2006: 192) describes the 'hybrid languages of Africa' as 'contact outcomes that have evolved at a time when African communities are coming to terms with the colonial and post-colonial situation that included rapid urbanization and a bringing together of different ethnic communities and cultures with a concomitant exposure to different ways of being. The youth are caught up in this transition; they are children of two worlds and want a way to express this duality, this new "ethnicity"'. Out of this mix, emerge new language varieties, such as 'Sheng', a Swahili/English hybrid, that provides urban youth with 'a way to break away from the old fraternities that put particular ethnic communities in particular neighborhoods/"estates" and give them a global urban ethnicity, the urbanite: sophisticated, street smart, new generation, tough' (Bosire, 2006: 192). This focus on emergent languages of the street brings to the fore the ways in which new varieties of language are forged as acts of identity.

Higgins' work takes up these challenges, destabilizing dominant conceptualizations of English as a distinct code, as a global language, as an entity bounded by particular domains of use. Instead, she suggests we need to grasp the implications of the hybridity and linguistic bricolage in which English so often participates. In a variety of ethnographic studies of multilingual practices in East Africa (mainly Tanzania), including work places, market places, popular culture (hip hop) and beauty pageants, this book draws attention to the multivocality of hybrid forms of multilingualism involving English. For Higgins, the Bakhtinian concept of *multivocality* offers a more useful way of understanding English use in these diverse contexts. Multivocality refers both to the different 'voices' present in a single utterance as well as the *bivalent* syncretism of language mixing, where multiple meanings are conveyed simultaneously. Multivocality establishes *multiplicity* as a starting point for the analysis of language, treating contexts of multilingualism as open-ended and creative spaces of language intersection.

For Higgins, therefore, English needs to be understood as part of multilingual practice. It is also a local language. A basic premise of much of the work on world Englishes is that English has its origins in the central, native-speaker countries (UK, USA, Canada, Australia) and then is localized as it spreads. The comparison is always based on domains where local varieties differ from the original. Higgins, however, relocates English in these local contexts of multilingual language use. The focus, therefore, is no longer on a variety of English answerable to the center but rather on the ways in which monologic uses of English occur in domains such as education (or, indeed, beauty pageants) while other domains such as popular culture (hip hop) and advertising use more multivocal forms of language. This focus on the multivocal sociolinguistics of hip hop is part of a new direction in research, bringing together cultural studies and sociolinguistics to show the dynamism of new, popular uses of language (see Alim *et al.*, 2009). As Higgins points out, these domains also draw on each other, so that politicians and AIDS educators will also draw on the multivocality of hip hop to get their message across.

A key strength of Higgins' work is the close ethnographic attention she brings to the different contexts discussed in this book. One important aspect of this is that she refuses to rely on text analysis alone without the interpretations of those who read the texts; nor does she claim that her analysis alone is the only interpretation. A problem that emerges in applied linguistic research from a critical perspective is that it often attempts to use ethnography and critical discourse analysis (CDA) together. While not incompatible, the difficulty here is that CDA tends to rely almost entirely on the processes and perspectives of the analyst. There may be a nod in the direction of text production and interpretation but by and large it is critical armchair discourse analysis (CADA) that holds sway (see Blommaert, 2005). In order to understand how hybridized English is interpreted, Higgins attempts to overcome this problem of researcher-centered interpretation by including the perspectives of the language users themselves. This is something that always needs to be kept in mind in research that attempts to give a critical account of language use: whose critical version is this?

Christina Higgins shows in this book how East Africans exploit the heteroglossia of language to perform modern identities. This focus on the performative nature of language helps us see how language and identity are produced by localizing global linguistic and cultural resources. Her work adds important insights to some of the newly emergent work on lingua franca English (LFE), when this is understood not as a 'system out there' but rather as 'constantly brought into being in each context of communication' (Canagarajah, 2007: 91). From this point of view, practice rather than prior language form is central: LFE is not so much an entity located in the minds of speakers as it is a social practice that is constantly being reconstructed in a specific locality. Higgins' work thus responds to Nakata's (2007: 39) critique of 'the inability of linguists to give primacy to language speakers', and takes up Canagarajah's (2007: 98) call for a 'linguistics that treats human agency, contextuality, diversity, indeterminacy, and multimodality as the norm'. She has confronted this dual challenge to address the locality of English in contexts such as East Africa and to rethink the ways in which language is constructed in such contexts. In a significant addition to our *Critical Language and Literacy Studies* series, Higgins has opened up a new space here for thinking about language, locality and multivocality.

Alastair Pennycook
Bonny Norton
Vaidehi Ramanathan

References

Alim, S., Ibrahim, A. and Pennycook, A. (eds) (2009) *Global Linguistic Flows: Hip Hop Cultures, Youth Identities, and the Politics of Language*. New York: Routledge.

Blommaert, J. (2005) *Discourse: A Critical Introduction*. Cambridge: Cambridge University Press.

Bosire, M. (2006) Hybrid languages: The case of Sheng. In O.F. Arasanyin and M.A. Pemberton (eds) *Selected Proceedings of the 36th Annual Conference on African Linguistics* (pp. 185–193). Somerville, MA: Cascadilla Proceedings Project.

Bruthiaux, P. (2003) Squaring the circles: Issues in modeling English worldwide. *International Journal of Applied Linguistics* 13 (2), 159–177.

Canagarajah, S. (2007) The ecology of global English. *International Multilingual Research Journal* 1 (2) 89–100.

Makoni, S. and Pennycook, A. (2007) Disinventing and reconstituting languages. In S. Makoni and A. Pennycook (eds) *Disinventing and Reconstituting Languages* (pp. 1–41). Clevedon: Multilingual Matters.

Nakata, M. (2007) *Disciplining the Savages: Savaging the Disciplines*. Canberra: Aboriginal Studies Press.

Chapter 1
Multivoiced Multilingualism

> *I ask myself this question*
> *But I don't have the answer*
> *The language we Tanzanians speak*
> *English-Swahili*
> *Let's add Chinese, even*
> *We'll keep coming up with names for it –*
> *It's currency and status*
> *Tanzanians, let's keep adding to Swanglish*
> Wakilisha, translated lyrics of 'Swanglish'

> *We do not need our tribal tongues in this age of increased mixed marriages and cosmopolitanism. Yet, English and Kiswahili do not define who we are. Sheng, that blend of many of the languages prevalent in Kenya, is who we are.*
> John Mugubi, lecturer in the Department of Literature, Kenyatta University, Nairobi[1]

> *Here, the problem is that many words are African and have been anglicized, anglicized – I should say they are words from here, but they have been postponed. Like in English, the word 'citizen' – you can't say it, you should say 'mwananchi' in a newspaper. We have anglicized it because we understand its meaning. It's been anglicized, so in sum, the standard of English is not the best.*
> Chief sub-editor of an English-medium newspaper in Dar es Salaam

In most of Britain's former colonies where English was installed as an official language, it is often assumed that English serves to connect local communities with the globalized world. In many nations, however, it is clear that the language of globalization also serves distinctively local needs and is used, in various forms, as a local language among locals. The photograph on the cover of this book illustrates a localized use of English in a suburban area of Dar es Salaam, Tanzania, where an enterprising storeowner has named his shop *2PAC STORE*, a name which combines the international popularity of deceased US rapper Tupac Shakur with the practical matters of selling rice and beans. The storeowner does not sell music or other retail goods associated with hip hop culture; instead, he markets two staples of many Tanzanians' diets by referring to a globally recognized popular culture icon. This example illustrates how English can serve a local sphere of material consumption through intersecting with a sphere of global cultural production. Moreover, it demonstrates how localized uses of English often creatively mix genres, in this case, popular music and marketing.

Of course, much of the time, localized English involves more than just English. For many multilinguals, English is a component of 'urban vernaculars', or ways of using language that are better described as amalgams rather than as codeswitches between languages (Makoni et al., 2007). These new codes are often characterized by an interplay of local and global cultural references, as in the case of 2PAC STORE, in addition to the creative and skillful use of several languages. For most multilinguals, such language use is part of everyday practice. However, speakers of urban vernaculars are frequently caught in an ideological tension about language and cultural identification that is often articulated through debates about the importance of language purity and mutual intelligibility. The above statements about language in East Africa[2] from pop artists, a university lecturer, and a newspaper editor illustrate the spectrum of attitudes about multilingualism involving English. Some are proponents of linguistic and cultural hybridity, but others lament the loss of language purity and view language mixing as a problem. These contrasting views towards mixed languages relate well to Bakhtin's (1968, 1981, 1984, 1986) conceptualization of language as a socio-historical, multifaceted and dialogical struggle over the meanings of signs, and they raise questions about how these multiple meanings are sorted out among speakers. For example, among the cultural and linguistic bricolage involving the language of the former colonizer, and now the language of a globalizing world, what socio-political meanings emerge? What new forms of meaning are created in localized forms of multilingualism that are not possible in monolingual, center varieties such as British Received Pronunciation (RP), or what Lippi-Green (1997) calls Mainstream United States English (MUSE)? And, to what degree do mixed language forms have validity or mutual understanding among speakers?

In considering the answers to these questions, this book explores the weighty issue of how multilingualism involving English is ordered in post-colonial, globalizing societies. Instead of investigating the linguistic aspects of local forms of English or the effect of English on local languages, my goal here is to develop a framework that theorizes how languages work together in multilingual societies by placing multilingual practices at the theoretical center. As Bakhtin (1981: 293) writes, 'For any individual consciousness living in it, language is not an abstract system of normative forms but rather a concrete heteroglot conception of the world'. Because of its colonial history and its current status as the world's dominant *lingua franca*, English is a central part of the *heteroglossic*, or multilanguaged, backdrop in East Africa. Many investigations of language use in Tanzania and Kenya have shown that rather than compartmentalizing their languages into distinct spheres of communication, speakers often take advantage of their multilingual repertoires within single domains of use such as school classrooms (e.g. Batibo, 1995; Brock-Utne, 2002; Muthwii & Kioko, 2004; Rubagumya, 1990, 1994), in casual conversation (Abdulaziz & Osinde, 1997; Blommaert, 1999a, 2005b; Myers-Scotton, 1993a), and in forms of popular culture such as song lyrics (e.g. Githinji, 2006). Of course, this phenomenon is not limited to East Africa since millions of speakers worldwide exploit English to produce different types of *hybridization*, a 'mixing of various "languages" co-existing within the boundaries of a single dialect, a single national language, a single branch, a single group of different branches or different groups of such branches, in the historical as well as paleontological past of languages' (Bakhtin, 1981: 358–359).

Beyond describing, cataloging and analyzing various types of hybridity, this book argues that we need to pay more attention to the manner in which forms of multilingualism are conditioned (though not determined) by *domains* of language use. As Chapters 3–6 aim to demonstrate, various forms of English are given different kinds of values depending on where they are used and who uses them with whom. In other words, each domain conditions, and is constituted by, different *speech genres* (Bakhtin, 1986), and the linguistic aspects of each genre are shaped by the specific nature of that particular sphere of communication. This becomes clear when comparing casual conversation with the domain of beauty pageants in East Africa, for example, as pageant judges and audience members typically only value contestants who speak a kind of English that is very standardized, internationally-recognized and mutually intelligible. This variety does not stray far from 'center' Englishes. However, in domains of casual conversation, popular culture and local commerce, a rather different assortment of Englishes and hybrid languages are allowed and given value. The relationship between domains and legitimate forms of language will be further investigated in this book, and special attention will be paid to the social, economic and political spaces surrounding these languages. As Blommaert *et al.* explain:

> Context (including space) does something to people when it comes to communicating. It organizes and defines sociolinguistic regimes in which spaces are characterized by sets of norms and expectations

about communicative behavior – orders of indexicality. Entering such spaces involves the imposition of the sets of norms and rules as well as the invoking of potentially meaningful relations between one scale and another (e.g. the local versus the national or the global). (Blommaert et al., 2005: 203)

A focus on context deemphasizes multilingualism or fluency in English as a property of the individual and reestablishes it more firmly as a property of situations. The domain-based approach to multilingualism taken in this book reveals both the affordances and the limitations that contexts create for various multilingual practices.

Theoretical Contributions of This Book

The main theoretical contribution of this book is to destabilize the dominant conceptualizations of English as a global language by drawing attention to the cultural and linguistic bricolage in which English is often found. This decentering challenges dominant understandings of 'English' as a distinct code, neatly bounded by diglossic language domains, and it problematizes the association of English with the expression of western and/or global cultural references. Hybridized languages often defy linguistic descriptions, as they shift and morph, sometimes into new languages, as speakers use them. They challenge prevailing notions of bilingualism as well, as many hybrid language speakers are not able to separate discrete languages from the spectrum of languages that they speak. Nevertheless, since most of the contexts in which hybrid languages involving English are spoken are also contexts that experienced British colonization, the populations in these settings are often described in reference to their English proficiency in terms like 'English-knowing bilinguals' (Pakir, 1991) the 'outer circle of English' (Kachru, 1986), and speakers of 'local forms of English' (Strevens, 1992). Clearly, references to 'Anglophone Africa' and 'English speaking nations' in the post-colonial world are at odds with the ways hybrid languages involving English are treated in the literature. Though codeswitching, localized Englishes and urban vernaculars have been widely analyzed,[3] this scholarship has often been excluded from theoretical discussions of the socio-politics of English as an international language. Scholars who examine the politics of English have advocated for greater consideration of linguistic hybridity as a central aspect of English in the world (cf. Canagarajah, 1999, 2006; Pennycook, 2003a, 2007; Fabrício & Santos, 2006; Makoni, 2003), but this remains a minority perspective in the vast literature on global English. Through a series of ethnographic studies of multilingual practices in East Africa, this book strives to engage with the prominent literature on global English, and to call for greater inclusion of hybrid forms of multilingualism involving English.

In bringing hybrid language practices to the center of discussions about English as a global language, I draw inspiration from Makoni's (1998, 2003; Makoni & Pennycook, 2005) work on the *disinvention* of languages. Building on Mudimbe's (1988) deconstruction of European categories in scholarship about Africa, Makoni uses this concept to dismantle linguistic boundaries and concepts, and he calls for a reconceptualization of language based on sociolinguistic realities among multilinguals. Makoni (2003) demonstrates how the South African Constitution, which now recognizes 11 official languages, perpetuates the colonial invention of languages such as Xhosa and Zulu by falling prey to the colonial ideology of linguistic fixity. He explains that the colonialists applied their own European worldviews onto African people and their languages, imposing their view of a one-to-one relationship between language and ethnicity. The result was that the interconnectedness of Zulu, Xhosa and other languages in South Africa was ignored, resulting in a false 'boxed' representation of linguistic and ethnic divisions. Hence, current language policy in South Africa is a legacy of the colonialist misrepresentation of the sociolinguistic reality of most Africans. Remarking on the speech of South Africans, Makoni (2003: 143) writes, 'In these urban centers, the "mixed" forms are themselves the linguistic norm, the starting point in the process of language socialization for most people, and at times the only version of language for everyday encounters'. Through describing language as it is used, Makoni asserts that we can develop more grounded starting points for analyzing the socio-politics of English and other languages in the 21st century.

This leads to the second major theoretical contribution of the book, which is to challenge the either/or tendencies that characterize much sociolinguistic research on English as a global language. A fairly identifiable dichotomy has developed that treats English as either an oppressive force or as a creative resource for previously colonized or currently globalizing societies. The 'oppressive' side of this dichotomy is often characterized by a focus on the hegemonic and imperialistic effects of English, and in this literature, historical associations with colonialism are quite prevalent (e.g. Kumaravadivelu, 2006; Phillipson, 1992). The 'creative' side of the dichotomy is occupied by a focus on the localization and appropriation of English in local communities and the types of creative expression that occur, often in hybrid forms (e.g. Bamgbose *et al.*, 1995; Kachru, 1986, 1992a). This body of research generally seeks to redress the strong claims made by those who view English as an imperialistic language through demonstrations of how the language has been altered by speakers around the world and made to fit local contexts and local registers.

A major goal of this book is to show how hybridization challenges both of these theoretical perspectives regarding the socio-politics of English, particularly since neither one can always account for what is found in language use among speakers in post-colonial societies. Instead, I propose that the Bakhtinian concept of *multivocality* offers a more comprehensive framework for interpreting the hybrid and transcultural language used in such societies. Using this concept, my intention is to show how the co-existence of lingering and recently developed forms of linguistic and cultural imperialism can be analyzed alongside appropriations and localization, and to explore how members of multilingual societies make sense of the linguistic *heteroglossia* (Bakhtin, 1981) and the multiple of meanings that surround them. The concept of multivocality refers to the several simultaneities that English can index in post-colonial and multilingual societies, including the dual nature of English as an imperialistic language and English as a language that has been reappropriated for its local contexts. Given its historical and contemporary status as the world's most hegemonic language, we need to know how ideologies regarding English emerge and adapt through hybrid language practices, and how they relate to current theories of global English. Next, I discuss multivocality and how it relates to current perspectives on global English that have become prominent in academic circles.

Multivocality

Multivocality refers to a set of interlinked concepts detailed in Bakhtin's writings on voice as well as the multiple perspectives, or speaking positions, articulated through language. The term describes the quality of linguistic utterances as 'contested terrains' (Holquist, 2002: 24) in which multiple meanings of utterances can be voiced, and where an indefinite number of interpretations are possible. Bakhtin's insistence on the multiplicity of language was a response to what he called the 'monologization' of human experience in academic thought of his time.[4] In particular, he challenged Saussure's scholarly work for its failure to address the plurality of everyday language, calling him an 'abstract objectivist' due to his concentration on shared aspects of *langue* (Holquist, 2002: 42). In contrast, Bakhtin promoted 'individualistic subjectivism' by emphasizing the disunity of speech, insisting on the difference and complexity of utterances. In his writings, he underscored the indeterminacy and unfinalizability of language, and he characterized social life and human existence as 'an open dialogue characterized by multivocality and the indeterminacy inherent when those multiple voices interpenetrate' (Baxter, 2004: 108).

In this book, I use the term multivocality in two interrelated ways that correspond roughly to an interlinked microlevel and macrolevel sociolinguistic analysis. Firstly, multivocality refers to the different 'voices' or *polyphony* that single utterances can yield due to their syncretic nature. Creative language forms are frequently produced when speakers intermingle the languages and language varieties circulating in their daily lives. The results of this multilingual practice are varied and can take the form of assimilation into a language (i.e. borrowing), language mixing (the use of two or more languages that produces no pragmatic effect), and codeswitching (the use of two or more languages that does carry a pragmatic effect, *cf.* Auer, 1999). Another possibility is that language mixing can result in a type of syncretism that retains the multivocal quality of the utterance and conveys all possible meanings simultaneously. Woolard (1998) describes these forms as *bivalent*, that is, belonging equally to two languages at once. Bivalent forms allow speakers to remain in the interstices of multivocality, rather than having to choose one code or another. As the chapters of this book show, bivalent multivocality allows for a range of double-voiced usages, including parody, word play and double entendres.

The concept of multivocality appears quite relevant for the study of language in multilingual environments, but it is important to highlight that multivocality is identifiable even in utterances comprised of single languages because of language's syncretic properties, the 'suppression of a relevant opposition under certain determined conditions' (Hill, 1999: 244). Hill illustrates this syncretism in the single word *niggardly*, an English word that has become the subject of debate due to its similar structure with a racial epithet, in spite of its very separate etymology. By taking a stance on whether or not *niggardly* is offensive, speakers control the meanings of multivocal utterances by selecting certain historical associations and suppressing others. Speakers achieve multivocality through inhabiting already-existing language and inflecting it with their own meanings. Bakhtin calls this *assimilation*, a process in which

> our speech that is, all our utterances (including creative works), is filled with others' words, varying degrees of otherness or varying degrees of 'our-own-ness', varying degrees of awareness and detachment. These words of others carry with them their own expression, their own evaluative tone, which we assimilate, rework and reaccentuate. (Bakhtin, 1986: 89)

Secondly, at a more macrolevel, I use the term multivocality to explore how various languages are voiced (and censured) in multilingual societies in response to centripetal and centrifugal forces. As Bakhtin (1981: 272) writes, 'Every concrete utterance of a speaking subject serves as a point where centrifugal as well as centripetal forces are brought to bear. The processes of centralization and decentralization, or unification and disunification, intersect in the utterance'. In East Africa, as in many places, centralizing, centripetal forces drawn from the pressures of globalization and internationalization promote the standardization and compartmentalization of language. On the other hand, decentralizing, centrifugal forces continue to construct linguistic forms of localness by drawing on the global resource of English, resulting in a fascinating range of hybridity.

Bakhtin's discussion of centripetal and centrifugal forces relates well to the paradigms of research on English as a global language, and the constant tension that is produced as a result of these competing forces demonstrates how important it is to include both aspects in research on multilingualism involving English. In the following sections, I summarize existing literature situated in each paradigm, and then I turn to a discussion of how multivocality has the capacity to address both perspectives.

Centripetal forces: Linguistic imperialism and counter-narratives to colonialism

Phillipson's (1992) book *Linguistic Imperialism* is the most prominent example of scholarship in sociolinguistics that treats English as an imperial and hegemonic force. Much research that operates in this framework investigates the effects of language policies and educational practices involving English and regional *lingua francas* from a macrolevel perspective, with particular attention to issues of pluralism and the unequal distribution of power and privilege through language resources (e.g. Batibo, 2000, 2005; A.A. Mazrui, 1975; A.M. Mazrui, 2004; Mazrui & Mazrui, 1998). The spread of English is viewed to have succeeded through *linguicism*, the term Skutnabb-Kangas (1988: 13) uses to refer to 'ideologies and structures that are used to legitimate, effectuate and reproduce an unequal division of power and resources between groups which are defined on the basis of language'. Linguists working in this area often share perspectives with post-colonial literary scholars such as Fanon (1961, 1967), Said (1978) and Spivak (1987, 1988), writers who critique colonialist discourses by producing counter-narratives of western imperial history. The aim is to show how imbalances in power and imperialist attitudes of superiority were discursively constructed and then inscribed onto cultures and languages, producing various forms of *symbolic violence* (Bourdieu, 1991). A common theme across this scholarship is the notion of the colonialist misrepresentation of the 'other', and the implication that an authentic representation is possible, yet buried under many layers of western discourses. As a follower of Aimé Césaire's *négritude* movement, Fanon sought to reclaim Blackness as a positive identity source, removing it from subjugation by Europeans. Fanon describes the need to reject past representations of Black people and to embrace one's true identity:

> I am not the slave of the Slavery that dehumanized my ancestors [...] I am my own foundation. And it is by going beyond the historical, instrumental hypothesis that I will initiate the cycle of my freedom. It is through the effort to recapture the self and to scrutinize the self, it is through the lasting tension of their freedom that men will be able to create the ideal conditions of existence for a human world. (Fanon, 1967: 230–231)

Just as Fanon's work envisions an 'authentic', proud vision of Blackness as a way to combat the oppression of Blacks, Said's (1978) *Orientalism* hints at a 'real' Orient in his efforts to dismantle the dominant discourses of cultural imperialism. Moreover, Barber (1995) points out that Spivak's (1988) question, 'Can the sub-altern speak?' also implies that something constituting an indigenous perspective exists and is being muffled, though she recognizes that Spivak is quite careful to avoid advocating for a nativist perspective which could produce further essentialized conceptualizations of local knowledge. Still, Barber goes on to say that Spivak's (1995: 5) 'critique is effective precisely because it uses the idea of alterity to provide a kind of virtual vantage point outside the western episteme, from which to gain leverage for its deconstruction'. Relatedly, Bhabha (1994: 114) makes reference to 'other, "denied" knowledges [that] enter upon the dominant discourse and estrange the basis of its authority'.

These deconstructionist perspectives resonate strongly with the work of Kenyan literary scholar, author, and activist Ngugi wa Thiong'o (1986, 2000), who takes the stance that the choice of local languages in literature produces counter-narratives which displace the west's grip on the representation of 'the other'. Ngugi views the use of local languages as a means by which Afro-centric worldviews can be preserved in the face of westernization. He writes,

> We reject the primacy of English literature and cultures. The aim, in short, should be to orient ourselves towards placing Kenya, East Africa and then Africa in the centre. All other things are to be considered in

their relevance to our situation and their contribution towards understanding ourselves. (Ngugi, 1986: 94)

Similarly, Ali A. Mazrui and Alamin M. Mazrui emphasize the need to dismantle Africans' 'lingo-intellectual dependency' on English (A.A. Mazrui, 1975, 1996; A.M. Mazrui, 2004; Mazrui & Mazrui, 1998, 1999). A.A. Mazrui illustrates this dependency by discussing the imbalance in the world's languages at the international level. He argues that

> A Japanese may win the Nobel Prize for works written in Japanese; a South Asian for masterly use of Bengali, Urdu or Hindi; a Frenchman for genius of expression in the French language; and an Egyptian for creative accomplishments in Arabic. However, for the foreseeable future, the Nobel Prize for Literature is unlikely to be awarded for brilliant use of an indigenous African language. (A.A. Mazrui, 1996: 5)

For A.M. Mazrui (2004), appropriation is an ideal concept for English, but it is one that has not been achieved in sub-Saharan Africa. He explains that English remains as a largely foreign voice since, excepting Liberia and South Africa, there is no significant constituency of African 'native speakers', and because the standards of correctness are still based on external models of English. He is skeptical that hybridity can transform the colonial language, and he argues that the theory of appropriation does not manifest itself in most people's actual language use, but rather, remains in the hands of the elite. He argues further that even in cases where language is transformed into the voice of the people, it is never enough to merely change the language – any linguistic transformations must be accompanied by changes in the social order.

A common viewpoint among all of these scholars is the idea that indigenous languages are necessary for their capacity to express indigenous and alternative worldviews. While the effects of colonization have surely had negative effects on language diversity and local forms of knowledge, the result of focusing on the disastrous effects of the imperial narrative is that appropriation and resistance takes a backseat to understanding how dominant discourses work and how hegemony operates at the level of textual (re)production. Little room is left for considering whether new meanings might result from the imposition of western languages, or for investigating the alternative worldviews that are assumed to be found in indigenous literature. In her discussion of this strand of post-colonial critique, Barber (1995: 5) writes, 'the theoretical effect is either to consign "native" discourses to the realms of the unknowable, or to imply that they were displaced, erased or absorbed by the dominant discourses'.

Centrifugal forces: Localizing and appropriating English

Instead of unraveling the relations between the colonized and the colonizer, research that focuses on the localization and appropriation of English explores the many ways that users of English index their *ownership* of the language (Higgins, 2003; Norton, 1997; Widdowson, 1994) through altering it to fit their local contexts and situated purposes. Though this research has developed a range of paradigms and theoretical bifurcations of its own, it is probably safe to say that appropriation shares perspectives with a set of post-colonial perspectives noted for a fairly optimistic spirit, namely those articulated in the seminal work of Ashcroft et al. (1989), scholars who emphasize the ability of the downtrodden colonial subjects to 'write back' using the language of the oppressor. In extreme contradistinction with Kenyan author and critic Ngugi, Nigerian author and critic Chinua Achebe (1966: 21) summarizes this view concisely: 'Can an African ever learn to use [English] like a native speaker? I should say, I hope not. It is neither necessary nor desirable for him to be able to do so. The price a world language must be prepared to pay is submission to many different kinds of use'.

In linguistics, the appropriation perspective is often associated with the work of Kachru (1965, 1986, 1992a) and the World Englishes (WE) paradigm, a framework that examines the forms and functions of English varieties outside of traditionally 'native' contexts such as Australia, Canada, the United States and Great Britain. While WE research has challenged the monolithic nature of English in significant ways, a major shortcoming is that the Englishes of the post-colonial world are often described as mostly monolingual in nature, often with an apparent interest in comparing their grammatical structures with those of center Englishes. Confusingly, however, Kachru (1992b) still refers to speakers in India as 'English-using bilinguals', and Sridhar and Sridhar (1992: 96) explain that 'English shares [a functional overlap] with local languages in a number of domains', and that 'code-switching and code-mixing are formal manifestations of this overlap'. Despite such acknowledgments, little research on WE has been devoted to the study of language hybridity. As Pennycook writes,

> the notion of world Englishes does little more than pluralize monolithic English. The notion of world Englishes leaves out all those other Englishes which do not fit the paradigm of an emergent national standard, and in doing so, falls into the trap of mapping centre linguists' images of language and the world on to the periphery. (Pennycook, 2007: 22–23)

Building on and also critiquing both the linguistic imperialism framework and the WE paradigm, Pennycook's (2001, 2003a, 2003b, 2007) work extends the idea of appropriation to investigate how English is used among speakers to perform transcultural and transborder identities. Characterizing the linguistic imperialism perspective as 'homogeny' and the WE paradigm as acritical support for linguistic 'heterogeny', Pennycook (2003b) advocates for a third position that will more thoroughly account for the hybrid, transcultural and translingual phenomena that are part of global English in the world today. Pennycook's (2007) work on *transcultural flows* recognizes that the identities performed through English are neither strictly global nor strictly local, but rather, are forms of a fluid, transcultural interplay, a framework compatible with the interconnectedness of languages discussed by Makoni (2003). Drawing on examples of hip hop language as a form of global English and as forms of localized practices, Pennycook (2007: 9) advocates for an approach that might 'account for the constant reciprocity between globalization and localization'. He discusses Japanese rappers Rip Slyme's lyrics, which blend hip hop language, Japanese and Japanese English, as well as excerpts from novels such as Zadie Smith's *White Teeth*, which features Bengali characters who use Jamaican accents, Bengali and English to produce a simultaneously local and global set of identities. Similar data can be found in studies that focus especially on hybrid forms of English in language play (e.g. Rampton, 1995), in classrooms (Canagarajah, 1999), and in various domains of popular culture (e.g. Adejunmobi, 2004a; Lee, 2006b; Omoniyi, 2006). Such examples challenge binary concepts such as locality or globalization since their meanings are produced as a result of border crossing and transcultural movements, rather than a strictly localized adaptation of a global resource. Pennycook (2007) makes sense of such data through exploring its *transgressive* elements across language, culture and semiotic modes. A transgressive theoretical approach focuses on how people break rules, go beyond established categories, and transcend their limitations. Pennycook (2007: 42) writes that transgression 'is not a project of random, pointless transgressive interruptions but rather a profound and methodical investigation of how to understand ourselves, our histories and how the boundaries of thought may be traversed'.

Rather than studying how people have resisted, rejected or adapted colonial modes, a transcultural approach is rewarding because it examines how people create new spaces, new cultures and new languages with their local and global resources. Using the example of global-local relations in hip hop, Pennycook (2007) describes how the 'global spread of authenticity' creates translocal identification with English through transcultural modes for 'keepin it real', that is, an expression in hip hop that refers to the need to speak from lived experience and to use creative expression as a way to critique social problems in one's immediate circumstances. He gives examples such as Singaporean rapper Shaheed who excludes references to smoking and drinking in his songs because of moral concerns, DJ Jun in Korea who raps about the 'Korean problem' of required army service for all Korean men and Malaysia's Too Phat who criticize American-style rap as inauthentic for the Malaysian context (Pennycook, 2007: 104–105). Pennycook explains that these efforts to keep hip hop real for local contexts is neither the effect of the global, nor are they fully local in character. Instead, they correspond to the 'constant tension between the global flow of an ideology and the local fixity of what authenticity means and how it should be realized' (Pennycook, 2007: 112).

Balancing Centripetal and Centrifugal Forces with Multivocality

The ways that people use language in East Africa often relate to Pennycook's description of transcultural and translingual practices since English does not systematically index the west or the foreign, and because 'local' languages such as Swahili do not consistently relate to only Tanzanian or Kenyan concerns. However, a focus on the transcultural does not always fully encompass the co-presence of centripetal and centrifugal forces that can be found. Pennycook (1998, 2003a, 2007) is sensitive to the fact that English has had an imperial role in post-colonial contexts, and he acknowledges that English has often been the language of 'discommunication', leading to inequality and injustice in many parts of the world. He also concedes that some elements of appropriation and full-on localization have certainly been documented. However, in his work on transcultural flows, he largely sets these issues to the side in his focus on transcultural practices such as the global spread of hip hop and English.

Instead of putting these issues to the side in order to examine the transcultural processes that are clearly part of the linguistic practices in East Africa, it is my goal to include these issues in the formulation of a theoretical apparatus that will be able to cope with the co-present and sometimes contradictory discourses in and about English. My views are similar to those expressed by Ramanathan who explains the apparent paradox involved in emphasizing hybridity and societal structures such as inequality:

> Postmodern views of cultures and peoples as being fluid and dynamic and of all identities being hybrid are most valuable, most especially

because they give us a way of talking about individuals in contexts. But social stratifications of class, caste, ethnicity, and gender in societies still exist and when languages – especially English and the Vernaculars in post-colonial contexts – seem to fall along those lines, then a critically and ethnographically oriented researcher has little choice but to address the chasms as well. (Ramanathan, 2004: viii–ix)

While imperialism and appropriation represent two extreme possibilities for relations between previously colonized people and English, my fieldwork in East Africa shows that these polar extremes are not commonplace. Sometimes, people hold both sets of views, as well as perspectives that move back and forth between these poles. Other times, multilingualism involving English is treated as unremarkable and is oriented to as a normative way of interacting. The multiple interpretations of English in East Africa suggest a need for a concept that deals with this ambiguity. This book argues that the concept of multivocality allows for an analysis of the multiplicity of meanings constructed through English that include aspects of linguistic imperialism and global hegemony, as well as resistance to imperialism in the forms of appropriation and transcultural hybridity.

In the chapters that follow, I investigate the values accorded to different kinds of multilingualism involving English across four domains of social life – casual conversation, beauty pageants, hip hop and advertising. Even though constraints do appear to operate on multivocality according to context, the centrifugal aspects of language seem to allow for transformative language use that challenges the boundaries of 'fixed' languages. Hill and Hill (1986: 399) write, 'For Bakhtin, heteroglossia in multilingual popular usage amplifies and opens the possibilities for meaning and freedom... Thus, Bakhtin sees syncretic speech as fundamentally liberating'. In certain domains, centrifugal forces produce locally valued language forms such as those described by Blommaert (2005b), who shows how local merchants in Tanzania make use of 'public English', a variety characterized by misspellings, novel morphosyntax and highly localized meanings that is used to advertise local goods and services. Merchants in Dar es Salaam who use language such as 'sliming food' to refer to diet food benefit from public English by marketing their products successfully. However, Blommaert points out that centripetal forces exist beyond East Africa. He explains that forms of public English 'are only meaningful locally, they do not count as "English" as soon as translocal norms are imposed on them' (Blommaert, 2005b: 410). While local merchants may not imagine their clientele to be international consumers, Blommaert's concerns bear out in other domains explored in this book. In the realms of beauty pageants and, to a lesser degree, in hip hop music, concerns about the transportability of language emerge.

Through the study of domains, I illustrate how space becomes central in allowing for multivocality in creating specific kinds of language variation and language diversity. Blommaert *et al.* (2005: 199) make a similar point through their conceptualization of *truncated multilingualism* as the 'linguistic competencies which are organised topically, on the basis of domains or specific activities'. The concept that language is conditioned by domain is strongly related to the notion of *indexicality* as well. As Blommaert *et al.* (2005: 199) write, 'indexicality forces us to look at social processes as culturalized, i.e. as turned into complexes of meaningful and understandable (indexical) items that offer semiotic potential to people'. In my examination of four domains of social life, we will see a range of indexicalities for English and English-infused multilingualism, including meanings which contradict and compete within the same slices of social life.

In sum, multivocality is an important concept for both microlevel and macrolevel types of analysis because it establishes *multiplicity* as a starting point for the analysis of language, and because it treats contexts of multilingualism as spaces where languages intersect with one another in creative and 'unfinalizable' ways. For Bakhtin (1981), language itself is a dialogue of multiple voices and speaking positions that interacts with centralizing (centripetal) and decentralizing (centrifugal) forces. Because heteroglossia steadily challenges the unification and standardization of language by providing establishing new meanings via innovative linguistic intersections, it is also a very useful concept for theorizing English in multilingual contexts vis-à-vis linguistic imperialism (a centripetal force) and theories of appropriation and transcultural flows (centrifugal forces).

Interpretive Authority in Researching the Politics of English

Pennycook's (2007) point that 'language identities are performed in the doing rather than reflecting a prior set of fixed options' emphasizes the situated nature of language and the multiple meanings possible in language. However, to fully appreciate his point, we need to know how various linguistic and multimodal performances are *interpreted* by members of the communities we examine. Hybrid languages are part of the increasing number of *new literacies* (Cope & Kalantzis, 2000; Gee, 2003; New London Group, 1996; Street, 1995) that multilinguals encounter in various modalities, including oral communication, popular music, written texts and electronic communications. These literacies require specific types of knowledge and exposure to particular communities of practice. However, little is known about how people of differing backgrounds with various degrees of familiarity with hybrid languages 'read' these modalities. In each chapter of the book, I address the question of interpretation through ethnographic methods.

Researchers working on English in post-colonial and globalizing contexts (e.g. Canagarajah, 1999; Lin, 1999; Makoni, 2003; Ramanathan, 2004, 2006) often make use of their 'insider' status and draw upon their own sets of 'local' and 'global' knowledges when examining the language practices of their respective contexts of inquiry. Importantly, the contributions of these authors expand the field by providing perspectives that are beyond the white, western-raised, western-educated experience. Canagarajah (1999) describes this work as the democratization of center discourses, as 'their oppositional subject position, outsider identity, marginalized status and alternate cultural traditions provide a critical interpretive perspective on Western discourses' (1999: 34–35).

At the same time, these scholars also struggle with the reality that all researchers, whether 'native' or not, are constrained by their own subjectivities in the act of doing research. Much interpretive work that employs ethnography is based on the premise that the researcher will be able to gain some distance from the context under study in order to identify and analyze various linguistic or cultural practices. Canagarajah writes that while 'defamiliarization comes easily to alien researchers, an insider has to struggle to adopt such a perspective. Being an insider does not guarantee an "accurate" or "correct" understanding of the different contextual and discursive forces at play during the research process' (Canagarajah, 1999: 54). Similarly, the view that one's position as an 'insider' will undoubtedly facilitate the interpretation of data does not fully acknowledge the multiple and complex nature of discourse communities.

As a white American who learned Swahili as a foreign language in university classrooms, it is fair to say that I experienced difficulty in comprehending the kinds of English and cultural references used in East Africa. I often encountered nonstandardized Swahili and language that involved code alternation and mixing, and I was a relative novice to this type of speech. Early in my research, I made the mistake of interpreting all hybrid language as meaningful code contrasts because of my own 'sociolinguistic biography' (Makoni, 2003), which made it difficult for me to view the use of two 'languages' as a singular code. As I soon discovered, the meanings of 'Swahinglish' speech were not equivalent to the combined meanings of English and Swahili. Through ethnographic methods including observation, retrospective interviews and semistructured interviews, I came to better understand how individuals interpreted the heteroglossia surrounding them.

It seems that reflection on the researcher's role in applied linguistics and sociolinguistics research is rare, particularly among white, western researchers who study cultures other than their own. A notable exception is Pennycook (1998), who is quite careful to limit his analysis to how contemporary white culture has represented the 'other' in discourses surrounding the teaching of English. Through focusing on the effects of colonialism as discursively constructed by Europeans, Pennycook explains that a critical form of reflexivity can be gained. He writes,

> While this may seem a strangely Eurocentric direction to take, I want to argue that it is important both because I, as a European, am looking critically inward to examine some of the cultural constructs that govern my and other European/Western lives, and because in so doing I am not trying to suggest on behalf of colonized people how they have experienced colonialism. (Pennycook, 1998: 66)

As one way to handle the 'over-representation of center-based perspectives' (Canagarajah, 1999: 46) in socio-politically oriented work on English in post-colonial contexts, I have made many efforts to focus on the perspectives of Tanzanians and Kenyans as the voices of interpretive authority in this book. Moreover, I have taken an ethnographic approach to the four domains analyzed here, drawing on fieldwork and analysis carried out from 2001 to 2007. I do not rely on text analysis without the interpretations of those who read the texts, nor do I pretend to be the only person whose interpretation matters. While I cannot and do not claim to have developed an insider's perspective, I can claim to have made extensive efforts to ground all of the analysis in the interpretations of those who live in and through the discourses I present. One of the benefits of this 'decentering' of interpretive authority is that the power difference between the researcher and the researched is reduced, and the culture is not represented by the outsider researcher alone.

Outline of the Book

Since 2001, when I began researching language in East Africa, four domains have emerged as fascinating sites for the study of dialogue between the local and the global, and these have become the four data-based chapters of the book. After providing an overview of the socio-historical aspects of English in Kenya and Tanzania in Chapter 2, I turn my attention to these four domains.

Chapter 3 investigates how English and Swahili are discoursed among office workers and journalists through a study of casual conversation in a newspaper office. Here, English is used as a language of neutralization when the staff use codeswitching between Swahili and English to mitigate what may be called 'Tanzanian' rules of politeness that require linguistic deference to one's elders. In the same office, however, the disjunction between English and Swahili is used as a resource for making jokes, to highlight punch lines, and to provide another 'voice' for the production of humor. While the office appears heteroglossic at the microlevel, the language these office workers use is an 'acrolectal' variety in the repertoire of hybrid languages in Tanzania. In speaking a variety that demonstrates one's monolingual abilities in both languages, the journalists can double-identify with the heteroglossia of urban, Swahinglish Tanzania and can claim membership in an elite/global world of transnational English speakers.

In Chapter 4, I explore the somewhat sordid world of beauty pageants in East Africa. In this domain, monologic forms of English are dominant and they seem to offer international identification for beauty pageant contestants who aspire toward international competitions. This identification carries over into beauty products and in descriptions of beauty contestants of the past, many of whom are very active in Tanzania's burgeoning celebrity lifestyle. While monologic forms of English and western beauty aesthetics provide a great deal of cultural capital for contestants in the pageants, these same practices are critiqued as 'selling out' in alternative beauty pageants and in newspaper articles about past pageant winners. These divergent but co-existing discourses about beauty, language and body aesthetics are responded to in carnivalesque humor in the form of parody, where pageants and beauty practices such as skin whitening, dieting and hair straightening are ridiculed. In the process, Africanist versions of beauty are presented as counter-narratives as well, which highlight Swahili as symbolic capital for local identification.

In contrast to the monologic qualities of language and cultural practices in discourses of female beauty, the domain of hip hop offers a breathtaking degree of heteroglossic liberation. Chapter 5 shows how the already counter-culture practices of west-based hip hop are reappropriated in Kenyan and Tanzanian rap. It also demonstrates the layering of meanings through multiple processes of re-entextualization. Rappers double-identify with the global hip hop nation and with their local fan base by using names and lyrics that simultaneously refer to the global and the local. Finally, the analysis of the re-entextualization of a Kenyan rap song into the domain of politics shows how the processes of reterritorialization result in new linguistic codes that not only produce localized English, but also relocalized African languages and cultural practices.

Advertising is the focus of Chapter 6. Here, I show how multilingual advertising involving English is symbolic of a new world order that is taking shape at both economic and linguistic levels, a new form of 'modern living' that challenges binary concepts of the global and the local. I analyze how English in multilingual advertising helps to construct both a new world order and a sense of the local by investigating how it is used as a commodity and as a source of creativity in Tanzania and Kenya. I examine many multilingual advertisements that double-identify with global English and local language varieties, and I turn to interview data to assess the kinds of new hybrid literacies that are developing in Tanzania. The chapter shows that hybrid language practices are often more powerful forms of communication than monologic varieties in advertising. Consumerist language seriously challenges prescriptive attitudes towards purity in language and the maintenance of boundaries between languages.

Finally, in Chapter 7, I relate the domains examined in previous chapters to other countries where similar research has been done. I then consider a final realm of social life that has thus far been rather impervious to heteroglossia – formal education. In comparing the possibilities for heteroglossia in education to other domains of social life, my aim is to probe what I see as a reluctance to recognize the hybridity that English generates in all societies in education, and to look for any promising signs of change. While formal education seems to be holding fast to the centripetal forces of monologism, the domains of life generated through popular culture have become increasingly heteroglossic, and this multivocality now includes mediated forms of education. Through multivocal hip hop, and to a lesser degree, advertising, I argue that educational dialogues about moral living, sexual health, the maintenance of cultural traditions and the integrity of political leaders are made available to the masses.

Notes

1. Retrieved October 6, 2006, http://www.nationmedia.com/dailynation.
2. 'East Africa' often includes Burundi, Kenya, Rwanda, Tanzania and Uganda (and sometimes Eritrea, Ethiopia and Somalia). I explore contexts in which Swahili and English are widely used, so Kenya and Tanzania will be the focus of the book.

3. For research on linguistic hybridity, codemixing, and codeswitching in sub-Saharan Africa, see Adejunmobi (2004b), Blommaert (1999a), Dakubu (1997), Finlayson and Slabbert (1997), Goyvaerts (1992, 1996), Higgins (2007, 2009), Makoni (2003); Makoni et al. (2007), Mesthrie (1992), Myers-Scotton (1993a), Omoniyi (2004), Satyo (2001), Scotton (1982) and Spitulnik (1998).
4. According to Holquist (2002), much of Bakhtin's writings can be read as arguments against the homogenization and monologization of cultural and political life in the Soviet Union.

Chapter 2
From Pre-colonial Beginnings to Multivocality

This chapter provides a basic overview of the development of multilingualism involving English in East Africa. While the term 'East Africa' can encompass many configurations of nation-states, I use it in this book to refer to Kenya and Tanzania, a choice shaped by my own experiences as a researcher and the sites of my fieldwork in these two countries since 2001. The bulk of my research has been on language in Tanzania, with the main focus on the urban context of Dar es Salaam. My discussion of the Kenyan context comes from one short period of fieldwork and access to popular publications and internet resources. Readers interested in a book-length discussion of the sociolinguistic history and present-day policies of East Africa should consult Mazrui and Mazrui (1999) and Mazrui (2004).

The Impact of Swahili on the Spread of English in Kenya and Tanzania

In a very dialogic manner, the present day use of English in East Africa is to a large degree shaped by the history and currency of Swahili in East Africa. Swahili has long been spoken in Kenya and Tanzania, in addition to the bordering nations of Burundi, Rwanda, Mozambique, Somalia and Uganda, but its use in each nation varies tremendously. The official status of Swahili in Kenya and Tanzania reflects the difference: Swahili is the official and national language of Tanzania while it is only the national language of Kenya. Many observers might even argue that English is the *de facto* national language of Kenya, as Swahili has been replaced in many contexts due to the perceived higher status of English (Michieka, 2005; Muthwii & Kioko, 2004). However, most Kenyans are not functionally fluent in monolingual forms of English (Mazrui, 2004; Michieka, 2005).

In contrast, the general nationalistic pride Tanzanians share in their use of Swahili in most linguistic domains points to a rather positive attitude toward the language. The differences in language use in these two East African countries can be explained by demographics, historical factors and political developments.

Demographics

In part, the proliferation of Swahili as a *lingua franca* in Tanzania encountered fewer obstacles than in Kenya due to the linguistic character of its population. Tanzania is a nation comprised of mostly small Bantu groups who are not in competition with one another politically; moreover, no single group dominates another in terms of population. Of the approximately 120 languages in Tanzania, 95% are Bantu while the remaining 5% speak Cushitic, Nilotic or Khoisan languages. Therefore, in Tanzania, Swahili makes for an ideal national language because of inter-ethnic contact. Since most speakers are not likely to have an advantage, it suits the role of a regional link language as most Tanzanians do not speak Swahili as their first language, but are indeed speakers of Bantu languages. In contrast, Kenya is much more heterogeneous than Tanzania in terms of linguistic populations. Of the approximately 32 languages in Kenya, 24 are Bantu (66%); moreover, less political harmony exists in Kenya among the varying ethnic groups, and many Kikuyu, Kalenjin and Luo speakers maintain their political power in part through language. Still, as in Tanzania, Swahili acts as a link language in Kenya, for it is seen as a neutral language not tied to one specific ethnic group.

Historical factors

Swahili was originally a language limited to the coastal regions of present-day Kenya. According to Nurse and Spear (1985), Swahili speakers dispersed north to southern Somalia and south to northern Mozambique from the 10th to 12th centuries. Centuries of contact with the Arab-Islamic world imbued Swahili with linguistic and cultural aspects of Islam, and the development of Islamic schools and mosques on the coast led to the development of a rich poetic tradition and writing in the Arabic script (Mazrui & Mazrui, 1998).

Since the Arabs commanded Indian Ocean trade, Swahili became important in economic domains as well. In Zanzibar, the increased need for ivory spurred the development of trade routes in Tanganyika (the mainland of present-day Tanzania) in the early part of the 19th century.

The beginning of American trade with Zanzibar increased demand drastically as a result of the independence of the colonies in 1776; between 1832–1834, 32 of 41 ships that arrived in Zanzibar's ports to trade were from the American colonies (Whiteley, 1969: 45). In addition to the demand from America came renewed demand from Germany and France in the 1830s after the end of the Napoleonic Wars. As a result, Sultan Seyyid Said developed Zanzibar's clove plantations and began to finance caravans inland to acquire slaves and ivory by 1840. The use of Swahili in Tanzania became necessary to the success of the caravans as many of the laborers used by Seyyid were from the coast. As the trade routes developed, settlements were established which helped to spread trade routes into the interior (Mkangi, 1985), bringing Swahili along with them.

In Kenya, the notorious hostility of the Maasai to caravans from Mombasa impeded the spread of Swahili. More importantly, the obstacle of the Taru desert and the lack of cooperation of the Kikuyu and Nandi tribes made it difficult to establish any long-lasting trade routes. No settlements were established on the northern route since few leaders cooperated with the Sultan's political alliance. As a result, Swahili failed to spread in the mainland of Kenya substantially. Gorman argues the lack of Swahili culture and Islam in inland Kenya reveals the historical facts: 'It is true to say, however, that in the area constituting present day Kenya, *Ustaarabu* – the coastal way of life and the language with which it is associated – never assumed the prestige with which it was associated in parts of Tanzania and the Congo, particularly in the early twentieth century' (Gorman, 1974: 401).

The missionaries to the coast also influenced the spread of Swahili differently. During the period between 1860–1880, missionary activity expanded and produced Swahili texts that made the further development of Swahili possible. The Anglican Bishop Edward Steere 1870 explains the usefulness of the language for proselytizing in his *Handbook of the Swahili Language*: 'For if the members of the Mission can go forth from Zanzibar, or, still better, can leave England already well-acquainted with the language, and provided with books and translations adapted to their wants, they will carry with them a key that can unlock the secrets of an immense variety of strange dialects, whose very names are yet unknown to us' (quoted in Whiteley, 1969: 54). Since the schools of the late 19th century were primarily operated by missions, the emphasis on Swahili by the Lutherans and the German Benedictine Church in most of southern Tanganyika helped spread Swahili as a language for education. The use of one *lingua franca* was much more economical than translating the Bible into over 100 vernaculars. Moreover, Swahili's infusion with monotheistic concepts and vocabulary from Islam facilitated the conversion to Christianity among many East Africans (Mazrui & Mazrui, 1998).

Colonial beginnings

The Germans were the first Europeans to occupy East Africa in the form of a protectorate over the Sultan of Zanzibar's coastal possessions in 1885. Three years later, the Sultan gave the British East Africa Company a royal charter and concessionary rights to the Kenyan coast, and Germany conceded its coastal holdings to the British in exchange for Tanganyika. The British occupied Kenya from the late 19th century, transforming Kenya from a protectorate to a British Crown colony in 1920; the Germans held Tanganyika as a colony from 1880 through 1919. With the advantage of a relatively widespread *lingua franca* due to the caravan trade routes, Swahili filled many roles under the German rule in Tanganyika, but English was used more in Kenya, particularly among the chosen elite who worked with the British government. Relatively fewer Germans were involved in the development of the country than were the British in Kenya. Kenyans were primarily used as a source of cheap labor for the white settler minority, whereas in Tanganyika, more Africans held administrative positions (Mkangi, 1985: 332). The dominance of Swahili in Tanganyika resulted from the Germans' creation of an African civil service that used Swahili as the *lingua franca*. They also built government schools using Swahili at Tanga in 1892, and by 1914, there were 83 government schools in various parts of the country. The German administration carried out its work in Swahili, reserving German for high-level communication (Batibo, 1995).

Swahili in Kenya did not benefit from the caravan routes in the same way as Tanganyika; therefore, the pre-colonial spread of Swahili was not as great. Mkangi (1985: 336) argues that the British felt that English should not be taught to Africans in schools in order to maintain their inferior status. Mazrui and Mazrui (1998) also explain that many settlers viewed the teaching of English as likely to lead to subversion of their authority. A similar attitude in Tanganyika prevailed towards the teaching of German. The efforts made by whites to learn Swahili in the two countries were quite different, however. In Tanganyika, colonists generally made sincere efforts to learn the dialects and grammar of Swahili well; in Kenya, the development of the Kisetla dialect shows the lack of interest by the British in learning Swahili proficiently. Mkangi explains their reasons for this attitude as socio-economic: 'For settlers to speak correct Kiswahili – for example, *mbwa mkali* ("fierce dog/hound") – would not only have been tantamount to demeaning themselves, but also to elevating Kiswahili to equal status with English' (Mkangi, 1985: 336).

Although Tanganyika was placed under British rule in 1919, it did not experience the same language policy changes as did Kenya in the 20th century. Because Britain was given Tanganyika as a mandate territory under the League of Nations, Britain was never as involved in the affairs of the country as in Kenya. A policy of indirect rule developed in Tanganyika which allowed Swahili to continue to develop as a cultural and political language that unified the country's development. In Kenya, the development of Swahili was quickly oppressed by the British when it became a unifying force politically. In 1919, Harry Thuku used Swahili to organize against the Kipande labor laws; the protest resulted in the 1922 massacre of workers in Nairobi. In the years following the massacre, officials discouraged the use of Swahili since it threatened their political authority. In 1929, the Governor Sir Michael Grigg declared, 'Every encouragement will be given to English which must be the *lingua franca* of this colony. There shall be no bilingualism in our institutions or courts' (Mkangi, 1985: 337). In contrast, Swahili is often viewed as one of the most important tools in Tanzania that was used for labor agitation, collective bargaining and participation in national politics prior to independence (Mazrui & Mazrui, 1998).

Language in Education

Not surprisingly, the use of Swahili in education under the colonial powers and the language policy enacted during colonialism impacted the future of English and Swahili differently in Kenya and Tanganyika. The eventual promotion of English in Kenya's education system developed as a result of linguistic and economic difficulties. Following the recommendations of several committees on education in Kenya, the report of the East Africa Commission stated that elementary stages of education were to be carried out in the children's first languages with Swahili as a subject, and English was to be taught at secondary and university levels (Gorman, 1974: 411). The report of the Calcutta University Mission in 1919 suggested the use of Swahili, Kikuyu, Luo and Luyia for the first languages, in accord with population. However, disagreement over how to implement such a multilingual educational system prevented solutions from being found. In addition, a general inadequacy of educational facilities, teachers and materials stymied the development of multilingual primary education. In 1929, the Hilton Young Commission noted other difficulties: 'The obvious difficulty in the way of adopting (Swahili) at present time is the very small percentage of Africans who are sufficiently educated to speak it with any fluency and the still smaller number who are qualified to teach it' (Gorman, 1974: 420).

As a result of difficulties posed by a general lack of proficiency in Swahili and the use of four indigenous languages in primary school, the decision to focus on English became inevitable in Kenya. In 1949, the Beecher Report recommended that English replace Swahili as a medium of instruction for the Kenya African Preliminary Exam and ended the teaching of Swahili in 1953. The East African Royal Commission of 1953 even declared that Swahili, 'as a second language, was a complete waste of time and effort' (Mkangi, 1985: 338).

Education in Tanganyika was more reliant on Swahili under colonial rule. Although English was taught as a subject, Swahili was typically the medium for instruction for primary school. In secondary schools and higher education, English was the medium for instruction, and for this reason, English was emphasized more in Grades 4–6. Despite the focus on English, the patterns of Swahili use that German colonialism had instilled in Tanganyika were highly influential when independence came in 1962.

Political and economic developments in Kenya and Tanganyika from the 1950s contributed substantially to the dissimilar evolution of Swahili in each country. Though the occupation of Kenya by Europeans had always differed from Tanganyika in terms of its more substantial number of settlers, this difference became a source of major economic differentiation from the mid-20th century. Partly as a result of the Mau Mau peasant war, British officials put forth the Swynnerton Plan in 1954 in order to promote private land ownership, which consequently created a landowning, elite class in Kenya (Mkangi, 1985: 338). This scheme presumably allowed British colonists to have control over the powerful groups in the African population of Kenya and limited the availability of power through dividing the haves from the have-nots. After World War II, growing resistance to British rule prompted policy-makers to replace Swahili with English in education to minimize intra-African contact at the level of the masses (Mazrui & Mazrui, 1995). By 1953, English had become a compulsory subject in the national exam after primary school and as the medium of instruction in intermediate schools. By 1966, 50% of all primary schools were taught in English, and Swahili did not figure on the national exams until the 1980s (Mazrui & Mazrui, 1995: 275).

In contrast, Tanganyika promoted unity and a leveling of economic opportunity among the population. From the time of the Maji Maji War in 1905 to the formation of the Tanganyikan African National Union, what would become the ruling party after independence, nationalistic movements required the use of Swahili as a unifying force. Once independence was achieved in 1961, the first president, Julius Nyerere, championed the use of Swahili in education, especially as a means for giving all Tanzanians the same opportunities (Nyerere, 1967). He argued that Swahili was a transmitter for Tanzanian values, and he argued that the adoption of Swahili as the official and national language of Tanzania allowed for the goals of socialism to be met. Nyerere pointed out that in addition to knowledge of arithmetic, history and knowledge of the government, Tanzanians needed to be able to read and write in Swahili in order to fit into and serve their communities. The teaching of English was noticeably secondary to these goals, as it did not factor into the country's *Ujamaa* ('familyhood') policies. Swahili became the official language of Tanzania in 1967 and was adopted as the medium of instruction for all primary schools as well.

Despite the moves made to create economic and cultural independence from the west, however, Tanzania never experienced complete Swahilization, and English remained as an official language in education and other domains throughout the socialist period. Blommaert (1999a) argues that renewed friendly relations with Great Britain were to blame for this state of affairs, due to years of economic hardship culminating in the Oil Crisis of the early 1970s. In fact, by 1974, Nyerere was quoted in *The Times*, promoting bilingualism. He stated, 'Tanzanians would be foolish to reject English. We are a small country. English and French are African languages, and so one we have. It is a very useful language' (quoted in Kihore, 1976: 50). In Kenya, the choice of Swahili as the national language was not as meaningful for the newly independent nation since Swahili was not as widely spoken. Despite President Kenyatta's proposals for the use of Swahili in parliament, English still dominates the governmental operations of Kenya. In non-Islamic urban schools, English is the medium of instruction from the beginning of primary school; Swahili has been allocated three periods a week in the primary school syllabi (Gorman, 1974: 442). As more Kenyans join the ranks of the middle class, children are exposed to English at a very young age in the home as well (Mazrui & Mazrui, 1998; Michieka, 2005). In rural schools, vernaculars are often used for the first few years of primary school before English is introduced, and Swahili is only taught as a subject (Bunyi, 2005). Similar trends are beginning to take hold in Tanzania as well, where the number of private English-medium primary schools has risen dramatically over the past decade (Neke, 2003). Currently, Swahili remains the medium of instruction for government-run primary schools, though changes in governmental policy now call for English to be introduced as a subject beginning in third grade (Vavrus, 2002).

Despite the label 'English-medium', instruction in both Kenyan and Tanzanian schools typically involves a great deal of multilingualism in the form of codeswitching (Brock-Utne, 2005; Bunyi, 2005; Merritt, 1992; Rubagumya, 1994). While some of this switching facilitates learning, some researchers assert that low achievement among students is directly related to students' and teachers' poor command of English, particularly among those who live in rural areas. In her research on Kenyan primary schools, Bunyi (2005) found that rigid, drill-based, rather tedious teaching practices dominated the classroom. She found high degrees of initiation-response-feedback (IRF), choral responses and strongly teacher-fronted lessons in both Gikuyu and English that yielded little opportunity for literacy development that would benefit students on exams. Similarly, research on private English medium primary schools in Tanzania by Rubagumya (2004) found very similar teaching methods to characterize much of the learning that takes place. In fact, many parents concede that their children are likely to learn better in their mother tongue or in a regional language such as Swahili rather than in English (Muthwii, 2004). In spite of this, however, many teachers, students and parents in East Africa prefer that English remain as the medium of instruction, citing the prestige of the language, their desire to move upward socio-economically and the need for English as a language of development.

Modern Day Multivocality

Auer's (1999) framework for language mixing and language alternation provides a very useful starting point for understanding multivocality in modern day East Africa. At the grammatical extreme are *fused lects* (FLs), varieties of bilingual speech that contain an invariable grammaticalized code (see Figure 2.1). Within FLs, speakers are obligated to use

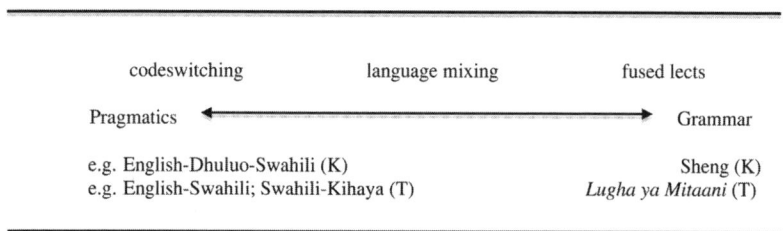

Figure 2.1 Continuum of multilingualism in Kenya (K) and Tanzania (T)

one 'language' or the other for specific grammatical constituents. Speakers are typically unaware of the etymologies of the languages involved and do not orient to the constituents from different languages in any particular way since, for them, all items are treated as grammatical constituents of the same communicative code. In this way, FLs can be viewed on par with creoles since these are language varieties in which the choice of language for lexical items has essentially become grammaticalized, and variable switching between languages is no longer allowed. Here is where Sheng in Kenya and a great deal of *Lugha ya Mitaani* ('Street Language/ Street Swahili') in Tanzania would be placed. Further along the continuum is *Language mixing* (LM), which Auer (1999) defines as the occurrence of variable switching that no longer contains meaning, as displayed by the speakers involved. In other words, the language alternation itself does not generate additional meanings for the speakers. In East Africa, language mixing can involve Swahili and English, Sheng and Swahili, Sheng and English, Street Swahili and English, and so on. At the pragmatic extreme of the continuum is *codeswitching* (CS), a form of speech in which language contrasts are oriented to as meaningful by conversational participants and which can be interpreted as indexing contextual aspects of the situation. Again, CS can involve any number of languages in East Africa. In Kenya, speakers frequently alternate between more than two languages, whereas in Tanzania, codeswitching usually involves Swahili and English or Swahili alternating with ethnic community languages such as Kihaya, Kichagga, and so forth. Auer's framework has been developed to examine bilingualism in naturally occurring conversation, but it provides a useful baseline for considering how the language use in any context might be understood.

Multivocality in Kenya

At Auer's FL end of the language alternation scale is Sheng. Sheng refers to S<u>wa</u>hili <u>Eng</u>lish and is understood to have evolved in Nairobi in the 1960s and 1970s as a language of solidarity and identification with the underclass. In terms of identity making, Sheng is a language that has often been described as a 'resistance vernacular' (Mazrui, 1995; Githiora, 2002), and its main characteristics are usually seen to be its ethnic neutrality and its ability to represent the voice of the urban underclass. Using Bourdieu's metaphor of linguistic markets, Githinji (2006) describes Sheng as one of the options in the linguistic marketplace. In urban areas in particular such as Nairobi, Kenya's national languages of English and Swahili compete with ethnic languages such as Kikuyu and Kalenjin. Though

Swahili can serve as a language of pan-ethnic solidarity in Kenya, it remains somewhat formal in its monolectal form for Kenyans due to its failure to spread as widely as it did in Tanzania during pre-colonial periods. Githinji argues that Sheng has stepped in to serve the function of solidarity among urban youth, for it provides them with an alternative linguistic market. Originally a symbol of resistance toward the elite, it is has become increasingly widespread among residents of the Nairobi area, and varieties of Sheng have also emerged (*cf.* Abdulaziz & Osinde, 1997; Githinji, 2006).

Though some have called it a creole, according to Githinji (2006), Sheng does not fit the standard definition of a creole language since Swahili was present when it evolved, and so there was no creole-based need for another *lingua franca*. While Sheng seems to defy categorization in many ways, it can be considered a FL in that the fusion of languages in Sheng produces altered meanings that are distinct from the meanings in the source languages. The following illustrate these new meanings (Mbaabu & Nzuga, 2003):

(1) *saikoro* 'old, out-dated' (< Kiluhya *msakhulu* 'old man, old husband')
(2) *chums* 'money' (< Swahili *chuma* 'iron')
(3) *mbuyu* 'father' (< Swahili *mbuyu* 'baobob tree')
(4) *dame* 'girl' (< English *dame*)

The following examples from Sure (1992) illustrate some of the grammatical aspects of Sheng, showing that they mostly follow a Bantu grammatical structure:

(5) *Atakam* = a-ta-kam = she/he-future-come 's/he will come'
(6) *Simlaik* = si-m-laik = I.neg-her/him-like 'I don't like him/her'

Sheng refers to a continuum of hybridity in language. Some utterances deemed Sheng are nearly all English or all Swahili, less a few words of Sheng. The first example in (7) is nearly all English, and it comes from *Pulse* magazine, a weekly entertainment magazine published with the English-medium *East African Standard* newspaper. The example in (8) is very heavily Swahili, and comes from hip hop lyrics from Dudubaya's song *Mpenzi* ('girlfriend') (Githinji, 2006: 41–42). Here, we have started to get a glimpse of how context might call for certain linguistic choices.

(7) Having lived in *stato* for a long time   Having lived in the **United States** for a long time
(8) *Nakupenda mpenzi usiyependa chapa*   I love you my girlfriend who doesn't like **money**

Nakupenda mpenzi	I love you my girlfriend
usiyependa **doo**	who doesn't like **money**
Tikisa!	Shake it!
Shore *wa kweli!*	The real **girl**!
Manzi *wa kweli!*	The real **girl**!

Githinji explains that one Sheng word in an otherwise-English utterance qualifies the entire utterance as Sheng, and several words of Sheng alongside Swahili in lyrics can also earn the label Sheng, rather than codeswitching. While some have characterized the former as Engsh, Githinji points out that all it takes is one word for an utterance to be labeled Sheng by Kenyans. Githinji (2006) documents the degrees of variation in Sheng along *baze* (neighborhood/street corner) boundaries. For example, in one *baze* Githinji (2006: 113–116) studied, the word for girl was *msupa* and in another, it was *spleng*, even though many words in common Sheng abound to refer to girls, including *manzi, shore* and *dem*.

Language mixing and codeswitching practices in Kenya have been the focus of Myers-Scotton's (1983, 1992, 1993a) scholarly work for several decades. In her markedness model, she draws on language data from Kenya and other African contexts to establish four types of codeswitching: (1) to present sequential unmarked choices; (2) to present an unmarked choice (a change in code between sequential turns); (3) to present a marked choice; and (4) to present an exploratory choice. The first and second types could arguably be classified as LM in Auer's terms, as they do not carry any particular pragmatic function in conversation, whereas the third and fourth types mark the interaction in a significant way through language alternation. Of course, speakers can also switch between types in single conversations, which may result in language mixing or codeswitching, depending on the typological switches. In Myers-Scotton's framework, the switching to a marked or unmarked choice depends on how the speakers view the context they are in. She explains that it is up to the speaker to make the choice to act upon a change in situational features in order to maintain or change the level of markedness. For example, Swahili-English CS in Nairobi that tends 'to avoid favoring any one ethnic group' (Myers-Scotton, 1992: 171) is the unmarked choice, whereas the use of a monolingual variety of English in the same setting would be marked. An example of this 'CS as an unmarked choice' appears in (9) below and is taken from a context in which seven young men who speak English and Swahili regularly are together in one of the men's homes. Myers-Scotton explains that such a conversation can be heard in other African urban areas, and is a common way of speaking among the educated in Nairobi.

(9) CS as the 'unmarked choice' (Myers-Scotton, 1992: 171).
1 G: *Hawo chicks hawakuwa* standard *ya* mine.
   (Those girls weren't of my standard)
2 A: *Halikuwa* a standard higher? *Sio?*
   (They were of a higher standard? Isn't that so?)
3 G: *Ben-si wewe ndio ulikuwa una*float *na* beer *yako kwa ile* corner *wewe?*
   (Ben, weren't you floating with your beer at the corner?)
4 A: *Haki ya mungu, pale siku*float. *Mimi nilikuwa na msichana* throughout.
   (I swear, I never floated at that place. I had a girl throughout)

While Myers-Scotton's work is admirable for its intent to provide an explanatory framework for multilingual conversations, the issue of how linguistic choices become marked or unmarked for certain contexts is not thoroughly explored her work. Other researchers such as Auer (1998) have critiqued Myers-Scotton's work for this very point, arguing that the significance of codeswitching itself is not something that can be established prior to a conversation since participants can use codes as conversational tools for managing interaction. I partly agree with Myers-Scotton's view since there is evidence that language choices in East Africa are legitimized (or not) in certain domains of social life; however, as the following chapters show, there is also evidence that speakers use their creativity to cross domain boundaries, usually for pragmatic effect. Her framework does not explain how or why codes change in their markedness across time or across domains, but the data I discuss in the next several chapters often illustrates that speakers appropriate unmarked multilingual talk to establish new, marked meanings, and they also re-entextualize marked and unmarked codes into new domains, thereby creating new indexicalities.

Multivocality in Tanzania

As a means of understanding the development of mixed languages in Tanzania, it is helpful to examine several varieties of CS and LM that have been well documented by Blommaert (1992, 1999a). Rather than viewing language mixing from a grammatical perspective, Blommaert chooses to see language use in multilingual societies as the performance of identities in relation to the distribution of power-related elements. He explains that 'the power that makes resources accessible to certain people also allows them to imbue these resources with power and exert power by means of them. Concretely: someone who speaks a "rare" or "exclusive" code (e.g. "high" English in Tanzania) can use knowledge of this code to include or exclude people from certain material or symbolic benefits' (Blommaert, 1999a: 163). To illustrate his points, he describes 'Campus Kiswahili' and 'Tough Talk', two distinct varieties of English-infused Swahili, to show how language differences index the disparity in levels of education and different kinds of identification among the speakers.

Blommaert calls 'Campus Kiswahili' a prestige variety of 'English-interfered Swahili', both because of its grammar, which he describes as the combination of standard English with standard Swahili, and because of its speakers, the educated elites at the University of Dar es Salaam (Blommaert, 1992; 1999a). Example 10 shows how Campus Kiswahili maintains a Swahili grammatical frame, and how words imported from English retain their grammatical subcategorizations, such as the static verb 'nationalized', and the use of English plurals which fit into a Swahili frame. In other words, the language mixing here does not disrupt the quite standard Swahili basis of the utterances.

(10) Campus Kiswahili (Blommaert, 1999a: 166)
Kana kwamba private schools zote baada ya kupata au baada ya uhuru
as though private schools pl.-all after getting or after independence
Azimio la Arusha zilikuwa nationalized?
declaration of Arusha they-pst.-be nationalized
'As though all private schools after independence or after the Arusha Declaration were nationalized.'

Though the switches are not obligatory, speakers of Campus Kiswahili often report experiencing difficulty in keeping English out of their Swahili, as the following quote from a Campus Kiswahili speaker attests (Blommaert, 1992: 61):

(11) Sisi tunasema practically Kiswahili sanifu.
We we-prs-speak practically Swahili pure
'We speak practically pure Swahili.'

Blommaert takes the view that the overall significance of the language alternation is not so much in what pragmatic work it might be doing, but rather, how it marks the people who speak it as elites. Despite the rhetoric about Swahili and the convictions held towards its value, Blommaert also notes that the university scholars' own language use is contradictory to the principles of the socialist period in Tanzania. He explains that Campus Kiswahili marks them as members of a group which has restricted access to high-status economic and linguistic resources. Campus Kiswahili distinguishes them from less educated speakers who use more hybrid forms, such as 'Tough Talk', which is closer to a FL in structure. Blommaert argues that this distinction is ideological in nature, and despite the ideological underpinnings of the socialist movement in Tanzania, the ways that the kinds of English are incorporated into the language among both groups reflects social class divisions.

What Blommaert (1999a: 174) calls 'Tough Talk' is the variety spoken by youths who have acquired English 'in bits and pieces, mainly from radio broadcasts of western music, records and cassettes, sometimes from publicity billboards or from a movie'. He explains that their bilingual speech marks their identity as belonging to an entirely different social class. Such language is also referred to as *Lugha ya Mitaani* (literally, 'street language') in everyday reference by Tanzanians. In their introduction to a rather comprehensive dictionary of this variety, Reuster-Jahn and Kießling (2006) describe Street Swahili as a language of the youth, created and spread through *daladalas* (minibuses) and in *kijiweni* (hanging out spots for unemployed, typically male, youth).

Popular culture and the media are prime sources for spreading forms of this language. Reuster-Jahn and Kießling explain that it is a marker of youth identity, but as is the case with Sheng, many words are known by the older generation, an indication of a shift in the status of this 'street' language to something more common. In terms of origins, Street Swahili is often the result of semantic shift and lexical elaboration of borrowings from English in addition to hyperbole, metaphors and language play involving Swahili and English. Reuster-Jahn and Kießling assert that Street Swahili is not the same as codeswitching, in spite of the many uses of English, since it is obligatory, rather than optional. For this reason, it qualifies most clearly as a FL, utilizing Auer's (1999) framework. Moreover, they argue that this language is distinct from borrowing since it involves such a high degree of transformation in meaning. The examples in (12) and (13) illustrate Tough Talk (Blommaert, 1999a: 173):

(12) *Unajipraudipraudi* = u-na-ji-praudi-praudi (you-pres-reflex.-proud-proud)

(13) *Nitacheki kwamba toto iko fresh* = Ni-ta-cheki kwamba toto i-ko fresh (I-will-check if child is-there fresh, 'I will see if there is a pretty girl')

In spite of the many similarities with Sheng, Reuster-Jahn and Kießling (2006) explain that Street Swahili is quite distinct from Sheng in its linguistic and social aspects. They explain that while *Lugha ya Mitaani* in Tanzania is based on manipulations of Swahili and, to a lesser degree, English, Sheng in Kenya is a hybrid of many local languages such as Kikuyu, Dholuo and Maasai, plus Swahili and English. Sheng involves more grammatical restructuring than Tanzania's street language, including many morphological innovations. They describe Sheng as 'the creative effort by the youth to do two things at the same time: to appropriate the ex-colonial official language English and to indigenise widespread Swahili to make it an acceptable medium for communication and identification to all Kenyan youth, irrespective of their partly antagonistic ethnic backgrounds' (Reuster-Jahn & Kießling, 2006: 74). On the other hand, since Swahili is a pan-ethnic language for Tanzanians, they claim that Street Swahili does not have to fill the function of an ethnically neutral code, as is the case with Sheng. Reuster-Jahn and Kießling argue that unlike Sheng, Street Swahili has not needed to perform the function of decolonizing English since Swahili fulfilled those functions from the time of Independence.

While there are differences in the language politics of Kenya and Tanzania, the apolitical quality of Street Swahili is highly debatable, and evidence of perspectives toward English as a colonial language can be found amidst neutral views toward the language. In the song 'Swanglish' by the Tanzanian pop group Wakilisha, for example, each of the singers in the group takes a different stance on English in Tanzania. In (14a), one of the singers praises the language for its creativity, using some forms of Street Swahili (in bold) but in (14b), a rapper in the group remarks upon its associations with the colonial past.

(14a) *Najiuliza hili swali* I ask myself this question
Sipati jibu kamili But I don't have the answer
Kimombo *Kiswahili* **English**-Swahili
Tuongeze basi Kichina Let's add Chinese even
Tuzidi pata jina We'll keep coming up with
 names for it –
Ni malipo nayo ni **mabobishi** It's currency and **status**
Wabongo *twamwaga* **Tanzanians**, let's keep adding
Swanglish to **Swanglish**

(14b) *Mkoloni katufilisi* The colonists bankrupted us
Kiuchumi na kiakili Economically and intellectually
Anataka tukiri They wanted us to concede
Tuna nuksi, tusishamiri We are under a spell, let's
 not be destroyed
Mababu zetu, walitekwa Our grandfathers, when they
 were captured
waliondoka wanalia They left crying
Siku hizi, ukipata viza These days, if you get a visa

Akiondoka unashangilia	When you leave, you celebrate
Tuitunze lugha yetu, ikibidi	Let's protect our language, it should
kuganga mara	be strong

The lyrics refer to slavery in mentioning how 'our grandfathers, when they were captured, They left crying'. The lyrics go on to criticize the enthusiasm for English in Tanzania as well, relating the idea of 'English without money' (i.e. development) akin to 'making racket'.

(14c)	Tunamfagilia mzungu	We praise the white man
	Sisi tuna shida tele	(while) we have plenty of problems
	Kiingereza bila hela	English without money
	Ni sawa na kupiga kelele	It's the same as making racket

Whether or not English is seen as a language of modern creativity or a legacy of the colonial past is a question the rest of the chapters in this book explore. Just as the lyrics in 'Swanglish' indicate, there is evidence that both perspectives co-exist.

The co-presence of forms like Street Swahili, standard Swahili, ethnic languages and English in Tanzania, and Sheng, Swahili, ethnic languages and English in Kenya allows speakers who have some fluency in any of these languages to exploit their multilingual knowledge in multivocal ways. Languages in East Africa do not tend to say in compartmentalized boxes of di- or triglossia. Instead, speakers, authors, politicians and artists blend them together, switch back and forth, and insert appropriate elements in what they deem to be the 'right' context. The next four chapters examine the result of this multivocality across a range of domains of use.

Chapter 3
Double-Voices in the Workplace

This chapter analyzes face-to-face interactions that involve Swahili and English among workers at a newspaper office in Dar es Salaam, Tanzania. I examine the data using an ethnographically informed and critically oriented approach to naturally-occurring interactions following work such as Blommaert (2005a) and Rampton (1995). I ground the analysis of conversation by starting with the microlevel aspects of interaction and, through interviews, observations and stimulated recall sessions, I investigate the layers of meaning tied to the microlevel of talk. In the situated context of the newspaper office, the conversational data show that the use of English among the journalists does not evoke the voice of colonialism or neo-colonialism. Instead, their use of the language is a hybrid alternative to the confining associations that speaking either 'pure' Swahili or 'pure' English would yield. Consequently, their speech provides a good example of what Pennycook (2001) has described as *post-colonial performativity*, wherein alternation between English and Swahili and hybrid forms of language resist and appropriate previously colonialist discourses tied to English. Among the journalists, the historically 'marked code' of English appears to be fully localized by its own community of speakers. From a Bakhtinian perspective, then, the journalists have *double-voiced* the language, thereby making it their own:

> The word in language is half someone else's. It becomes 'one's own' only when the speaker populates it with his own intention, his own accent, when he appropriates the word, adapting it to his own semantic and expressive intention. Prior to this moment of appropriation, the word does not exist in a neutral and impersonal language (it is not, after all, out of a dictionary that the speakers gets his words!) but rather it exists in other people's mouths, in other people's contexts, serving other people's intentions: it is from there that one must take the word, and make it one's own. (Bakhtin, 1981: 293–294)

Double-voicing is found in the ways that language mixing is used to create new meanings in *Swahinglish*, a term Tanzanians often use interchangeably with *Swanglish* and *Swingereza* (< Swahili + *Kiingereza* 'English') that describes a way of speaking which encompasses mixed language forms, including Blommaert's 'Tough Talk' and 'Campus Kiswahili', as well as English-infused Street Swahili (described in Chapter 2). Swahinglish is distinct from Sheng in that it is typically based on Swahili and English, whereas Sheng draws on these languages and more including Dholuo, Kikuyu and Kalenjin. In addition to Swahinglish, the workers at the newspaper office made use of monolectal forms of English and Swahili, which afforded them a three-way distinction in codes that they could use to achieve interactional goals. Though English does not appear to carry meanings of the 'other', the journalists used strategic contrasts between Swahinglish and English, Swahili and English, and Swahinglish and Swahili.

On rare occasions, I recorded interactions in the office involving ethnic languages such as Kichagga and Kihaya, which were sometimes used monolectally but other times mixed with the journalists' other codes. Hybridity involving the workers' ethnic languages shows that hybridization is not limited to languages brought to Tanzania during the colonial period. Of course, indigenous language mixing is a common phenomenon in multilingual societies (*cf.* Blom & Gumperz, 1972; Wolfson & Manes, 1985). However, since the bulk of the journalists' conversations did not involve ethnic languages, and because of my own linguistic limitations, I chose to focus on interactions comprised of Swahili, English and Swahinglish.

The workers frequently juxtaposed two or more of their languages to manage their social relations, as we will see below. However, unlike what Myers-Scotton (1993b) has proposed, I will argue that English is sometimes used as an unmarked choice among the journalists and is treated as one of their local resources for managing their social relationships in harmonious ways. To make this point, I first present excerpts from the corpus that illustrate how the journalists employ a great deal of monolingual English in their greetings to one another. Drawing on ethnographic information, I argue that when the journalists switch to English to greet one another, they establish a social order in the office that suits their situated needs. In addition, I show how the journalists exploit the contrasts between English and Swahili in various forms of language play, often creating humor. This language play establishes a jocular atmosphere, alleviates boredom and fatigue, and it also mitigates acts involving criticism of one another's professional work. Both kinds of strategic use of English in this workplace reveal multiple 'in-group' functions and provide strong evidence that these journalists experience *ownership* (Higgins, 2003; Peirce, 1995) of English, rather than oppression in the form of imperialism. Hence, in this particular context, English cannot be said to represent the voice of the 'other'.

While there are solid arguments for reappropriation of English among the journalists, the larger context in which these journalists live and work also plays a role in determining the meaning of their speech. After all, even though they spend many hours working together, they also spend time outside of the office walls. In considering the larger heteroglossic context of Swahili and English in Tanzania, it is easy to see that the multivocality in the office is limited by the values accorded to different kinds of mixed language in Dar es Salaam. The result is that the journalists contribute to *elite closure* (Myers-Scotton, 1993b), the establishment of sociolectal boundaries within a society based on speakers' access to education, social mobility and steady employment. Therefore, this chapter demonstrates how English has been reappropriated for its local context, yet on a macrolevel, continues to reproduce class divisions inherited from the pre-independence period. In speaking a variety that demonstrates one's monolingual abilities in both languages, the journalists participate in micro and macrolevel multivocality, as they can double-identify with the heteroglossia of urban, Swahinglish Tanzania while also claiming membership in an elite/global world of transnational English speakers.

The Tanzanian Gazette

For six months in 2001, I spent three to four days a week at the office of *The Tanzanian Gazette* (a pseudonym), a daily English-medium newspaper published in Dar es Salaam, Tanzania. My fieldwork included observations and field notes, interviews, recordings of conversation (video and audio) and stimulated recall sessions with the journalists. As might be expected of people in the newspaper business, all of the staff were incredibly busy people who spent a great deal of time with one another, as they worked 10 and 12-hour days regularly, six to seven days of each week. The demands on their time created a quite cohesive, homogeneous group of participants who all knew one another very well and provided a setting where conversations were likely to take place about a range of topics, including personal matters. The ethnographic nature of my fieldwork required me to fully immerse myself in the lives of the employees. The recordings of natural conversation took place in the office, but I also attended meetings and events with journalists around the city when possible.

The newspaper office was in the city center, surrounded by a large printing business on one side and a set of offices including a copy shop, a book publisher and several cafés on the other. The office employed over 70 people, counting those who worked in advertising, circulation, the business office, the manager's office, typesetting and the newsroom.

After an initial month of observation without recording, I began to place my digital camera in a corner of one of the three rooms after the daily post mortem meeting, and then I would then leave the room. Most of the conversations I analyze below come from the 'sports room', where the majority of the computers were placed for typing up stories. The sports room was the office where the editor of the sports page was stationed, and it was also the room where many of the staff writing stories on sports and entertainment spent their time. It was the place to go if workers wanted to be loud or if they wanted to relax. In an interview with one of the junior male journalists, Chema, described the sports room as *kijiweni*, a 'street' Swahili way of expressing the street corner, the front stoop, or any suitable place to hang out and chat. Indeed, this room proved to be a great site for capturing a multitude of conversations, only some of which were about work.

In Search of Contextualization Cues

To examine how the range of codes employed by the journalists and editors helped to produce a heteroglossic environment, I analyzed *contextualizaton cues*, a concept that Gumperz (1982; Blom & Gumperz, 1972) developed in his work on interactional sociolinguistics. Gumperz (1982: 162) defines contextualization as 'the identification of specific conversational exchanges as representative of socio-culturally familiar activities'. The surface structures of linguistic messages are the cues which signal the context and are a way to alert participants to the social and situational context. Gumperz explains that people learn how to interpret the meanings of contextualization cues through interactions with one another and socialization in a community. Contextualization cues may occur at all linguistic levels, from phonetic to syntactic, and they may be extra-linguistic, involving gestures and gaze. In his work on bilingual speech, Gumperz (1982) shows how language alternation in a variety of contexts and involving a number of languages does the contextual work of signaling the use of reported speech, qualifying messages, emphasizing and specifying the addressee.

Building on these functions, I examined the corpus of Swahili-English speech to determine what sorts of meanings were contextualized through language switching or language choice. I was particularly interested to find interactions that would indicate how the speakers were producing their local interpretations of specific contexts. I also turned to ethnographic methods to uncover additional meanings produced by language mixing.

Interpreting the Data

As a cultural outsider to Tanzania, I have found that the use of ethnographic information is crucial for my understanding of the pragmatic effects of codeswitching and hybrid language use. Although I can see for myself how language alternation aligns with conversational work or pragmatic functions, my restricted cultural knowledge limits my ability to interpret the linguistic or social significance of such language alternation, especially when that significance may be unspoken. As Gumperz (1982: 99) states, 'Codeswitching provides evidence for the existence of underlying, unverbalized assumptions about social categories, which differ systematically from overtly expressed values or attitudes'. Therefore, I turned to retrospective interviews involving stimulated recall as well as interviews with the journalists in order to rely on their perspectives as much as possible in interpreting the meanings of their talk. I found that it was necessary to use stimulated recall methods (SRM) to uncover some of these unverbalized assumptions, and to see whether the participants would even notice the switches and comment upon them as carrying meaning.

I based my SRM on approaches taken by scholars such as Erickson and Schultz (1982), Rampton (1995), Tyler (1995), and Pomerantz et al. (1997), researchers who asked the actual participants to review the data in which they participated. During the sessions, I showed the participants video recorded interactions in which they participated, and I asked them comment on them. These sessions gave me insight into what types of linguistic phenomena were occurring, and the social significance that the participants might have extracted from the language use. During the sessions, I asked the participants very broad questions such as 'What's going on here?' and 'Can you tell me what you think about the language use in this example?' I encouraged the participants to do the majority of the talking and refrained from giving my opinions as much as possible, though it became necessary to ask more pointed questions with some of the participants. I recorded these sessions using an audio recorder and later transcribed them as well.

Swahinglish Conversations in the Workplace

The different forms of language use in the office created a heteroglossic environment that involved varieties of Swahili and English, as well as hybrid combinations of the two. Many of the conversations among journalists involved heavy use of English insertions, and can be characterized as 'English-interfered Swahili', very similar to what Blommaert (1992) described in his study of Campus Swahili at the University of Dar es Salaam. This kind of language mixing does not appear to contextualize the situation in any specific pragmatic manner, but instead, is an unmarked form of LM (see Chapter 2 for a discussion of these terms). This way of speaking is often described as *Swahinglish* by Tanzanians themselves. The first example below comes from a conversation between two senior journalists who are discussing a recent anti-globalization rally and the prospects of writing an investigative report about the event. For the sake of showing the degree of English in the dialogue, words with English origins are in bold for Excerpts 1–3 (see Appendix for transcription conventions following Atkinson & Heritage, 1984).

(1) Swahinglish in a discussion of yesterday's news

1   Irene: **The whole world**   *walikuwa*   *wana***contest**   **against globalization**
             the whole world   they-pst-be   they-prs-contest   against globalization
             'The whole world was protesting globalization'
2   Luther: *Ehe* **globalization** *ya nini*,
             yes globalization of what
             'What kind of globalization?'
3   Irene: *Hii* **world globalization** *unajuwa.*   (*Ina***print**)   **capitalism**
             this world   globalization you-prs-know   it-prs-print   capitalism
             'This world globalization, you know? This (newspaper) says capitalism,'
4   Luther: **Okey.**[1]
             'okay'
5   Irene: *Kwa maana   ina***privatize**   **the betterment** *ya wafanyakazi wote duniani*
             for meaning it-prs-privatize the betterment of pl-worker all world-loc
             'Because of privatizing, the betterment of workers' conditions all over the world'
6   Luther: **Okey.**
             'okay'
7   Irene: *Yaa   kwa sababu labda   kwenye nini   kwenye* **international** news *ya leo.*
             yeah, for reason maybe in   what in   international news of today
             'Yeah, so maybe you could write a story about it for the international news section today'

The use of English words in (1) should not be attributed to a lack of equivalents in Swahili. In my discussions with Irene and Luther, both told me they know *utandawazi* ('globalization'), *ubepari* ('capitalism'), and *privatize* ('kubinafsisha'), but they described this way of speaking as 'ndivyo ilivyo' ('how things are') in the office.

Another example of Swahinglish in the office comes from a conversation involving the giving of advice. In (2), Kalembo is advising Chema about how much time to spend in a meeting. Like previous studies of English-interfered Swahili have shown (e.g. Blommaert, 1992, 1999a), English words are integrated into the Swahili morphosyntax, as in line 1, where the verb 'to brief' is inserted where a Swahili verbal root would appear. In line 2, we see the use of an English adverbial phrase that also does not alter the basic Swahili structure of the sentence.

(2) Advice-giving at work

1 **Chema:** *Inawezekana   mimi huenda   sikuwa***brief**   *vizuri.*
  it-prs-possible I   hab-go   I.neg-pst-them-brief well
  'It's possible that when I go I don't give them enough information'.

2 **Kalembo:** *Lakini Chema, mimi nafikiri*   **to be safe** *budget*   *mimi- ikifika kumi na mbili   kasa robo*
  but Chema I   I.prs-think to be safe, budget   I-   if-it-arrive ten and two less quarter
  'But Chema, I think to be safe, you should budget, I – if it gets to be 11:45,

3   *itafaa.*
  it-fut-do
  'it will suffice'

Another excerpt from the sports room shows a similar degree of mixing without performing any sort of pragmatic function. In (3), a photo has prompted a conversation among the journalists about a group of Tanzanian soccer players who imitate western fashions without an understanding of their western contexts, such as the need for gloves during cold winters in Europe. Swahili equivalents of all of the English words are available in the journalists' lexicons, but they choose a more hybrid code.

(3) Swahinglish in a discussion of soccer players

1 **Leonard:** *hawamwelewi*   hh. *wanasema   nini   kwa hiyo hao wakimwona   mtu*
  they.neg-obj-understand hh. they-prs-say what for   that they they-if-obj-see person
  'they don't understand and they say what, therefore, they when they see someone'

2   *amevaa*   **gloves** *anafikiri*   hh. *ni*   **style** *kumbe wale   wamevaa*   **gloves**
  s/he-has-wear gloves s/he-prs-think hh. it.is style wow   they-there they-have-wear gloves
  'wearing gloves, they think that it's a style to follow,   and all of a sudden they decide to wear gloves too'.

3   *wakati wa wakati ..hh bari- wa* **winter** *kule*   *kuna   baridi hh.*
  time   of time   cold- of winter   over.there   there.is cold
  'During, during the cold peri- during winter it is cold   there (in Europe)'.

((talk omitted))

7 **Peter:** *Hilo   wala   si   kwa wachezaji   tu   sema* **majority** *wa   Tanzania.*
  it-dem nor   neg for   players   only say majority of   Tanzania
  'This isn't for sports players only; admit it, it's the   majority of Tanzania'.

While much of the English-infused Swahili conversation resembles (1) through (3) above in that no particular contextualizations are performed through the hybrid code, at other times, the journalists' use of English constructs meaningful social relationships. In the next section, I present excerpts that demonstrate how longer English insertions were used to manage the local social order of the office.

Local Social Order through Language Alternation

In addition to Swahinglish, another aspect of heteroglossia that can be found in conversations is *layered codeswitching* (Meeuwis & Blommaert, 1998) between Swahinglish and Swahili-English. Use of English in greetings was particularly noticeable among the journalists. In most Swahili-speaking contexts, greetings are considered to be very important for showing one's respect to others and for establishing appropriate social relations (Yahya-Othman, 1995). Outside the realm of contexts such as busy newspaper offices, greetings often take many minutes, involving a series of ritualized question and answer sequences regarding the well-being of one's family, one's farm and one's neighbors. Many people who live in Dar es Salaam often employ English in their greetings, and the use of English can be seen as a contextualization cue that indexes their identities as urbanites who live in a fast-paced society. It comes to no surprise that the constantly busy journalists use English quite frequently, as shown in the excerpts below.

In (4), the sports editor, Gideon, has walked in the door and greets everyone present in the sports room by making a comment about the passing of time. The journalists are often concerned with the time of day given the pressing deadlines they face. Gideon's greeting here is a commentary on how long everyone has been working, including himself, and this sentiment is affirmed by Leonard in line 2. In line 3, Gideon greets Leonard in a more personal manner, calling him 'Simba friend', a reference to his knowledge that Leonard is a fan of the Tanzanian soccer club named *Simba* ('lions'). The greeting also makes sense in the sports office, where many articles and features on Simba and other soccer teams have been written, edited, and discussed with great interest by all (as exemplified in Excerpt 3 above).

(4) 'How are you Simba friend?'
1   Gideon: Is it good morning afternoon or evening?
2   Leonard: All together.
3   Gideon: *Simba* friend. (.) How are you *Simba* friend? ((to Leonard))

4		*Eti Chema alikuwa hapa?*
		hey, Chema he-pst-be here
		'Was Chema here?'
5	**Fulgence:**	Ehe yeah yeah.
6	**Gideon:**	*Ameenda wapi. Kwenye mkutano?*
		he-pfc-go where to meeting
		'Where did he go? To a meeting?'

Sometimes, the journalists would use the common Muslim greeting used in all parts of the Islamic world, *Salaam Aliekum* ('peace be upon you'), and its pronunciation variants. However, in the examples that occurred in my corpus, English would follow such greetings rather quickly, cutting short the niceties. In (5), Baraba greets his fellow Muslim colleague Kwaro using the Arabic-origin greeting, and quickly moves on to the business at hand of finding 'the big man', that is, the chief sub-editor. Kwaro takes the opportunity to play with the ambiguity of Baraba's question, counting himself as one of the 'big' men in the office. The interaction is soon interrupted, though, when Baraba's attention is pulled away by the news editor, and Swahili reframes the activity.

(5) Greeting 'the big man'

1	**Baraba:**	*Salaam waliekum.* Where is the big man here, Mister Kwaro.
		'peace unto you'
2	**Kwaro:**	The other one.
3	**Baraba:**	Another big man is there.
4	**Abdul:**	(Baraba),
5	**Baraba:**	*Nakuja eh.*
		I.prs-come eh.
		'I'm coming, alright'.

Similarly, the journalists in (6) use a common Swahili salutation to greet one another. While Luther's line 3 seems to indicate that a lengthy greeting may be on the horizon, Mbwilo's response in English is fairly successful at curtailing it.

(6) Swahili to English greetings

1	**Luther:**	*Mambo?*
		things
		'How are things?'
2	**Mbwilo:**	*Safi.*
		clean
		'Fine'.

3	Luther:	*Za saa hizi.*
		of hours these
		'How have you been recently?'
4	bwilo:	Fine.
5	Luther:	How is everything?
6	Mbwilo:	Not bad.

Excerpt (7) displays how the main business of producing a newspaper is carried out in Swahili and Swahinglish, and how greetings take the form of asides through their linguistic mediums. One of the sub-editors, Mwema, is involved in a negotiation with his colleagues about the use of a particular photo. Gideon enters the room and greets him, entirely in English.

(7) Greeting as interruption of work

1	Mwema:	*Mtaturuhusu kuweka hizo picha* about military armaments.
		you.pl-fut-us-allow to-put these pictures about military armaments.
		'Will you allow us to put these pictures about military armaments'.
2		*Aloo huyu anaitwaje =*
		Hello, this.person s/he-prs-call-psv
		'Hey, what's this person called?'
3	Gideon:	= Mwema.
4	Mwema:	Yes.
5	Gideon:	A man behind the Tanzania Gazette success.
6	Mwema:	Yes.
7	Gideon:	Recent success.

In other interactions, the journalists would greet one another through asking a question or making an observation about the work being accomplished in the office that day in English, rather than explicitly greeting their colleagues. This sort of greeting appears to allow speakers to maintain the pragmatics of Swahili, which requires speakers to acknowledge one another's presence or absence whenever entering or leaving a room, but in an indirect and quick manner.

(8) Indirectness in greetings

1	Mwema:	How is the business of reading? ((carries on with his work))
2	Ntabile:	*Ehee.*
		((acknowledgment token))

I reviewed some of the above excerpts with Gideon to ask him why so many greetings in the office were done in English when it was obvious that everyone knew how to greet one another in Swahili. I was particularly interested in his answer since he was one of the main users of English for greetings in the office. In responding, he remarked upon the deference system involved in Swahili greetings, which requires that younger people use the respectful *shikamoo* (literally, 'I hold your feet'). I was quite familiar with this greeting and tended to overuse it myself in order to avoid any possible pragmatic gaffes. Gideon expressed that he is not comfortable with the hierarchical relationships that this greeting creates, no matter if he is in the lower or higher position. In the excerpts below from the stimulated recall sessions, the original data is first reproduced, followed by a translation. English elements of the talk remain un-italicized in the original and underlined in the translations.

Wengi wanapenda kutumia Kiingereza hapa. Wengi wanaogopa kuamkia watu 'shikamoo' kwa sababu, kwa mfano mimi naona kumwambia mtu 'shikamoo' namwambia 'good morning sir'. *Inanipa heshima zaidi yaani inaonyesha kwamba siku-. Kama yule bwana anataka nimsalimie kwa sababu ni mkubwa lakini na sasa sipendi kumwambia 'shikamoo' na yeye hapendi 'shikamoo' kwasababu tuna- ni marafiki* we are friends. *Tunakaa sehemu tunakunywa wote yeye anaona nikimwambia 'shikamoo' namzeesha sana. Vile vile hapendi 'shikamoo' anasema tunamzeesha anakuwa mzee.* I don't like to look old I want to look young, so just say how are you.

Many people like to use English here (in greetings) because many are afraid of greeting people with 'shikamoo', because, for example, I think to tell someone 'shikamoo', I tell them '<u>good morning sir</u>', it gives me more respect. In other words, it shows that I have not – like if a person wants me to greet him because he is older, but – now if I don't like greeting him with 'shikamoo', and he doesn't like it either, because we are friends, <u>we are friends</u>. We sit together, we drink together, and so if I tell him 'shikamoo', I make him seem very old. Even he might not like it and will tell me that I'm making him old, he's like a really old man. <u>I don't like to look old I want to look young, so just say how are you.</u>

Gideon's resistance toward Swahili cultural norms through the use of English is an interesting case of reappropriation of English. Although it could be claimed that he has been indoctrinated by a western culture that devalues hierarchical relationships, he is clearly making use of a local resource to contextualize the situation as he desires.

Humor through Codeswitching

Heteroglossia was frequently produced through talk involving humor in the office (also see Higgins, 2007). Switches into English seemed to help contextualize the situations as playful, light-hearted and jocular. The journalists enjoyed teasing whenever possible, a practice which surely alleviated their stress in producing articles day in and day out with tight deadlines. Mbwilo, a senior journalist, and Gideon (referred to in the transcript by his family name, Nderumo), the sports page editor, often joked around. Sometimes this teasing was an indirect way to criticize Mbwilo's work as a novice photojournalist. In the following excerpt, Mbwilo has just given Gideon some photos of a recent flood in the city in which the people pictured are smiling, rather than looking distressed. It is clear that the photos were not taken of people 'in the moment', which is apparently what Gideon had expected.

(9) The best picture

1 Gideon: *Halafu Mbwilo hizi picha za kupanga hizi bwana siyo nzuri Mbwilo.*
and.then Mbwilo these photos of to-plan these sir/friend neg. good Mbwilo
'Now Mbwilo, these staged photos my friend, these are no good Mbwilo.'

2 Mbwilo: *Hivi Nderumo ushukuru Mungu hawa ndiyo wa mwisho kuingia*
this.way Nderumo thanks god these indeed of end to-enter
'Now Nderumo, I thank God that these last people to enter were there'

3 Gideon: Of course [actually

4 Mbwilo: [*Tulikuwa tumelambwa* [*tu*
we-pst-be we-pfc-lick-psv only
'We had been defeated (in our quest to get good photos of the flood)'

5 Gideon: [*basi ngoja nikuambie,*
enough wait I-you-tell
'Alright, let me tell you'

6 Mbwilo: *Eeh.*
'go ahead'

7 Chema: [*Tumeshachelewa,*
we-pfc-late-psv
'We're already late'

8 Gideon: [*Kwa* information *hii ndiyo imeonekana tangu uingie* Gazette *hapa*
for information this yes it-pfc-appear since you-enter Gazette here
'For your information, indeed, it seems that since you have worked here at the Gazette',

9 this is the best picture you have done

10 ((Laughter))

11 Noreen: *Lalalalalalalalala* ((high pitched))

A stimulated recall session with Gideon confirmed the scolding and yet simultaneously joking tone of his 'compliment' to Mbwilo. He emphasized the bad judgment Mbwilo used in staging the photo, but he agreed it was a form of *utani* ('teasing') in the end.

Sasa wale wamepatwa na shida yaani maji yameingia kwenye nyumba itakuwaje? Wacheke kwanza kumimina hivi halafu wanacheka siyo rahisi. Wanacheka inaonyesha aliwaambia chekeni basi kidogo akawapiga. Sasa akaambiwa umewapanga watu ndiyo maana ... ilikuwa ni utani.

Now for those people who have got problems, meaning the water has really entered the house, how will it seem? Maybe they laugh when the water trickles in, but to laugh isn't easy. Their laughing shows that he told them to laugh a little so he could take a photo. Now, (in the video), he was told 'you have staged the photo' meaning that ... it was teasing.

In (10), junior journalist Mary asks Mbwilo to read the article she has drafted. Using Swahinglish, she admits that she copied a great deal of the article, and Mbwilo responds in English. Here, humor is achieved in part through metaphorical language framed by a switch to English, perhaps to make the advice more secretive. The switch also seems to mitigate the (very soft) reprimand that Mbwilo is giving Mary for her admitted plagiarism.

(10) 'If you are sweeping'

1	Mary:	*Naomba usome yote.*
		I.prs-beg you-read.sbj all
		'Please read this entire article'
2	Mbwilo:	*Haya.*
		'okay'
3	Mary:	*Nikukabidhi.*
		I-you-entrust
		'I entrust you with it'
4	Mbwilo:	*Haya.*
		'okay'
5	Mary:	*Kwa sababu nime*copy *kote bila* xxx
		for reason I-pfc-copy all without
		'Because I've copied it all without'
6	Mbwilo:	<If you are sweeping (.) don't allow your broom to go too far under the bed. (.) You
7		might retrieve unwanted objects.>
8	Mary:	((Laughter))

The next two excerpts show how English is juxtaposed with Swahinglish in order to encourage one another at work. These excerpts also resemble the praise in (5) and (7) where greetings are carried out through complimentary language. In (11), Chema encourages Kalembo, who is under pressure to meet a deadline. On this particular day, Chema had been made acting sports editor by Gideon. Chema's encouragement here, and his switching into English, help to contextualize this temporary identity for Chema. Through what he says and how he says it, he takes on the role of the person in charge.

(11) 'A commendable job'

1	Chema:	Hallow mzee, kamati walimwamini nanii hapa ndani?
		hello elder committee they-pst-obj-trust um here inside
		'Hello my man, did a committee entrust someone in here (with authority)?'
2		Kalem, you are doing a commendable job though. Keep it up!
3	Kalembo:	Just wait.
4	Chema:	Wee endelea tu.
		you continue just
		'Just keep going'

In (12), Chema expresses his concern to Kalembo about the need for a long article to fill up the sports page which he is in charge of for the day. He encourages Kalembo, calling him 'our lead man' in line 3, and then tells Kalembo that he hopes that the article will be as long as an Anaconda snake. The article Kalembo is writing is about a sports team which does not appear to be doing well at the time. In the midst of Chema's playful language and encouragement, Kalembo tries to interrupt, using Swahinglish to do so. Chema continues with his train of thought, and Kalembo responds by expressing that the story is not a very long one, which is not good news for Chema. Chema switches back to Swahili in line 10, announcing *'Imemstua jamaa!'* ('the team has shocked him'), which refers to an imagined situation in which the team Kalembo is writing about becomes formidable players. The switch, along with the content of the utterance and its emphatic delivery, contextualizes this turn as playful and funny. Chema then continues with his Swahinglish recommendation that Kalembo include predictions about an upcoming sporting event in order to lengthen the story. He finishes up with an English-medium utterance in line 11 in which he recommends that Kalembo make a ridiculous prediction about the team. The silliness of the talk is oriented to through the laughter, but Kalembo re-contextualizes the mood through a return to Swahinglish and an orientation to the team's lack of popularity.

(12) 'As long as ... an Anaconda'

1	Chema:	*Nanii* Kalembo-man?
		'um Kalembo-man'
2	Kalembo:	*Hallow.*
		'hello'
3	Chema:	So that is our lead man,

4	**Kalembo:**	((Laughs))
5	**Chema:**	I hope it is very long one of the longest ((referring to Kalembo's article))
6		As long as the snout- snake.
7	**Kalembo:**	Yeah. *Hallow sasa nanii,*
		'yeah hello now um'
8	**Chema:**	Anaconda snake.
9	**Kalembo:**	It is just a ten para.
10	**Chema:**	*Imemstua jamaa.* Suppose it take on this long *ukasema na* it seems *kwamba*
		it-pfc-him-surprise person suppose it take on this long you-cns-say and it seems that
		'The team has shocked him. Suppose the story becomes really long, you could say it seems that'
11		these guys are going to win this game.
12		((Laughter))
13	**Kalembo:**	*Wengi wako against them sasa [nasikia kwamba-*
		many they-loc against them now I.prs-hear that
		'Many people are against them now, I hear that-'

Excerpt (13) shows how the workers would often use English in making requests of one another, but in a coy manner. In the conversation, Luther and Mshule are both standing by the tea and coffee station in the office, and Mshule is pouring himself a cup of tea. In line 3, Luther asks Mshule to pour him some tea as well, tacking on 'as a friend' at the end of his request. Mshule is one of the eldest men in the office, and he is the newspaper's librarian; Luther is a college-educated senior journalist. Though these two men chat regularly in the office, their relationship is limited to a working relationship. Hence, Luther's use of 'as a friend' in (13) appears to be a rather explicit contextualization which mitigates the imposition of his request on his more senior colleague.

(13) 'As a friend'

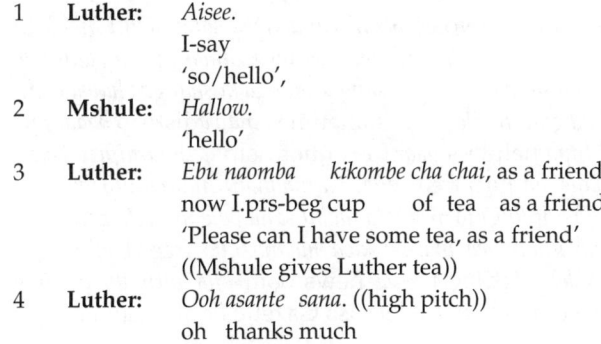

1	**Luther:**	*Aisee.*
		I-say
		'so/hello',
2	**Mshule:**	*Hallow.*
		'hello'
3	**Luther:**	*Ebu naomba kikombe cha chai,* as a friend.
		now I.prs-beg cup of tea as a friend
		'Please can I have some tea, as a friend'
		((Mshule gives Luther tea))
4	**Luther:**	*Ooh asante sana.* ((high pitch))
		oh thanks much
		'Ooh, thanks a lot'

Finally, we see the use of English alongside very explicit forms of teasing one another just for the sake of alleviating stress in the office. In (14), the journalists had been working a long day, and it was clear that Chema in particular was a bit 'punch-drunk' from having worked so many hours. After a Swahili-medium greeting, Chema abruptly tells Frankie 'I want to kiss you', an utterance that is followed by hearty laughter. Kalembo, who joined in during the laughter, immediately gets on with his work and recontextualizes the mood of the talk in the next turn, however, when he complains aloud about the article he is writing in Swahinglish.

(14) 'I want to kiss you'
1   Chema: *Mambo.*
              things
              'how are things?'
2   Frankie: *Poa.*
              cool
              'fine'
3   Chema: I want to kiss you. ((to Frankie))
4   All: ((Laughter))
5   Kalembo: *Hata* first para *inabidi   niwapigie hesabu.*
              even first para it-prs-demands I-them-hit math
              'I better count (the number of words) even in the first paragraph'

In an interview with Chema, one of the biggest jokers of the office, I learned that the Gazette was considered to be a special place in comparison with other newsrooms around the city. Chema explained that it was unique for its friendly atmosphere, and for the freedom the workers had in expressing themselves in the office. His comments, all in Swahinglish, emphasize the lack of restrictions on talk, similar to the atmosphere of the *kijiweni* he had mentioned earlier.

> Yeah we laugh we talk *kwa* voice *yaani tunaongea sana lakini hiki kitu hukuti ofisi nyingine kazi kazi basi. Mambo ya toka zamani pale yaani zile* small talks *zinatawala sana tunaongea sana unaweza kushangaa hawa watu wanafanya kazi muda gani na ile kelele* sometimes *inawa*disturb *baadhi ya watu. Lakini mimi nipo* helpless *yaani* I cannot help *lazima nipige kelele nikiingia pale na najisikia nipo* free *sana. Na nadhani nitapata taabu hata kama kufanya kazi ofisi nyingine nitapata taabu sana pale nimeshazoea sana unaongea ovyo ovyo unaongea matusi kwa maana upo* free. *Lakini hata* Observer *hamna kelele. Ukiingia kule* newsroom *kila mtu yuko* busy *kidogo labda wanaongea taratibu. Lakini* sasa Gazette *ile* atmosphere *sijui tuseme* friendly *sana.*

Yeah, we laugh we talk loudly, but you don't encounter this kind of thing at other workplaces. In the past, small talk was forbidden and now we talk a lot, it's really surprising. You think, 'these people, when do they do work?' and the noise, sometimes it disturbs other people. But me, I'm helpless, I mean, I cannot help making noise if I enter there, I feel free. I think I will have trouble working any other place because I've become accustomed to speaking without thinking, crudely, insults, whatever – it means you are free. But at the Observer there is no noise. If you enter there in the newsroom, every person is very busy. Maybe they speak very quietly, but here at the Gazette the atmosphere is, let's say very friendly.

The above excerpts show how heteroglossic language alternation can be a powerful contextualization cue by which speakers can alter the frame for interpreting talk. The use of language switching by itself did not appear to create the humor, however. Instead, it was the contrast that the switches provided which contextualized the playful mood of the utterances. Chema's switch from Swahinglish to English, followed by Swahili and more English in (12) also indicate that directionality is not what creates humor. This is not the case in other studies of humor in bilingual talk, such as Woolard's (1988) study of Eugenio, a comedian who switched between Catalan and Castilian, transgressing the sociolinguistic rules of these languages by using them together in the same domains. While Woolard (1988: 71) describes his comedy as 'a fictional world [...] where the two languages have a peaceful coexistence' (1988: 71), we have seen that Swahili, Swahinglish and English do more than just peacefully coexist among the journalists. The heteroglossia produced by these languages actually enhances their social relationships.

Multivocality in Microlevel Performance and Macrolevel Ideologies

Throughout the preceding discussion, the journalists' use of English within mostly Swahili turns of talk reveals that they use English for a variety of in-group purposes, which makes it difficult to assert that English is a language which is still imbued with a sense of 'othering' wrought by colonialism. Instead, these journalists employ English within their mostly-Swahili talk to express solidarity, to joke, and to align with one another in positive ways. In the next section, I examine how interview data helped me to see whether the journalists recognized any elements of their own heteroglossic speech as including legitimate forms of the global language. Their comments revealed a strong awareness of the sociolects involving English in Tanzania and showed how their own forms of hybrid language were at the top of the status scale. In the interviews, the journalists categorized themselves as belonging to the group who is of a higher social class, the result of a high level of education and certain linguistic capital. They demonstrated their awareness of their own prestige variety of Swahili-English, and yet, they still held the view that the English language as spoken in Tanzania was a deficient form of the language.

Elite closure

The journalists and editors can be described as part of the elite stratum of Tanzanian society, by virtue of their relatively high level of education (most have post-secondary training), and their employment at an English-medium newspaper office.[2] Their speech styles are a good example of *elite closure*, a type of 'socialization mobilization strategy by which those persons in power establish or maintain their powers and privileges via linguistic choices' (Myers-Scotton, 1993b: 149). This type of language use limits the access of non-elites to positions of power, and thereby has the effect of drawing boundaries around the social classes.

I should point out that my use of the term 'elite' here is used in a similar fashion by Blommaert (1992, 1999a) and Myers-Scotton (1993b) to refer to East Africans who are educated, white-collar workers. An important difference between Myers-Scotton's use of elite closure and my own, however, is that my study is limited to talk that takes place among journalists who work together, and hence, my focus is on a group of people who do not differ *prima facie* from one another significantly by way of social status. Nevertheless, the concept of elite closure is still important on a macrolevel since an examination of the journalists' ways of talking with one another can help produce an analysis of how they construct their identities within the context of their own workplace, and for an analysis of the methods they employ for (potentially) reifying and reinstating their identities as educated, white-collar workers among one another. Their identities as elites are further enhanced through their experiences traveling in and outside of Tanzania, their ability to use English monolingually with non-Swahili speakers, and their lifestyles. They have unlimited access to sporting events, embassy openings, music shows, political meetings, and so on. In fact, many of the journalists were often featured on the nightly television newscasts while appearing at a press conference or other newsworthy event. The consequence of their access to such privileged positions grants them a special status in Tanzanian society. It grants them a great deal of cultural capital (Bourdieu, 1991) by positioning them alongside those with much greater amounts of economic capital.

Discourses indicating awareness of membership in an elite sociolect

One of the views expressed in the interviews was the notion that language alternation was commonplace in East Africa and elsewhere in the continent, without regard to social class or socio-economic barriers. Mwema, a middle-aged sub-editor, explained that language alternation occurs across Africa.

(15)

> *Vinaenda pamoja kila mahali Africa wanafanya hivyo kila mahali. Hata ukienda Nigeria wanaongea Kiingereza wanaingiza lugha ya kienyeji labda Kiyoruba au Kihausa wanatumbukizatumbukiza maneno ya Kihausa kule ndani.*

> The languages go together everywhere in Africa, they do that, everywhere. Even if you go to Nigeria, they speak English and they insert local languages, maybe Yoruba or Hausa is dropped into it here and there, Hausa words are there in it.

Later in the interview, however, Mwema did report an awareness of sociolects, citing his language use when communicating with his father. He contrasts this with the way that the journalists communicate at the newspaper office, and his comments point to the cohesive nature of the office in his use of the term 'family' to refer to his colleagues who also employ a specific type of language in their daily conversations.

(16)

> *Halafu vilevile inategemea unaongea na nani kama baba yangu akitoka kijijini aje hapa ambaye najua hajui Kiingereza kabisa anaongea Kiswahili peke yake siwezi kufanya hivyo unaelewa sasa inategemea na mtu unayeongea naye*... Yes yes this is a family *wamekuwa pamoja* for so many years *unaona bwana.*

> But in the same way it depends who you are speaking with, like if my father if he came from the village and if he should come here I know that he doesn't speak any English, he only speaks Swahili and I can't use both languages, you see? So, it depends on the person who you are talking to ... Yes, yes <u>this is a family</u>; they have been together <u>for so many years</u>, you see, friend.

The family that Mwema points to in (16) is incredibly cohesive, as the journalists and editors all do spend quite a lot of time together, and their abilities to speak English, Swahili and bilingual varieties of language appeared to be fairly equivalent to me. However, when asking about the practice of mixing English and Swahili, I discovered that some of the journalists had a sense of competition about their language skills. In (17), a junior journalist, Peter, commented about the ways that English has created another means for drawing boundaries, as those who are considered to use a high degree of language mixing are also viewed as winning a competition of sorts. Peter explains that language mixing is a way of showing one's position on 'the ladder' of social class.

(17)

C: *Ee kwa mfano umesema kwamba labda watu wanatumia kuonyesha kwamba wameelimika sana lakini labda ni kwa ajili ya watu wengine ambao hawafahamu vizuri au kujidai kidogo lakini hapa ofisini wote ni sawa kwa hiyo sijui.*

Peter: *Yaa wote ni sawa lakini tumezidiana kidogo kidogo hivi hivi kwa mimi naweza nikawa najua kingereza lakini kuna mwingine ataajua zaidi na mwingine anataka kuonyesha anajua zaidi. Kwa hiyo ile nini* ladder *bado ipo hata japo wote tupo sawa lakani tunazidiana.*

C: Yeah, for example, you have said that perhaps people use [language mixing] to show that they are very educated, but, maybe for other people who don't understand well or maybe they are showing off, but here in the office, all are equal, so I don't really understand [why they mix languages with each other].

Peter: Yeah, all are equal but we are more and less equal. For example, I can act as I know English but another person knows more and another wants to show s/he knows even more, So that <u>ladder</u>, it's still here, even though all are the same, we compete with one another.

Most of the time, the journalists' interviews pointed to discourses of social class when they described their own language use, or their reason for mixing English into their Swahili. One of the youngest journalist, Chema, explained that English marks speakers as sophisticated, and for young men, this quality is often employed in strategic ways for the purpose of impressing young women. His comments also indicate that English may be used as a marker of high social standing, despite actual economic status of the individual.

(18)

Yeah kuna wengine wanatumia ile yaani kuonyesha wanaonyesha lakini wengine inakuwa bahati mbaya inatokea wala wala hawafikirii chochote lakini kweli ipo class *ya watu wanataka waongee ili wale watu ambao wa*raise P. Peers *jamaa mjanja maanake hapa ile* misconception *kwamba mtu anayejua Kiingereza ina maana ndiyo ujanja si unajua tena yaani kwamba labda ndiyo kasoma ana* exposure *kaenda nje labda. Kwa hiyo unakuta akiongea Kiingereza sasa unajua atapata* baby *mzuri sana kwa sababu watamwona mjanja sana. Ungekuwa mitaani humo hata kama una hela ndogo lakini wewe unapiga sana hiki wasichana wanakuona upo* so sophisticated *sasa ile wasichana wengi wanapenda* sophistication *fulani yaani anaweza mtu baadhi ya wasichana hapa anaweza kuji*boost *kwa* friends *sasa jamaa yangu yule anaongea Kiingereza wanaweza kusema ah jamaa anaongea Kiingereza na hata hana hela lakini anaona ile lugha kwamba ni* mark *ya juu sana.*

It is true there is a class of people who want to speak so that they will raise their P (i.e. raise status in the eyes of others). Here there is a misconception that a person who knows English is clever, understand? Again it's as if maybe he or she has studied, he has exposure, or has gone outside the country for a while. So when you see a guy like this speaking English you know that he will get a pretty baby because they will view him as very sharp, very clever ... if you're on the street there even if you don't have much money but you use English a lot the girls think you are so sophisticated and many of them like that sort of sophistication because some girls here can boost themselves, raise their own social status through their friends. My friend he speaks English and the girls say ah that guy speaks English and even though he doesn't have money he speaks the language that is the mark of high class.

To reference the group of journalists within Dar es Salaam's social order, an intern, Derek, offered the following characterization of which type of people would be likely to mix English into their Swahili.

(19)

*Ina, ina, inategemea vitu vingi kwa mfano inategemea uwelewa wako wa lugha na pia inategemea umekulia wapi, ni vitu kama hivyo labda umesomea wapi kwa hivyo nafikiri hivyo ndiyo vitu ambavyo vinachangia labda una*interact *na watu wa aina gani.*

It, it it depends on many things, for example, it depends on your understanding of the languages and also where you were raised, and on things like where you have studied, so I think these are really the things that contribute to the way one interacts with various people.

My interview data also pointed to the participants' knowledge that the language alternation that characterized their daily speech with one another is not universally understood in Tanzania, or in Dar es Salaam, for that matter. Several participants explained how language alternation resulted in miscommunication. Chema described a failed relationship with a young woman who was living in Dar es Salaam, blaming their incompatibility on their language differences:

(20)

> *Alikuwa yaani hata neno moja Kiingereza anachojua ni* 'good morning' *basi yaani hawezi kuunganisha sentensi anajua labda hiyo* window, chair full stop *lakini ukimchanganyia sijui* 'where are you going?' *hajui kitu ukimwambia* 'Hi baby how is everything?' *hajui kwa hiyo inakuwa* problem *sasa yeye anakuambia mbona unaniambia maneno yasiyofanana* yeah ... *ni ni kama hivyo ah mimi mwenyewe nika*surrender. Yeah *vitu kama hivyo yaani tulikuwa hatu*mechi *kabisa. Yaani tulikuwa dunia ya pili tofauti pamoja na wanachanganya wanaelewana?*

> She was able to say one or two English words at a time, like <u>good morning</u> but she can't join sentences. She knows the word for <u>window, chair, full stop</u>, but if you mix with her I don't know, like '<u>Where are you going</u>?' she doesn't understand. If you say to her '<u>Hi baby how is everything</u>?' she doesn't understand therefore it became a <u>problem</u> and she was telling me 'Why do you speak to me in words that don't match up?' ... It was that way, so I decided I would <u>surrender</u>. <u>Yeah</u>, that kind of thing, I mean, we just didn't <u>match</u> at all. I mean, we were from two different worlds and we were together. People from two different worlds, if they interact, will they understand each other?

My interview with Chema revealed that language alternation created obstacles for making friends and feeling comfortable on a personal level. He explained that his use of Swahinglish can cause problems with certain Tanzanians, particularly because he finds that he has to translate for those who cannot understand the meaning when languages are alternated:

(21)

> *Kuna baadhi ya wakati inabidi mjitenge yaani kwamba ile nini. Yaani moja hawa*fly together birds with same feathers *sijui nini* fly together. *Baada ya muda mtatofautiana sana mtakuta mazungumzo hayaendani vizuri kwa sababu kila ukiongea inabidi u*clarify *tena, ah samahani nilikuwa namaanisha sasa ile inakufanya uvunje* discussion *na mtu wa aina ile ambaye kila*

unachoongea haelewi ... *maanake kila siku unaweka maneno mengi kwa siku sentensi nyingi za Kiingereza zinaingia kwa siku sasa ni kwamba kila ukiweka u*clarify *ah samahani. Ina*bore *sana.*

Some of the time [differences in language use] make it so that you separate yourselves, I mean, that one – they don't <u>fly together, birds with the same feathers,</u> I don't know, <u>fly together.</u> After a while, people differ from each other a lot. You will encounter conversations not going well because every time you speak you have to <u>clarify</u> again and again, saying 'Sorry, I meant so and so'. So, doing that breaks the flow of <u>discussion,</u> with a person of that kind who doesn't understand each thing you say ... meaning that each day if you use many English words or English sentences each day, then it becomes necessary to <u>clarify,</u> 'Oh, pardon me.' It's really <u>boring/tiring.</u>

In (21), Chema's language use is doubly meaningful as, in his explanation of the divisions caused by language use, he employs an English proverb (birds of a feather flock together) which does not have an equivalent form in Swahili involving the same referents. Others indicated an awareness of the various abilities of Tanzanians to understand heteroglossic speech. Participants such as Fulgence, a young journalist, expressed a need to make judgments regarding others' language abilities before mixing languages. He mentioned that he mixes more in the Gazette office than any other place, however. His comments point to the sense that in Dar es Salaam, there are certain expressions which everyone knows, despite their social class:

(22)

C: *Unaonaje unafikiri wewe unafanya hivi mara nyingi tu hapa ofisini na nje ya ofisi wewe mwenyewe?*

FN: *Nafikiri mara nyingi zaidi ofisini kuliko nje. Nje inabidi uangalie na watu uliokuwa nao. Mara nyingi ukichanganya sidhani kama wanaweza wakakuelewa labda au wakapata ugumu kuelewa lakini huku kuna baadhi ya maneno unaweza ukayaelezea vizuri kwa kutumia Kiingereza kwa sababu unajua kila mtu atakuelewa kwa mara moja.*

C: What do you think? Do you think you mix languages a lot only in the office here or also outside the office?

FN: I think I mix more often in the office than in other contexts. Outside, you have to determine whether you mix based on the people you are with. Often if you mix languages, I don't think that they could understand, or maybe they would have a hard time, but here [in Dar es Salaam] there are many words that you can say, using English, because you know every single person will understand you immediately.

'The Standard of English is Not the Best'

In spite of the microlevel evidence that displays strong forms of appropriation of English, most of the participants indicated that their own varieties of English were substandard, and they pointed to the forms outside of Tanzania as superior. Interestingly, (23) reveals an awareness of Tanzanian varieties of English, including varieties which contain Swahili, as examples of local Englishes. Mwema refers to English which contains 'anglicized words' from Swahili such as *'mwananchi'* ('citizen') to describe the English used in Tanzania, but at the same time, he rejects this variety as 'not the best'.

(23)

> *Sasa* language *iliyo hapa* much better *than* language *ya zamani. Kuna* improvement *kubwa sana. Lakini hii haina maana ni kwamba ni kwenye* level *ambayo ni* acceptable. Grammatically syntax *na nini* it's not up to the highest standard *Kiingereza unachofahamu lakini* generally it is agreeable *ukisoma utaelewa*. English. *Na hapa tatizo hilo lipo halafu kuna vilevile maneno ambayo ni African nanii siyo* anglicized anglicized I should say *maneno ni ya hapa lakini wameya*postpone *kama ni ya Kiingereza kwa mfano neno* citizen *hauwezi ukasema mwananchi katika gazeti lile mwananchi ni Kiswahili utakuta tunalitumia hapa tumeli*-anglicized *kwamba sisi wenyewe tunaelewa maana yake*. The ruling party *tunaweza kusema* Tanzania Revolutionary party, *Chama Cha Mapinduzi lakini utakuta tunaandika Chama Cha Mapinduzi tumeli*-anglicized *kwa hiyo kwa kifupi* standard *ya Kiingereza* is not the best.

Now the <u>language</u> which is here is <u>much better</u> than the <u>language</u> of the past. There has been a big <u>improvement</u>. But this doesn't mean that it's at an <u>acceptable level</u>. <u>Grammatically syntax</u> and whatever <u>it's not up to the highest standard</u>. It's English you understand but <u>generally it is agreeable</u>, if you read it you will understand. <u>English</u>. And here the problem is that many words are African and have been <u>anglicized, anglicized I should say</u> they are words from here but they have <u>postponed</u>, like in English the word '<u>citizen</u>' you can't say it, you should say 'mwananchi' in a newspaper. You'll find 'mwananchi' in newspapers here – we have <u>anglicized</u> it because we understand its meaning. Or, '<u>the ruling party</u>', we can say '<u>Tanzania Revolutionary party</u>' which is 'Chama cha Mapinduzi', but you will only find 'Chama cha Mapinduzi' (even in an English newspaper). It's been anglicized so in sum, the standard of English is not the best.

Moreover, the journalists viewed other Englishes as superior to Tanzanian English, expressed by their remarks that nations in Africa such as Kenya were more suitable contexts for schooling, primarily because of the 'better English'. These comments indicate a rejection of local standards because of their perceived inferiority. Abdul, the news editor, described how those with the means send their children to Kenya for education precisely because of Tanzania's 'poor English'.

(24)

Wengine wanapeleka hata watoto wakasome Kenya au Zambia au Uganda yote ni kutafuta apate basis *ya Kiingereza sasa kule shule zote zinafundisha Kiingereza sana apate* basis *na kwa sababu akiwa pale bweni. Wale watu wa Kenya hawajui lugha nyingine wanazungumza Kiingereza tu. Sasa atapate* practice *hata na kweli watu wanaosomesha watoto wao wakirudi hapa wana msingi mzuri wa Kiingereza kwa hiyo tangia miaka ya themanini imekuja kutokea hiyo adhi kwamba ipo haja ya kujifunza tena vizuri Kiingereza.*

Some send their children all the way to Kenya, Zambia and Uganda in order to get a good English basis, there all the schools teach in English so that they get a basis and because if the child is there in the dorm. Those Kenyans don't know another language, they speak English only. Now he will get a lot of practice and people who send their children abroad for studies, when they return here they have a good English foundation.

When I asked Edward, the assistant news editor, about the need for English, he began to discuss his choice to send his child to a private English-medium primary school. He explained that his child would benefit from English at the school, and would learn Swahili at home and elsewhere. He reported that not knowing English would lead to disadvantages because of the assumption that in higher education, his child would eventually have to interact with others from foreign countries, and without English, his child would not be able to communicate or to understand the lessons.

(25)

Kuhitimu darasa la saba akiwa hawezi hata kuongea sentensi moja ya Kingereza ambayo ni inaleta kwake yeye ni nanii ni disadvantage *kwamba akienda baadaye kwenye* high education *akachanganyika na watu wengine kutoka nchi nyingine yeye anaweza kufeli sababu tu ya uwezo wake mdogo wa kuandika au kuongea Kingereza.*

To graduate from seventh grade without the ability to speak even one sentence of English would be a disadvantage because when one goes to higher education one will interact with others from other countries and one could fail to understand or to do well in school because of one's poor ability to write or to speak English.

The data also revealed that for many, economic success was bound to global travel, and hence, bound to English. Economic stagnation and a lack of development or advancement were associated with Swahili in an interview with Leonard, a young journalist. His comment 'If you know Swahili you can't go anywhere' constructs countries outside of East Africa as the only desirable destinations for Tanzanians, and excludes Swahili-speaking nations like Kenya, Uganda, Rwanda and Burundi as worthwhile places. By various accounts, Swahili is estimated to be the seventh-most comonly spoken language in the world, so this perspective fails to engage with the sociolinguistic reality of Swahili as a significant international language.

(26)

> *Sasa hivi huwezi kufanya biashara vizuri bila kujua Kiingereza. Pote ukienda Marekani ukienda hata Japan hata Ujerumani pamoja Ujerumani hawaongei sana Kiingereza lakini* at least *ukijua Kiingereza kitakusaidia zaidi kuliko usijue Kiingereza ukajua Kiswahili huwezi kufika popote.*
>
> These days you can't do business well without knowing English. Everywhere, if you go to America, if you go to Japan or even Germany, in Germany they don't really speak a lot of English but at least if you know English it will help you more than if you don't know English. If you know Swahili you can't go anywhere.

Finally, (27) offers a perspective on how deep the dominant (elite) ideology of the necessity of English has reached. Among the workers at the newspaper office, I focused primarily on journalists and editors, though other employees were of course part of the context. In an interview with a secretary (who had only graduated from primary school and who did not display any ability to use English, even in Swahinglish), the power of the belief in English as a means to economic success was evident.

(27)

C: *Kwa hiyo baada ya kujifunza Kingereza hata Kenya hapa watu wanaweza kufanya nini hasa kuliko watu ambao wamesoma Kiswahili tu?*

Rita: *Sasa ukisoma Kiswahili tu kwa kweli sasa hivi ajira, ajira zinakuwa ngumu kama unajua Kiswahili tu hujui Kiingereza sasa hivi kazi itakushinda*

C: Kweli inategemea kazi.
Rita: Mtu huwezi ukaajiriwa labda kazi ya kupiga deki ndiyo utaajiriwa kama hujui Kingereza.
C: Therefore after learning English, what can people can do better than people who only study Swahili?
Rita: Now, if you study only Swahili it's true that these days, employment, getting a job is very difficult if you know Swahili only and you don't know English. These days you won't get a job.
C: Maybe it depends on the type of work?
Rita: A person can't get hired. If you don't know English you might get hired to wash floors.

Conclusion

In this chapter, I have examined how white collar workers in a newspaper office use their linguistic repertoires to manage their social relationships with one another. I have related their language use with macrolevel tensions in Tanzania through a discussion of elite closure, drawing on interview data. As the interviews indicate, English is not always clearly divorced from its associations with the 'other' or the ongoing system of socio-economic stratification in Tanzania, at least at the metalinguistic level. This level is very powerful, as it influences decisions on schooling and opportunities for employment, and those with economic resources will always have more access to better English. At the microlevel, the journalists produce linguistic hybridity that displays their abilities to produce languages that carry a great deal of cultural capital, that is, monolectal forms of Swahili and English. Through alternating between standard English and standard Swahili, they succeed in setting themselves apart from those who only speak Tanzanian languages, and thereby mark themselves as members of a privileged group.

Still, the interactions reveal that the workers are most comfortable switching between their languages, and that they are expert at doing so. They can shift from unmarked mixing to monolingual forms of language in order to interrupt, to frame activities differently and to give encouragement. They can use English to invoke equality through greetings, to mitigate friendly requests and to joke around. The hybridity in their linguistic repertoires give them the tools to manage their social relationships at work, and they appear to use the centrifugal forces of language mixing frequently to destabilize office hierarchies, often combining humor with acts of linguistic creativity.

In the next chapter, I compare the journalists' linguistic hybridity with the language found in the domain of beauty pageants, a sphere of communication in which prescriptive attitudes that value monolingual forms of language dominate. However, the discourses surrounding the pageants are filled with heteroglossia at both a linguistic and an ideological level. This domain of social life allows us to observe the limits of linguistic and cultural hybridity when it is put on a stage.

Notes

1. Words like 'okey' and 'yaa' are actually bivalent (Woolard, 1998, see Chapter 1 for further discussion). The spelling of these words is based on the recommendations of Tanzanian research assistants who helped me transcribe my data.
2. My observations of two Swahili-medium newspaper offices and television offices made it clear that the degree of hybrid language use among the *Gazette* journalists cannot be tied directly to the fact that the office produced an English-medium newspaper. In my observations of half a dozen Swahili and English newspaper offices, all journalists used a very similar kind of speech with one another no matter where they worked.

Chapter 4
Miss World or Miss Bantu? Competing Dialogues on Female Beauty

The cover of a 1999 volume of *Kingo*, a magazine published in Tanzania with a circulation in Kenya and Uganda, asked a provocative question: *Yupi Miss TZ?* ('Which one is Miss Tanzania?'). The cover presents its audience with cartoon drawings of two diametrically opposed versions of Tanzanian beauty (Figure 4.1). A dichotomy is established through hairstyles (braided vs. straightened), clothing (traditional *kanga* vs. bathing suit), skin color (darker vs. perhaps chemically-altered light skin), and footwear (barefoot vs. high heels). Their differences are also apparent in the physical positioning of the women, as the full-figured woman's backside is the focus of attention, while the slender woman is presented frontally.

The cover forces readers to consider their preferences for East African beauty in its challenge to choose one woman as the best representative for Tanzania. The drawing presents a clean dualism that falls along the lines of tradition and modernity, and which symbolizes the sets of dichotomies that colonialism has produced in post-colonial societies – and particularly, that of the *self* and the *other* (Said, 1978). Figure 4.1 can also be read as resistance to the influence of western beauty norms for African women, as the presence of the full-figured, dark-skinned and traditionally-dressed woman as a viable option challenges a history of discourses in East Africa about women's appearance and the betrayal of African culture through straightened hair and western dress (Stambach, 1999). Interestingly, the men in the audience (who are judges) appear to be drawn to the full-figured woman, while the sole female judge looks perplexed by the dilemma in front of her. This dilemma is symbolic of a sometimes uncomfortable dichotomy that exists in East Africa in regard to the role of beauty pageants

Figure 4.1 *Yupi Miss TZ?* ('Which one is Miss Tanzania?') *Kingo*, Vol. 14, 1999. Reproduced with permission of Gaba Ltd

and other related phenomena in social life involving judgments of beauty, appropriacy and changes in gender roles.

This chapter examines the ways that English, hybrid Swahili-English and varieties of Swahili are used to discursively construct claims about beauty in East Africa alongside semiotic symbols such as body size, hair texture and skin color. Through examining popular culture texts about beauty and beauty contests, this chapter examines how English and Swahili are made to compete in the same space, and how these languages help to constitute the discursive debate about the place of local traditions, global modernity and cultural hybridity. Beyond offering an analysis of language use and semiotic forms, this chapter investigates how East Africans manage and make sense of the multivocality that indexes the multiple forms of beauty and the competing discourses surrounding appropriacy and authenticity. A key strategy for coping with this tension is to resort to humor, and particularly, to use parody and *carnivalesque* humor (Bakhtin, 1968, 1984). As illustrated by the cover of *Kingo*, the co-presence of westernized and Afro-centric forms of female beauty creates a duality that challenges East Africans to choose one aesthetic norm, an impossible task in a society where

Competing Dialogues on Female Beauty   67

both global and local discourses and ideologies of tradition and modernity are in constant dialogue. At the textual level, parodies of westernized and Afro-centric perspectives emerge as one of the coping mechanisms for this multivocality. Such texts may be seen as critical toward westernization and cultural imperialism via beauty pageants, and therefore, can be interpreted as acts of resistance.

This chapter examines the newspaper and magazine articles and advertisements for beauty pageants that take place in Kenya and Tanzania from May through August of each year, as well as discourses in advertisements that come from newspapers, beauty products and beauty salons. The data are from Swahili and English-medium newspapers published in Kenya and Tanzania, field notes and photographs of two beauty pageants I attended in Dar es Salaam in 2005 and 2006, and photographs I took of beauty products available at local shops and advertisements in Tanzania. Drawing on critical discourse analysis, cultural studies and semiotics (Fairclough, 1995, 2001; Hall, 1997; Van Leeuwen, 2005), the chapter examines the semiotic and linguistic forms that help to socially construct the range of discourses for East African women's beauty practices. Specifically, and because I am interested in questions of imperialism and resistance through appropriation and cultural hybridity, I explore the *social processes of production* (Fairclough, 1995) involved in the making of texts that discursively construct *systems of representations* (Hall, 1997) that relate to the concepts of self and other. The chapter explores how semiotic resources are used in 'specific historical, cultural and institutional contexts, and how people talk about them in these contexts – plan them, justify them, critique them, etc'. (Van Leeuwen, 2005: 3). I use interviews with Tanzanians of various ages and interviews with cartoonists and journalists to provide insights into the social processes of production in making these texts and the interpretation of the double meanings that these texts contain.

English, Social Mobility and the Beauty Market

Thus far, the study of global English has largely neglected the linkages of language with other semiotic forms such as body size, clothing and appearance. In East Africa, English is part of a package of globalized promise that offers young people in developing nations an avenue for success. It may be assumed that educational institutions are the primary contexts in which English is learned in the process of striving for success. In the developing world, however, English-medium educational systems hardly guarantee socio-economic mobility to those who graduate with secondary diplomas, including those who possess advanced-level diplomas (Mazrui & Mazrui, 1998: 137). This is partly because many schools do not have the resources to produce well-educated students, and largely because the economies of Kenya and Tanzania are relatively weak. Vavrus (2002) provides clear evidence that very few Tanzanian high school graduates in the Kilimanjaro region obtain steady employment after completing high school, even though they experienced English-medium instruction. Similarly, while the general public in Kenya views English as a marker of good education and of modernity (Michieka, 2005), such attitudes have been shaken recently, given the increased level of poverty and unemployment of the highly educated (Sure & Webb, 2000).

Beyond educational contexts, it is important to examine domains in which people use English for social mobility and economic success. For young, single women, one avenue for this possible success comes in the form of beauty pageants, as winning a national pageant may afford them the opportunity to seek employment outside of their home countries, where they can experience the benefits of more economic opportunities. English is part of this promise as well since it is viewed as a necessary language for international competitiveness in the pageant world. Even though competitions such as Miss World provide interpreters for contestants, the East African media repeatedly report that fluency in English can make or break a contestant's chances for success, both in East Africa and internationally. Moreover, the promise of economic opportunity is linked with the power of English in very practical ways, for many former Miss Tanzanias and Miss Kenyas are currently residing in Britain and North America, where economic opportunity is greater. As Cecilia Mwangi, the 2005–2006 Miss Kenya explains, working in Kenya does not afford young women the salaries needed for the right diet, exercise regimes and stylists. She says, 'It is a bit expensive to maintain yourself. Whatever we get on the [modeling] show is peanuts'.[1] Of course, many contestants also remain in East Africa, where they enjoy celebrity status and the opportunity to benefit from endorsements. Others take advantage of their opportunities to study abroad and return to their homes, wielding the cultural capital of degrees and more internationalized English from the outside.

Because pageants are associated with social mobility that may lead to opportunities outside of Swahili-speaking East Africa, the kind of English that contestants use at beauty pageants tends to be monolingual in nature, rather than the more common codemixed or hybrid forms of Swahili used by those with some level of education (Blommaert, 1999a, 2005b; Higgins, 2004, 2007). The contestants who opt to use Swahili in the pageants also employ quite standard forms of the language, making special effort to avoid mixing languages (*cf.* Billings, 2006). However, the responses to beauty pageants in the media and in popular culture texts tend to contain language mixing, East African forms of English and Street Swahili (see Chapter 2 for more detailed descriptions of these languages).

Beauty Pageants in East Africa

Kenya began its history of beauty pageants as British East Africa through its participation in Miss World in the 1950s, when Caucasian women were sent to represent the colony. The final Caucasian to represent British East Africa was Jasmine Batty, who participated in the contest in 1960. No one was sent again to compete until 1967, when Zipporah Mbugua, a Black woman, attended the contest, representing the Republic of Kenya for the first time. Kenya's changing political landscape towards independence in 1963 and factions in the government through the 1970s most likely kept Kenya preoccupied with matters of politics and economics. No one from Kenya was sent to Miss World again until 1984.

Pageant history in Tanzania is more complicated given its more explicit opposition to political and cultural forms of westernization after independence. Prior to independence, British-ruled Tanganyika participated in the contest for the first time in 1960, when a Caucasian woman represented the colony. Tanganyika became independent in 1961, and beauty pageants were discontinued until 1967, when Theresa Shayo, a Black woman, was crowned Miss Tanzania and sent to the Miss World pageant. Shortly after Miss World 1967, the Tanzanian government banned beauty pageants in the country, and no further contests were held until 1994. As Billings (2006) points out, this ban was part of the ideological movement of the socialist movement in Tanzania, as outlined by the Arusha Declaration of 1967. Central to this movement was a rejection of all things western, including economic policies, clothing styles and even language. Beauty pageants were one of the cultural practices that were seen as 'peddling foreign culture' (Tagama, 2003: 60), and hence were outlawed. Language also became a semiotic symbol for building the nation. Though Swahili was made the national language at independence in 1961, it became the language of instruction in primary schools after the declaration, and the government promoted Swahili as the language best suited to transmit African values among Tanzanians. Ethnic languages and ethnic cultural practices (such as Maasai traditional dress) were forbidden (Ivaska, 2002), all in the name of encouraging the development of a united Tanzanian populace.

The Winning Strategy of Speaking English

An explicit way in which English is intertwined with western forms of beauty in contemporary Tanzania can be seen in mainstream beauty pageants during the self-introductions by contestants and in question-and-answer sessions with the top five contestants. During these moments, the contestants have a matter of seconds in which to impress the judges, and sometimes more importantly, the audiences. Women who make verbal mistakes or who take too long in answering their questions are usually heckled by the audience through excessive clapping and overt comments that highlight their apparent inabilities. In Tanzania, contestants are given the choice of English or Swahili for introducing themselves and for answering questions during the interview session, if they make it that far. However, it is clear that the contestants who answer in fluent English have an obvious advantage over those who choose Swahili. Billings's (2006) research on beauty pageants in Tanzania shows a strong correlation between contestants' decision to speak in English and their placement in the pageants. In her study, data from eight pageants involving 50 contestants showed that 32 chose to answer questions directed at them in Swahili. Billings's analysis of the less regional pageants revealed greater degrees of English, and contestants in the regional pageants located in more urban areas also chose to answer in English more frequently. At the highest level of competition, Miss Tanzania, the top five winners all chose to use English. The choice of English is also noted by journalists. The English-medium *Sunday Citizen* (26 June 2005) described the language choices of the winner and the first runner-up for a regional pageant in Tanzania, making special point to compare them with the other contestants: 'Immediately after the evening wear parade a number of questions were asked to contestants Kessy and Ntanga who answered in English while the rest spoke in Kiswahili.'

It makes sense that contestants who have an eye on the international pageants or the international modeling market would need English in order to succeed, and hence, would choose it as their mode of communication at pageants. Moreover, because the prescribed standard of beauty in these domains is drawn from western ideals of beauty, it also makes sense that the women who would view themselves as having potential to succeed would be those who are unusually tall and slim. However, because the pageants are situated in Kenya and Tanzania, the contestants' language use and their physical attributes also need to make sense in their local contexts for local audiences; therefore, they are open to debate. Although most Kenyans and Tanzanians are well aware that many contestants expect to compete at the international level, there is a substantial degree of public dialogue regarding what should qualify as authentic African beauty and whether the 'Misses' truly represent Kenya and Tanzania. The discourses surrounding the pageants offer fascinating sites for exploring ideological constructions of local and international identities, and they shed light on how East Africans view language as well.

Contesting Authentic Forms of Beauty

For the urban populations who participate in the discourses of beauty pageants as readers of English-medium newspaper articles and as audience members in the VIP seats at the pageants, authentic East African beauty may well be that of slender, tall, fair-skinned, standard English speaking women. This seems to be a normative representation of beauty in urban areas like Nairobi and Dar es Salaam among the younger population. However, this is not an uncontested claim to beauty in East Africa. Many onlookers interpret the actions of these women as *kuiga* ('imitating') a foreign practice. Other phenomena often associated with this imitation include dieting, chemically lightening one's skin and dressing in styles considered too revealing.

The popular Tanzanian weekly *Rai*, a Swahili-medium newspaper that focuses on lengthy opinion pieces, devoted an entire article to these issues in July of 2006. The article is an interesting example of how some writers point to historical discourses and 'authentic' Africans in order to make claims about what is a 'true' representation of a female African identity. Author Maggid Mjengwa compared the contestants of a recent beauty pageant in the Dar es Salaam area to 17th century Queen Nzinga Mbande of Angola, a woman who found ways to remain equal in the eyes of the Portuguese who occupied present-day Angola. In a famous tale often told about Mbande, a Portuguese ruler placed a mat on the floor for her to sit, which implied a subordinate status. Not willing to accept this state of affairs, Mbande sat on her servant's back, making herself equal to the governor. Mjengwa laments, 'I tried to see if there are any beauty contestants who have the ability to represent the African woman in a way similar to Queen Nzinga Mbande and her followers. No, I didn't see anyone who approached her.' Mjengwa goes on to explain that 'many of the girls had hair that was not real, straightened hair', and 'some appeared to be unnaturally light-skinned', indicating that they had altered their skin color with bleach. 'It seemed clear that some of them were trying to look like white women.' He concludes his article by advising beauty contestants to embrace their natural skin and hair and to be proud of their African beauty.

Though criticism of the preference for fair-skinned women in East Africa is fairly common in commentaries such as Mjengwa's, fairness is strongly endorsed in advertisements and a multitude of beauty products. This endorsement co-occurs with monolingual forms of English, creating an indexical relationship between non-localized forms of the language and products that lighten dark skin. This indexicality is complexified by Mjengwa's reference to Queen Mbande's resolve to be treated as an equal in the presence of the colonialist Portuguese, and by his comparison of the pageant contestants with the Queen's behaviors. In short, he accuses the contestants of cultural betrayal while honoring Queen Mbande as a 'true' African.

Interestingly, the English word 'Lightness' is an increasingly popular name for girls in Tanzania and was the name of a contestant in a major pageant in the Dar es Salaam area in 2006. Figure 4.2, a billboard advertisement for skin cream, illustrates the adherence of English to the discourse of beauty through lighter skin. The name of the product is in English ('Skin Glow'), lighter skin is promised in English, after '6 weeks', and the safety of the product is ensured in a stamp of approval involving both English and Swahili. The Swahili explanation at the bottom of the

Figure 4.2 Advertisement in Dar es Salaam for Skin Glow, a product that promises *Weupe kwa njia salama* 'fairness/whiteness in a safe manner'

billboard, *Weupe kwa njia salama* 'fairness/whiteness in a safe manner' summarizes the message for the non-English readers, as does the set of photos which capture the skin transformation. Many women use these creams even at the risk of skin rashes, scarring and skin cancer due to the mercury and hydroquinone in the creams. Latifa Myinyikwale, a hairdresser in Dar es Salaam who used to use the creams, explained, 'You hear that if you want to look beautiful, then you have to look like a white person and to look like a white person you have to use these creams. Of course it is natural that women want to be beautiful.'[2] Although the Tanzanian government began to remove 83 brands of banned creams from stores in 2004, it is believed that many women still have access to creams that contain harmful elements.

Critiques of skin lightening practices also appear in Kenya's media, some of which also take the form of arguing for a specific representation of African beauty. In his popular Sunday column in the English-medium *The Nation*, Wahome Mutahi, aka Whispers,[3] the late journalist, author, playwright and humorist, ridiculed the emergence of what he called the '*mkorogo* ("mix") skirt wearer', the sort of Kenyan woman who 'has a face that has the colour of Fanta orange. Her hands and legs have the same colour. The rest of her body has the colour of Guinness' (www.nation.com). As in Tanzania, such women are accused of imitating foreigners. Mutahi writes, 'The Fanta orange faces and Guinness stout bodies are not the work of gods gone crazy in their laboratories of creation but of determined chemistry by the skirt wearers in their efforts to become a *Mzungu* ("white").' In another part of the column, skin lightening is associated with beauty pageants: 'The *mkorogo* face sometimes forgets that she has a Fanta face and a Guinness stout body and wears a mini skirt. What you see then is something that reminds you of a creature that has been half boiled, half roasted and then left in the sun. The *mkorogo* face pretends that Miss Universe has never looked better and so she walks all the same as if she has oiled hips.' Finally, *mkorogo* is tied directly to language:

> Something called mother tongue does not forgive those who like to pretend that they can't speak it. For that reason, it keeps interfering with the tongues of those who try to twang. The likes of Whispers Junior calls that interference by mother tongue or native language in the business of twanging, 'shrubbing'. Shrubbing simply means the village interfering with the city. As a result and much to the annoyance of the *mkorogo face*, she will say something that will betray her roots. Thus she will twang and say: 'I dan like babuliki transport.' Only a person from miraa[4] land that is Meru can say 'babuliki' when she

means 'public', and so this Fanta face pretending to be from Atlanta soon finds herself telling the world that she comes from a village called Kangeta where miraa is had for breakfast, lunch and dinner.

Mutahi was loved for his ability to entertain, and for his incisive observations about changes in Kenyan society. He was also well known for his use of Sheng and other Kenyan languages in his otherwise mostly English-medium columns. His article helps us to see how cultural betrayal and Kenyan authenticity are discursively constructed through references to language use. The interference of the '*mkorogo* face's' mother tongue with her English is treated as authentic and Kenyan, but only because her 'twang', which is described as approximating an accent from the southern United States, is proven to be false. The *mkorogo*'s 'slip' into localized English is presented as a sign of true identity, and the language itself does the work of identifying the 'imposter' as a Kenyan. Whereas Swahili marks people as authentic Tanzanians, in Kenya, one's ethnic language is more salient for marking a speaker as Kenyan, and as African. Her use of localized English, which bears the traces of her ethnic language, casts her as an authentic Kenyan as well. In Mutahi's funny tale, the *mkorogo*'s inauthenticity as a speaker of American English parallels her inauthenticity as a light-skinned woman. She is an imposter on two fronts.

While these examples show that some newspapers such as *Rai* and *The Nation* make space for critiques of practices deemed as imitation of the west, they more often provide a forum for pageant organizers to promote their business as a legitimate activity, a choice which may well be the result of the money spent on newspaper advertising for the contests and the business relationships among newspapers and promoters of beauty pageants. During the 'high season' of June through August, Tanzanian newspapers feature announcements for pageants on an almost daily basis. Newspapers often sponsor the pageants, and the newly crowned winners are named with the newspaper name first, followed by the regional area they represent (e.g. *Dimba* Miss Sinza; *Komesha* Miss Upanga). Features on beauty pageants and promoters are common, and they often emphasize the legitimacy of the pageants and the good that they can bring to young women with few options in life. In a two-page spread, *Dar Leo* (25 June 2005) featured Charles Maige Hamkah, an organizer for several beauty pageants in the Dar es Salaam area, offering him the opportunity to explain that pageants are not '*sanaa ya kihuni*' ('vulgar forms of art', akin to prostitution) and that they are not '*kinyume na maadili ya Kitanzania*' ('against Tanzanian morals'). In Tanzania, such statements are necessary given the amount of resistance to the pageants and accusations that they are a form of moral decay. In fact, Zanzibar banned all pageants in 2002, claiming that the contests were in opposition to the culture of the islands and to Islam. Similarly, in Kenya, some Muslim politicians also called for the end of beauty pageants because of threats to morality.

Though critiques of pageants are somewhat uncommon in mainstream papers, pageant organizers are found defending their work. In Kenya's *The Nation*, Hashim Lundenga, the manager of several major pageants in Tanzania, defended the entry requirements for the Nokia Face of Africa competition, a continent-wide pageant. To qualify, contestants had to be at least 68.5 inches tall, and their hips could not measure more than 36 inches. In response to the claims made that the contest was too dismissive of African forms of beauty, Lundenga was quoted as saying, 'I want to dispel the mentality that African men love fat women. Not all African men want to marry a fat woman' (*The Nation*, 9 December 2006). Drawing on pragmatism, Lundenga explained further, 'There are no laws banning short, fat women from competing in the Miss World contest. They can register and participate but would probably not win.'

Discourses of Competition

In addition to English and preferences for light skin, discourses of competition are strongly present in reports on beauty pageants. From a historiographic view (Blommaert, 1999b: 5–6), these discourses have a 'chronological and sociocultural anchoring which produces meaning and social effects in ways that cannot be reduced to text-specific characteristics alone'. These discourses are in stark contrast with the (now largely defunct) discourses of unity and brotherhood from the socialist *Ujamaa* 'familyhood' movement in Tanzania of the 1960s and 1970s, as well as the *Harambee*[5] ideology of Kenya's post-independence period that embodied ideas of 'pulling together' to build community self-reliance. These discourses of the past help to contextualize the degree of change in East Africa since economic liberalization, and as we will see in the examples below, they provide a resource for the construction of 'traditional' female identity.

The newspaper articles that report on upcoming beauty pageants and also on the outcomes of these contests focus on the material gains of the winners and use language with a strongly competitive and individualistic tone. These articles are published in the section typically called '*Michezo*' ('Sports'), a section which also reports entertainment news. They act as announcements for the pageants and function more like advertising than any sort of investigative or feature reporting. The articles tend to follow quite predictable format: those which announce upcoming pageants start with a paragraph about where the pageant will be held and the entrance fee, followed by a paragraph which lists the names of all of the contestants. Next comes information about the entertainment and the sponsors of the pageant.

In reporting on the upcoming competitions, it is striking how often the newspaper reporters use the word *kusaka* (literally, 'to hunt') in their descriptions.

> *Leo ndio leo wakati vimwana **wanaosaka** taji la Miss Magomeni watakapopanda jukwaani* (*Dar Leo*, 25 June 2005)
>
> Today is the day when the darlings who **seek/hunt** for the crown of Miss Magomeni will step onto the stage
>
> *Mashindano ya **kumsaka** mrembo wa kitongoji cha Ubungo 2005 yatafanyika Julai 8* (*Mwananchi*, 16 June 2005)
>
> The competition to **seek/hunt** the beauty for the hamlet of Ubungo 2005 will take place July 8
>
> *Zawadi ya fedha taslim Sh 1,000,000 itatolewa kwa atakayekuwa mshindi wa kwanza katika kinyang'anyiro cha **kumsaka** Miss Dar City Center 2005 leo kwenye Ukumbi wa Diamond Jubilee mjini.* (*Mwananchi*, 24 June 2005)
>
> A money prize of 1 million shillings will be given to the first place winner in the competition to **find/hunt** Miss Dar City Center 2005 today on stage at the Diamond Jubilee in the city.

Out of a corpus of two months' worth of newspapers, only a handful announced an upcoming competition using a different word to describe the purpose of the event. For example, in reporting on Miss Pwani ('Miss Coastal Region'), *kutafuta* ('to find') is used, a word devoid of connotations with bloodthirsty competition or cut-throat sport.

> *Mashindano ya **kutafuta** mrembo ya Kitongoji cha Pwani 'Miss Pwani 2005' yanatarajiwa kufanyika Julai 2.* (*Mwananchi*, 24 June 2005)
>
> The competition **to find** a beauty to win the coastal region 'Miss Pwani 2005' is planned for July 2.

My interviews with journalists in Tanzania revealed that *kusaka* has become quite popular for describing beauty contests, as well as other events in which competition is involved. One journalist gave the following example from soccer as a comparison: '*Katika klabu ya soka ya Simba na Yanga watakuwa wakim_saka_ mchawi wao*' ('In the Simba and Yanga soccer clubs, they will be looking for/hunting a star player'). Figurative language is invoked through *kusaka* and also in *mchawi* (lit. 'witch doctor', but here used to mean 'star player'). This kind of language use is often referred to as *Kiswahili kigumu* ('difficult Swahili') for its many metaphors and often, opaque meanings. A previous editor of a daily paper agreed that *kusaka* carries associations with hunting and may connote that the person being searched for has done some misdeed. In Swahili, he explained, 'The word means to hunt, and in looking for a pageant winner, it's like hunting. It's similar to the way policemen hunt for a thief who has broken into a home, for example, the home of the prime minister.'

Usage of *kusaka* is part of a larger discourse imbued with metaphorical language involving competition normally associated with sports; this discourse positions the pageant contestants as hungry competitors who are ready to duke it out over a crown. Examples include the headline '*Miss Utalii kutoana jasho*' ('Miss Tourism [contestants] make each other sweat') and a report on the outcome of the 2006 Miss Arusha contest: 'Amanda managed to wrestle the beauty crown from a total of 12 participants' (*This Day*, 8 June 2006). I interpret this discourse as one which embodies western forms of individualism and capitalism in which desire for material goods reigns supreme. This interpretation cannot be too far off the mark if one also considers the consistent patterning of the newspaper articles that report the prizes won by the contestants. The prizes and their monetary values are often listed before the details of the pageants, implying an order of importance for readers. The examples below taken from the first paragraphs of the newspaper articles that report the outcomes of the pageants illustrate this ordering, no matter whether the articles are in English or Swahili-medium newspapers:

> She is aged 19 and lives in Themi Hills area of Njiro. Amanda Alfred ole Sululu will also need a driving license now that she has just won a brand new saloon car, a Toyota Mark II, which is valued at Tsh. 7.4 million. By the way, Amanda is the Miss Arusha 2006 crown holder and the car was won at the beauty contest held over the weekend. (*This Day*, 8 June 2006)

> *Shindano la Miss Modern Arusha 2006 ambalo mrembo wake atazawadiwa gari jipya aina ya Mark II linafanyika leo kwenye Ukumbi wa Triple A jijini hapa.* (*Mwananchi*, 2 June 2005)

> The Miss Modern Arusha competition 2006 whose winner will be awarded with a new Mark II car will take place today at the Triple A Hall in the city.

Miss Chang'ombe anayetarajiwa kesho ukumbi wa Sigara (TCC Club) ataibuka na zawadi zenye thamani ya sh. milioni 2.3 na kupata tiketi ya kushirika mashindano ya Miss Temeke 2005. (*Majira*, 30 June 2005)

The one who wins Miss Chang'ombe tomorrow at the Sigara TCC Club Hall will emerge with prizes having a value of 2.3 million shillings ($2300) and will get the chance to participate in the Miss Temeke 2005 competition.

Moreover, in reporting on the results of pageants, many writers choose to express the prizes with the words *kunyaka* ('to grab/snatch') and *kujinyakulia* ('to snatch for oneself'), which connotes a sense of a free-for-all in which the winner is the most cunning player, rather than a well-organized contest in which prizes are awarded in an orderly fashion. No beauty pageant I have attended or which has been reported on in newspapers contains a description of any such melee among contestants at the end. Instead, the winners are announced and prizes are often given out on stage, to ward off accusations that the winners never received the prizes. In spite of what may actually happen on stage, the women are depicted as greedy and selfish, two characteristics that could not stand in further opposition to the discursive construction of Kenya's and Tanzania's socialist pasts, both of which emphasized communal principles through the spirit of *Ujamaa* and *Harambee*.

Nani atanyaka dola 500 Miss Kilimanjaro leo? (*Mwananchi*, 2 June 2005)

Who will **grab** $500 at Miss Kilimanjaro today?

Kwa ushindi huo, Caroline alijinyakulia zawadi ya masofa yaliotengenezwa kwa ngozi tupu yenye thamani ya Sh milioni 1.2, kabati la nguo lenye thamani ya Sh 800,000 na fedha taslimu Sh 200,000 (*Mtanzania*, 19 June 2005)

For winning, Caroline **won (lit. 'snatched for herself')** a prize of real leather sofas with a value of 1.2 million shillings (approximately $1200), a bureau for clothing worth 800,000 shillings ($800), and 200,000 ($200) in cash.

*... kimwana Parminda Raj, usiku wa kuamkia jana alitawazwa kuwa Komesha Miss Upanga 2005, baada ya kufanikiwa **kutwaa** taji la shindano la urembo la kitongoji cha Upanga na **kuwabwaga** warembo wenzake 10.* (*Nipashe*, 4 July 2005)

... darling Parminda Raj, late in the night was given the throne of Komesha Miss Upanga 2005, after succeeding in **capturing** the crown for the hamlet of Upanga and after **beating (lit. 'throwing down')** her fellow 10 beauties.

Responses to Western Discourses of Beauty

The above analysis of texts reveals how west-based versions of beauty are re-entextualized with English, preferences for light skin, and discourses of competition for material goods. Socio-economic success in the global marketplace is also tied to these pageants, and the necessity for success in international pageants creates a strong rationale for the use of English and the preference for slim and tall women at local pageants. In effect, it seems as though these pageants are domains in which localization is sharply delimited by global pressures.

One possible example of resistance toward total adaptation may be seen in the *vazi la ubunifu* 'creative wear' phase of the Tanzanian pageants during which contestants model clothing made from traditionally African fabrics. Like many western pageants, contestants participate in evening gown and bathing suit competitions that look much like those in other parts of the world, except for the fact that Tanzanian women must wear sarongs or shorts to cover their thighs. In contrast to these two parts of the pageant, the creative wear phase speaks directly to Afro-centric beauty. Billings (2006) draws attention to other features of the pageant which are also Tanzanian at heart:

> While certainly the overall framework of the competitions in Tanzania is based on an international model, ample opportunities arise for local interpretation. The Miss World formula is filtered through multiple people and passed on to contestants and organizers by title-holders, some of whom themselves have had only indirect access to the international model. More important though, is the fact that the phenomenon of the Tanzania beauty pageant, while inspired by and linked with western events, is simultaneously deeply local; the substance and trapping of the pageants, from the décor, entertainment, and prizes, to the specific ways in which contestants present themselves and are judged, must make sense to Tanzanians. (Billings, 2006: 134–135)

The creative wear phase of the mainstream pageants is indeed local in that the audiences and contestants are involved in a Tanzanian performance, for the clothing draws on the traditional dress of Tanzanian cultures. The most popular ethnic style that appears in the creative wear is that of the Maasai, a highly visible group in East Africa, which, by many accounts, is often deemed one of the most 'traditional' groups in all of sub-Saharan Africa (Hodgson, 2001; Lewinson, 2003). Contestants often make use of the trademark beads and the red and blue wool blankets worn by the Maasai in their reinvented outfits (see Figures 4.3 and 4.4).

Figure 4.3 A contestant at Miss Upanga in the creative wear phase of the contest

On the face of it, the choice to incorporate incontestably 'African' elements into the pageant looks like localization and resistance to imperialism through the reinforcement of African perspectives and the creation of hybrid fashion, a blend of Maasai and stylish modernity. However, it is important to consider the *invention* (cf. Makoni, 1998, 2003; Mudimbe, 1988) of this modern African identity. Many African 'traditions' were invented by colonialists and missionaries, including the invention of tribes such as the Maasai.[6] More than a few scholars of Africa have shown that the Europeans' own enthusiasm for maintaining traditions disposed them toward identifying, classifying and creating categories and traditions in colonial Africa, which have since been reproduced among Africans, leading to a deep attachment and sense of authenticity (e.g. Appiah, 1992; Fanon, 1961; Makoni, 1998; Mudimbe, 1988; Oyewumi, 1997; Ranger, 1992). Very similar points can be raised about the valuing of English and African *lingua francas* such as Swahili

Figure 4.4 Another contestant at Miss Upanga wearing Maasai-inspired creative wear. She won first place.

over other languages (*cf.* Makoni & Pennycook, 2005), and the ensuing linguistic hierarchies that result in the highest values for English at beauty pageants such as 'Miss East Africa'.

Miss Bantu and Jimama: Afro-centric Pageants as Multivocal Resistance

Another way in which East Africans claim authenticity is through promoting 'traditional' female beauty at alternative beauty pageants. Miss Bantu and *Jimama* (literally, 'big mother') are beauty pageants in which women are judged based on how well they fit a 'traditional' conceptualization of Tanzanian values and beauty, so they offer the opportunity to see how authentic African identity is established through texts. First held in 2001, the Miss Bantu pageant allows women of all ages and body types to enter. This is unlike typical beauty contests such as Kenya's 'The Smile of

Africa', a contest in which women must be aged between 18 and 27 years, have a minimum of secondary education, and a height of at least five feet nine inches. At Miss Bantu, the contestants' answers are expected to have an 'African' perspective, and the women should 'explain precisely their roles as African women in society and how they can impart these values to the next generation' (Tagama, 2003: 60). In contrast with the more individualistic orientation of the regional and national pageants, contestants in Miss Bantu are expected to show pride in their families, advocacy for women's issues and the economic development of their country. Compared with the winner of the Miss Tanzania contest, who is typically awarded a new car worth at least $3000, a modern apartment in Dar es Salaam and a monthly stipend, the winner of Miss Bantu is awarded 500,000 Tanzanian shillings (about $500). While Miss Tanzania can earn a profitable living off of her celebrity status, Miss Bantu winners are not likely to find such opportunities.

Other contests that promote indigenous forms of beauty make certain to emphasize the use of Swahili rather than English, thereby creating a strong indexicality between local identity and the Swahili language. The *Mrembo wa Kiswahili* ('Swahili beauty') pageant was held for the first time in December 2006 in Tanzania, with the goal of eventually producing a regional pageant across Swahili-speaking East Africa (darhotwire.com). The pageant's slogan, '*Lugha yetu Kiswahili, Fahari ya Tanzania, Fahari ya Afrika*' ('our language is Swahili, the pride of Tanzania, the pride of Africa') clearly advocates for Swahili over English; in fact, contestants must be able to recite Swahili poetry as part of the pageant. In addition, the only clothes allowed are the *buibui* (long black gown worn by Muslim women), or clothes made of *kanga* and *kikoi*, locally produced textiles. Furthermore, contestants are only allowed to use incense, *mdaa* (a black dye used for eyeliner) and African perfumes to adorn themselves.

Since the initial posting for this event was online (darhotwire.com), it afforded readers the opportunity to respond in an online forum. Of the four responses posted one day following the announcement, two were positive and two were negative. One reader was enthusiastic, asking for more information on the competition, while another was not able to tell if it was a non-humorous joke.

> *Jamani nimefurahi mnoooooo kusikia hili shindano ambalo si tu litakuza na kusamabaza lugha yetu bali pia utamaduni wetu hasa sisi watu wa mwambao! ... Nipeni maelekezo jamani tafadhali!!!!!!!*
>
> Friends I am sooooooo happy to hear about this competition which will magnify and make known our language and moreover, our culture, especially we people of the coast! ... Give me more information people, please!!!!!!!

Competing Dialogues on Female Beauty

> *Hiiki* [sic] *ni kichekesho au habari ya kweli. Mbona sasa sio April mosi? Ungetuambia nani ana-organzi* [sic], *yatafanyika lini?* ... *Unajua hapo nyuma tulishaona Miss Bantu: ilituweka kweney* [sic] *cart ya vimbwanga duniani, sawa na mbwa aliyetwa* [sic] *immigration na kupatikana kwa ngozi ya binaadamu.*
>
> Is this a joke or for real? Is it April first? Would you tell us who is organizing (this event) and when it will happen? ... You know in the recent past we already saw Miss Bantu: it put us in the hawkers' cart of the world (i.e. it sold us like property), like a dog who had gone through immigration and was made to look like a person.

Clearly, people are divided over how to interpret alternative pageants that promote Afro-centric beauty. It seems that the degree of localization of western norms for Africa and efforts to show pride in African beauty continue to exist in opposition to one another, rather than developing new and hybrid modes. Interestingly, however, the two different reactions to the idea of a Miss Swahili pageant also contain rather different language use. The positive response uses standard Swahili only, and through supporting the pageant, it discursively bonds 'pure' Swahili with enthusiasm for a contest that supports 'traditional' beauty. The negative reaction contains a fair degree of English, in words such as '*ana*-organzi [sic]' ('is organizing'), 'cart *ya vimbwanga*' ('hawkers' cart') and 'immigration'. The hybrid language becomes intertextualized with negative feelings about 'traditional' beauty. The difference between the two respondents is rather stark.

In the next section, I examine how producers and readers of texts manage these stark differences of opinion on female beauty through humor. Drawing on Bakhtin's (1981, 1984) writings on polyphony and heteroglossia, I show how parody becomes a key strategy for coping with competing discourses.

Managing Tensions through Humor

As the excerpts from Mutahi's column on the *mkorogo* phenomenon show, humor is one of the ways by which East Africans make sense of competing forms of beauty and competing claims to African authenticity. In his comical yet acerbic critique, Mutahi presents the *mkorogo* as a misrepresentation of reality through his claims about 'real' African identity, based on judgments of certain ways of speaking and specific skin tones. Similar claims are also made by the entry requirements for the Miss Bantu and *Jimama* contests, though humor is not an intended aspect of these pageants. Other texts use humor to call attention to the multiple discursive claims to reality in a more Bakhtinian sense through highlighting their *polyphony*, or presence of multiple voices, in the same texts and contexts. Often, these texts are parodies that make use of *carnivalesque* humor, a concept that Bakhtin (1968) developed in his analysis of French writer Rabelais's depiction of folk life at carnivals during the Renaissance. This humor challenged official views of reality by creative a festival for mocking authority figures, promoting the grotesque and lewd, and foraying into the typically off-limits domains of physical debauchery – in short, carnival was the world turned topsy-turvy. These two very different tactics to challenging western imperialism, claiming inauthentic representations and revealing polyphony, raise 'the key epistemological question as to whether one is dealing with a view of language and the world in which there is a reality that can be represented in language or whether one is working with a view that sees realities as produced through language' (Pennycook, 1998: 164–165).

In the end, it can be argued that both strategies constitute forms of resistance to imperialism since both challenge the prevailing view that western beauty is the only or the most appropriate model for beauty in Kenya and Tanzania. However, the texts that present the multiplicity of representations seem to better represent how people grapple with the development and reproduction of ideologies, including the ideologies of beauty and language. Again, polyphony is important in the process of this *ideological becoming*, where 'an intense struggle within us for hegemony among various available verbal and ideological points of view, approaches, directions, and values' (Bakhtin, 1981: 346). In sum, texts that exploit polyphonic meanings do not ask readers to uncover the 'truth' about reality; instead, they can be interpreted as an opportunity to ask readers to consider the humor in the co-existence of competing discourses about modernity, tradition and African identity.

Some scholars (e.g. Morson & Emerson, 1990) have argued that carnival is in essence contrary to the concept of heteroglossia because it seeks to disrupt prevailing orders of truth, implying that real 'truths' can be uncovered through laughter. Because carnival creates an opposition between the authorities of church and state and the masses, it has the potential to create a binary opposition between those in power who claim a particular version of reality and those who are subject to this power who can, through humor, uncover truth. My reading of Bakhtin's writings on laughter and carnival interprets these concepts as making space for multiple presentations of reality, rather than as a form of misrepresentation by the authorities. Sedgwick's account is similar: 'Instead of arguing for a polarised conception of authority and subversion through the juxtaposition of carnival and officialdom, Bakhtin seems to emphasize their ambiguous proximity [...] It is, it follows, an ambivalent phenomenon which is closely affiliated with the world of officialdom, from which it offers temporary release' (Sedgwick, 2002: 15). For Bakhtin, laughter is 'directed toward something higher – toward a shift of authorities and truths, a shift of world orders' (Bakhtin, 1984: 126). This shift need not be in the direction of 'truth', but rather in the direction of recognizing multiple claims to truth. His work on *Rabelais and His World*, also suggests this line of thought, as he argues that the carnivals held in the Middle Ages in Europe were a form of life that allowed people to be free from singular official feudal, religious, and political forms of domination. Bakhtin writes, 'carnival celebrated temporary liberation from the prevailing truth and from established order; it marked the suspension of all hierarchical rank, privileges, norms and prohibitions' (Bakhtin, 1968: 10).

Parodies of the Female Form

Though parody may be viewed as a somewhat trivial element of social life, it can be an important site for the study of gender identity, as it allows us to see how identities are contested and negotiated *vis-à-vis* the performance of other identities. Hall (2005: 126) illustrates how parody creates identities for speakers through their exaggeration of 'aspects of self that they perceive to be foreign to their own, positioning themselves as normative over and against the projected oddities of the other'. In her work on the third and fourth gender groups in India, Hall explains that the fourth gender *koti* claim their identity through parodying third gender *hijras*' lewd and sometimes non-standard Hindi. *Kotis* avoid identifying as gay men by mocking the conservative Hindi-English speech used in the gay community. In other words, by establishing who the 'other' is, the *koti* population linguistically produces a space in which they can claim a distinct 'self'. Hall's work also shows how parody is used to cope with the multiple forms of sexuality and competing discourses over third sex identities. She writes, 'linguistic parodies of the bawdy Hindi-speaking *hijra* and the prudish English-speaking patron serve as a commentary on the ever-growing tension between older and newer queer identities in urban India, themselves divided along lines of class as well as language' (Hall, 2005: 126–127).

In turning to the East African context, there are many humorous texts that can be read as parodies in the carnivalesque sense. Perhaps the most explicit example that has cropped up in the past few years is that of the comic entertainers who make a living performing at weddings, community bonanzas and other large parties. Though they can be hired for their services, they often work on the basis of tips, and they tend to show up

Figure 4.5 An entertainer at Leader's Club, Dar es Salaam, Tanzania (2005)

wherever large groups of people congregate in the evening. Among these entertainers are men who dress as women, placing two volleyballs on their backsides to emulate a well-endowed woman (see Figure 4.5). To earn big tips, these entertainers dance with men, as pictured in Figure 4.5, exaggerating their pelvic movements in order to make the volleyballs jiggle as much as possible. These performers entertain at events where people are likely to have a little extra spending money, such as outdoor music concerts, and for this reason, most audiences are comprised of educated, middle-class patrons, a social group who is likely to have a great deal of exposure to 'modern' versions of female beauty along the lines of Miss Tanzania. While the patrons are listening to live music and watching young and fit female dancers gyrate to the music onstage, entertainers such as the men dressed as women circle around the periphery in search of tips. These men create a disjuncture between the object of imitation and the performance. One onlooker at such an event remarked to me *'wanachekesha sana kwa sababu wanaiga vibaya'* ('they make people laugh because they imitate so poorly'). Unlike other populations of men who dress as women,[7] these entertainers are transparent males who are exaggerating one aspect of women's bodies, and hence, their performances can be interpreted as parody rather than some other phenomenon.

Columns in gossip-oriented newspapers are another source of carnivalesque humor. In a June 2006 edition of *Sani*, a Tanzanian newspaper whose slogan is *Burudisho la wasomaji* ('entertainment for the readers'), one of the headlines read *'Jimama lamdatisha Miss Tanzania!'* ('A large woman trips up Miss Tanzania!'). The article was about a former Miss Tanzania, Angela Damas, and particularly her reaction to a *Jimama* Taarab[8] singer who danced provocatively in front of her at a music awards show *'kwa staili inayojulikana kama "vaibresheni"'* ('in a style known as vibration'), which involved shaking her backside for an extended period of time. This dancing style is the 'authentic' version of what the men-dressed-as-women imitate, as discussed above. The article is a good example of how such texts can point out the competing discourses of appropriate or conventional female behavior through humor. The article presented the scene as if Damas was 'caught' by a video monitor with her mouth open and her finger pointing at the Taarab singer. Damas is presented as a novice to the world of Taarab, which marks her as 'untraditional'. This construction of her and other women who participate in beauty pageants is extended when one of the audience members is quoted in Swahili, saying, 'She's never gone to a Taarab concert, that one. These misses go to clubs and other places. If she sees Jimama Rose and other Taarab singers, she'll get totally confused.' The quote positions Damas as an outsider to a domain in which 'being female in Tanzania' and 'being Swahili' are central aspects of belonging to the Swahili culture associated with Taarab music. Damas is one of the 'misses' whose cultural activities are clearly different from Taarab entertainment. Importantly, the article does not condemn Damas for her ignorance of Taarab, however, but pokes fun at how she lacks the insider knowledge that the other women possess. Rather than claiming that she misrepresents Tanzanian women, what is claimed is that she symbolizes another version of female identity.

The article continues to highlight the multiple forms of female beauty in the domain of Taarab by reporting on how one of the emcees of the night, Nancy Sumari, Miss Tanzania 2005, was also constructed as an outsider by the other emcee, a male. After the *'vaibresheni'* episode, Sumari was asked by her fellow emcee if her own lack of *'makalio makubwa'* ('a large backside') would interfere with her ability to dance to Taarab music. Sumari replied that she could if she tried, and the emcee followed up with *'Utatingisha nini?'* ('What will you shake?'), which caused the crowd to burst into uncontrollable laughter. Like Damas, the article shows how Sumari is treated as 'Tanzanian' and 'female' by virtue of being asked about her ability to perform the dance, but she is depicted as an unsuitable female Tanzanian for this particular domain because of her body type (tall and slim). Though Sumari claimed knowledge of this practice, the audience's reaction clearly categorized her as an imposter for this particular domain.

Not surprisingly, cartoons are another source of polyphonic parody. Beginning in the 1990s in Tanzania, many Tanzanian cartoonists used exaggerated imitation in their depictions of *washamba* ('hillbillies', people from rural areas), juxtaposing them with city dwellers in order to achieve humorous effects (Lewinson, 2003). By the end of that decade, however, more attention was paid to the ways that Tanzanians were adapting to global culture, including that of beauty pageants. *Kingo*, the magazine referenced in Figure 4.1, is one of the few outlets for societal critique widely available in Uganda, Kenya and Tanzania.

The 1999 volume of *Kingo* (also depicted in Figure 4.1) took up beauty pageants as a theme and humorously examined the Tanzanian response to western forms of beauty alongside Afro-centric concepts. In the pages of the magazine, the answer to the question on the cover, 'Which one is Miss Tanzania?', unfolds through carnivalesque humor. The final two contestants (depicted in Figure 4.1) participate in evening gown and bathing suit competitions, followed by a series of absurd pageant tasks that highlight the urban and rural differences of the contestants, including a race to collect water in which the women are thwarted by a dysfunctional spigot, a common problem in Tanzania due to inconsistent water supply. The woman from Mtwara, a rural region in southern Tanzania, quickly resolves this problem by taking water from a nearby stream using a bucket (Figure 4.6).

The talent competition follows. Miss Mtwara rides a bike loaded with many heavy gunnysacks, while Miss Dar es Salaam shows off her ability to jump on a moving public bus while wearing high heels. Next, Miss Mtwara demonstrates her ability to carry a young child on her back without need of a blanket to secure the child with, and Miss Dar es Salaam illustrates her skills at hiding herself under a table after having enjoyed several beers with an older, well-dressed businessman in order to avoid the bill. Her behavior is a classic example of why Dar es Salaam is known nationwide as *Bongo* (< *ubongo*, 'brain'), since she uses her ingenuity for her own benefit here. Importantly, both women are depicted as having

Figure 4.6 An excerpt from *Kingo* which shows the two beauty contestants' very different strategies for filling a bucket of water. Reproduced with permission of Gaba Ltd

talents, albeit talents associated with very different domains of life. Intriguingly, it seems that no judgment is passed on the specific skills that each woman possesses. In fact, in the end, the emcee announces a tie, both women are awarded the title of Miss Tanzania, and the prize offered to both women is a new car, which Miss Mtwara promptly exchanges for a large amount of corn.

While a tie has never been the outcome of a Miss Tanzania contest, this result is a perfect example of multivocality, as it proposes acceptance of multiple kinds of women and multiple kinds of beauty in modern Tanzania, in addition to the entertainment being offered. In fact, in an interview about the beauty pageant issue with James Gayo, the cartoonist for *Kingo*, he explained that his magazine was not meant only to be funny, but rather to make people think about '*mambo yalivyo siku hizi*' ('the way things are these days'). Bakhtin writes about this same goal in his work on carnival: 'Combined in the act of carnival laughter are death and rebirth, negation ... and affirmation. This is a profoundly universal laughter, a laughter that contains a whole outlook on the world. Such is the specific quality of ambivalent carnival laughter' (Bakhtin, 1984: 126).

Conclusion

This chapter has examined how the female form is presented in popular culture and in the media, with a focus on beauty pageants. Compared with Chapter 3, the language used by contestants at beauty pageants imposes stricter controls on language mixing, although the discourses surrounding pageants are just as hybrid as in the newspaper office. In Dar es Salaam, modern, elite identities are typically constructed through English-Swahili language mixing, so the constraints against this way of speaking create artificiality. Though inauthentic for the local context of Tanzania, this way of speaking is valued because of international beauty pageants and global opportunities. While conceding the importance of the global stage, some East Africans remain uneasy about the artificiality of these performances, and they express their concern through mocking these 'misses', as Mutahi does in his article about the *mkorogo*, and as the Taarab singers do in their interaction with a former Miss Tanzania. Others respond by establishing pageants which promote indigenous beauty, thereby producing a counter-discourse and a claim to 'true' African beauty. Nevertheless, the reality on the ground is that multiple claims to beauty are present in Kenya and Tanzania, and the result is a multivocal and multimodal representation of womanhood. To facilitate a better understanding of how competing discourses can co-exist within the same domains, I analyzed how one of the common responses to competing forms of multivocality is carnivalesque humor, which seeks to destabilize monolithic and official perspectives on authentic beauty for East African women. As a coping mechanism, parody is an interesting form of dialogism in itself since it continually challenges the possibility of finding one 'true' representation of beauty by continually disrupting claims to authenticity.

My analysis also sought to assess the degrees of imperialism and localization of western norms for beauty. Clearly, some texts, such as Mutahi's article about the *mkorogo*, or the announcement for an upcoming Miss Swahili pageant in a Tanzanian newspaper, make explicit claims about authentic African beauty as Afro-centric, rather than as form of cultural hybridity with western aesthetics. However, these texts are relatively meager, at least in comparison with the prevalence of discourses that unquestioningly promote what is perceived as a western version of African beauty. Moreover, because western-style beauty pageants are increasingly viewed as a means to socio-economic success among young women in East Africa, discourses of social mobility through the adoption of western aesthetics, and western modes of beauty as a pathway to material wealth seem to muffle these discourses.

All of the ink dedicated to discussing women's bodies and women's language raises the question of why so much attention is paid to this topic. The answer may lie in the fact that in nearly every society, women's social and sexual behaviors are more closely monitored than men's behaviors on a whole (e.g. de Beauvoir, 1953; Friedan, 1963; Wolf, 1991), and that the unequal attention to women's bodies and women's language is a form of social control (Cameron, 1995; Weedon, 1987; Wolfson, 1984). From this perspective, in the East African context, this social control has an added facet since global and local aesthetics are also in dialogue, potentially leaving East African women exposed to a form of 'double-oppression' (Oyewumi, 1997; Spivak, 1985, 1987; Suleri, 1992) as post-colonial subjects and as women. However, the nexus of these multiple representations of womanhood and beauty may also offer them a means by which they can remain ambivalent about their own gendered identities, thereby resisting all forms of oppression in the process.

Notes

1. From 'Catwalking'. Available at dailynation.com (14 October 2006).
2. From 'Tanzania counts cost of "white skin"'. Available at http://news.bbc.co.uk (23 November 2004).
3. Apparently, Mutahi developed the nickname 'Whispers' because he takes on topics which most Kenyans only feel comfortable whispering about. Unfortunately, Mutahi died in 2003 due to surgery complications, but his son has taken over the column with the pen name Whispers Junior.
4. *Miraa* is a stimulant herb that is widely used in Kenya and other parts of East Africa.
5. *Ujamaa* refers to African socialism as implemented in Tanzania in the post-independence period. *Harambee* is a parallel concept in Kenya that refers to community-based efforts for self-reliance and development.
6. For tragic reasons, the most well known case of tribal invention is probably that of the Hutu and the Tutsi groups in present day Rwanda and Burundi. In pre-colonial times, these terms were used to refer to social status (Lemarchand, 1996), but under colonial rule, they became used to demarcate Africans on an ethnic basis. Tutsis were considered to be more Caucasian in appearance, and hence, were usually treated with greater respect than the Hutus.
7. Armory (1998) reports cross-dressing as ritual performance for harvest festivals, by cross-dressing entertainers who sing at *mbenda* (wedding) ceremonies, attended only by women and by some gay men.
8. Taarab music developed on the Swahili-speaking coast of East Africa and is a domain strongly associated with women and with the maintenance of Swahili culture. While the musical instruments are normally played by men, the most famous singers are women. The songs are full of metaphors and often contain euphemisms about sexual behavior and warnings to other women about their potential misdeeds (Askew, 2002).

Chapter 5
The Polyphony of East African Hip Hop

> *Tukianzia uzuri tu,* she gotta gwan
> *Tabia, heshima ndio du,* she gotta gwan
> *Mpaka kwa masista du yeeh nabaki tu kusema*
> uuh she gotta gwan
> Girl you gotta gwan
> You are my number one
> *Mama* get busy *twende kwenye* dance floor
> Ngwair, 'She Gotta Gwan'

> Gidigidi big name, am saleable
> *Kama pilipili,* yes am terrible
> Kanyamwa Homabay *ng'ama chalo koda*
> Do you know Gidigidi is unbwogable
> Gidi Gidi Maji Maji, 'Unbwogable'

These two excerpts of lyrics by East African hip hop artists represent the multiple languages used by artists in Tanzania and Kenya, and they also illustrate the varying types of localization that are taking place in this domain of social life. Some hip hop artists produce lyrics that are much closer to the linguistic and cultural references of west-based hip hop, even utilizing stock phrases from African American English (AAE). The lyrics from Ngwair's song above include direct borrowing of AAE *get busy* ('let's go', also euphemistic for 'have sex'), while the title and refrain of the song, '*She gotta gwan*', illustrates simultaneous localizations and globalizations of hip hop. These three words are both a Tanzanian-ized form of the AAE phrase (she got it goin' on), and a globalized expression due to the use of Jamaican Creole *gwan* ('gonna')[1] to mean something like 'this woman is really beautiful/sexy'. Other artists imbue their messages heavily with local languages such as the Kenyan duo of Gidi Gidi Maji Maji, who sing in Dholuo, English, Swahili and Sheng. Artists in Tanzania do the same, such as Mr Ebbo and Xplastaz, artists who blend Maasai into their otherwise Swahili and Swahinglish rhymes. More than appropriation of a cultural form from African American rappers in the United States, these lyrics represent linguistic, social, and even political processes of syncretic indigenization that produce various forms of multi-voiced expression. In this chapter, I examine this heterogeneity in hip hop lyrics and in other domains of youth culture where hip hop language has spread, including Internet sites that cater to East African consumers and text messages that are published in local newspapers in the form of shout-outs. In taking up East African varieties of *hip hop nation language* (Alim, 2004; Alim *et al.*, 2009; Osumare, 2007; Smitherman, 1997), I argue that East African youth are participating in what has become the global hip hop nation, and I show that they are relocalizing both English and African languages in the process.

Rather than focusing solely on localization, the exploration of multivocality in this domain goes beyond what many examinations of language and globalization focus on – transformations that English undergoes when removed from its 'native' context. In the domain of East African hip hop, we do not see a unidirectional adaptation of an outside linguistic/cultural form for the local context, but rather, multiple kinds of transformations taking place that involve both local and global resources. Kenyan and Tanzanian rappers 'reterritorialize not only major Anglophone rules of intelligibility' (Mitchell, 2003: 3) but also the African languages that are part of the mix.

The concept of *re-entextualization* (Bauman & Briggs, 1990; Silverstein & Urban, 1996) describes the processes of linguistic and cultural reterritorialization very well. Re-entextualization describes how speakers 'take some fragment of discourse and quote it anew, making it seem to carry a meaning independent of its situation within two now distinct co(n)texts' (Silverstein & Urban, 1996: 2). This concept borrows theoretically from Bakhtin's (1981) notions of intertextuality and polyphony in that speakers' utterances are never uniquely authored, as each word has its own social history, imbued with the many meanings acquired from previous speakers and listeners. The previous meanings of the utterance are not lost; instead, they become a sort of palimpsest on which new meanings are sedimented. (Re)-entextualization is a useful context for the intertextual aspects of musical performance on many levels, as it describes the art of sampling, the practice of extracting parts of older tracks and layering them with new beats and new rhymes to create a new form of artistry. It also describes how artists exploit the earlier re-entextualizations of particular words and phrases to mean anew, and it explains how youth use the global capital of hip hop language alongside street savvy codes to create a simultaneously global and local identity for themselves.

I first examine various kinds of re-entextualizations that are taking place within hip hop by examining the multivocality and double-identifications in hip hop artists' names and bivalency in song names. Then, I turn my attention to re-entextualization processes involving references to women in lyrics from Tanzanian hip hop, and I make use of ethnographic interviews to show how music fans are taking these re-entextualizations in. Finally, I explore an example of the re-territorialization of hip hop into other domains of life by examining how the 2002 presidential campaign in Kenya used Sheng hip hop lyrics for political gain, thereby changing the meanings of the language. The discussion of re-territorialization continues into Chapter 6, where hip hop language surfaces in the domain of advertising as well.

Multivocality in Naming Practices

Names of hip hop artists are crucial sites for identity making. While the practice of naming oneself 'MC' or using high-status labels such as Queen, Master and Prince might at first be taken as mimicry of west-based hip hop, these naming practices are arguably just as African in origin. In her study of global hip hop, Osumare (2007) asserts that naming is part of the power of the word, the center of African artistic expression that forms the 'African aesthetic' at the center of all hip hop. This aesthetic is an extension of artistic expressions emanating from Africa such as verbal word play and storytelling. Naming is part of this aesthetic and is an empowering process that serves to re-capture one's identity from oppressive circumstances. Like the African trickster figure in storytelling traditions, the hip hop artist uses language to dupe through verbal artistry, a feat perhaps most clearly recognizable in verbal 'battles' in which the audience chooses the most talented emcee. Rappers reinvent themselves through their names as a way to project their desired traits and skills, and some rename themselves with regularity (e.g. American artist Sean Combs has renamed himself Puff Daddy, then P. Diddy, followed by Puffy).

East African hip hop artists also reinvent themselves through their names, but their multilingual contexts provide them with additional resources they can exploit to resonate with the world of global hip hop while also re-capturing these references at a local level. For example, the popular Tanzanian artist King Crazy GK produced several songs featuring the group East Coast Team, and both aliases link to bivalent identifications relating to the global and the local. In King Crazy GK's name, the use of 'Crazy' relates to the AAE usage 'silly, fun, wack'; it is no coincidence that an African American rap artist named Krazy exists. GK refers to Gwamaka Kaihula, a strongly Bantu-sounding name, but in its abbreviated form, it fits the structure of many global hip hop aliases. The featured group, East Coast Team, creates a globalized indexical tie to the historical tension between the East Coast and West Coast hip hop scenes in the United States. As Tanzania is on the East Coast of Africa, this reference illustrates the double identification of hip hop pointed out by Pennycook and Mitchell (2009: 40), who write that 'Global Hip Hops do not have one point of origin (whether that be in African griots, New York ghettoes, Parisian suburbs, the Black Atlantic, or Indigenous Australia) but rather multiple, co-present, global origins'.

In a similar vein, several names in Kenyan hip hop doubly (and sometimes, triply) identify with the hip hop conscious state of California in the United States, and California Estate, a residential area in the Eastlands section of Nairobi. While the origins of the estate name are unclear, Calif Records is a production company located in Nairobi that focuses entirely on *Genge* ('mob') music, urban music that blends hip hop, dancehall and traditional African music styles. One of the best-known artists signed on Calif Records is the company's co-founder, Jua Cali (aka Paul Nunda). His name identifies with the record label (and through intertextual ties, with California, USA), as it translates from Swahili as 'know Cali', or, 'get to know Calif records'. *Jua* is the root of the Swahili verb for 'to know', and it is also a homonym with the Swahili noun for 'sun' in the Swahili phrase *jua kali* ('hot sun'), an idiomatic expression that is often used to refer to the idea that life is difficult, especially for those who have little education and therefore labor in the hot sun.

Other names are tied to more generically global identifications alongside Kenyan roots. For example, the Kenyan rapper born as Issa Mumar used the name E-Sir in his brief but vibrant career, cut short by a car accident in 2003. As Mwangi (2007) argues, the alteration of this Muslim artist's name from Issa to E-Sir goes beyond anglicization and suggests globalization due to affiliations with other forms of e-technology. It also recalls west-based hip hop artists' names that make use of the title sir, such as Sir Mix-a-lot and other markers of nobility (Jam Master J, Master P). It may be the case that these secular indexicalities offered the artist alternative identities which may have made him more marketable in a country in which terrorism has frequently been attributed to Muslims.[2] Either way, his alias simultaneously references his Islamic heritage and the global age in which he lived.

Sometimes, artists exploit the multivocality available to them to produce song titles whose multiple readings challenge local politics, or to get away with sexual explicitness. One of Kenya's most well-known artists, Nononi, of the very popular group Necessary Noize, has produced several song titles that have double (and triple) meanings, at least one of which is scandalous in some manner. His 2003 song *Wee Kamu* is a Sheng title meaning 'You just come' or 'come please'. However, as Mwangi (2007) explains, because the song was released right after the ruling party had been defeated after 24 years of dictatorial rule, the words were often interpreted by listeners as the euphoria that Kenyans felt because of this victory. Although the song has sexual overtones and is about a young man asking his lover to meet him unaccompanied in a house, the song 'conveys orgasmic fulfillment and bliss, which signal the hope that greeted the new government' (Mwangi, 2007: 323). Similarly, Nononi's 2006 song *Furahi Day* carries a dual meaning (as English *Friday* and Swahili *furahi*, 'happy'); Mwangi explains that though the song is apolitical on the surface, it is interpreted politically as a critique of the current government due to the song's discussions of illicit sexual activities that happen on Friday nights that are based on lying and infidelity. These dishonest acts are simply metaphors for other dishonest acts of politicians.

In the East African diaspora, websites can also display double identifications with west-based hip hop and East African street-consciousness in spite of being distantly located from the African continent. A good example is wakilisha.com, a website based in Raleigh, North Carolina. The name of the site indexes East Africa through the Swahili word *wakilisha* 'represent', and it points to the global hip hop English meaning of 'to represent', that is, to perform well, to speak for the people, and most importantly, to speak for the streets. Interestingly, while the site is managed in the United States, the subheading of the site is 'Representin' urban Kenya worldwide'.

Naming practices are just one aspect of hip hop in East Africa (and the diaspora) that are rich in multivocality. Music lyrics are another site within the domain of hip hop for multivocal performances, and in the next section, we see how the use of English words in Tanzanian hip hop produce quite different meanings, depending on the lyrical content that surrounds them.

Re-entextualizing and Relocalizing Hip Hop

In this section, I investigate how English-derived words become indexical in a new manner, that is, how they gain their appropriated meanings, and how those appropriated meanings then continue to undergo change in *Bongo Flava*, Tanzanian hip hop. This phrase makes use of Street Swahili *Bongo* (< *ubongo*, 'brain'), which is a pithy reference to Dar es Salaam, Tanzania's largest city – and most certainly a place where one has to use one's head to survive. Beginning with the lyrics in Ngwair's 'She Gotta Gwan' as a starting point, I examine the reterritorialization of English-derived words that refer to young women in Bongo Flava. I first illustrate how these English-derived terms are used to relate to a man's fantasy world where women are mostly sex objects. Then, I devote the remainder of my discussion to exploring how male artists use these terms within Swahinglish lyrics to critique these lifestyle choices. In making sense of the multiple languages used in Bongo Flava, I turn to interviews with fans.

Masista du and Mademu as sexual starlets in Bongo Flava

Bongo Flava is impossible to characterize in any unified sense since the artists who contribute to this genre vary from the likes of Mr II (aka 2 Proud, Sugu), Professor Jay and Mwana Falsafa ('Mr Philosopher'), artists who rap about social problems like corruption and poverty, to Mchizi Mox, Ngwair and Dully Sykes, artists best known for songs celebrating alcohol, partying and sex. This latter strand of Bongo Flava is known as party music, and its lyrics tend to focus on living the 'high life', characterized by the enjoyment of material and sexual pleasures. Rappers use varieties of English and Swahili in reference to social and sexual behaviors associated with a free and easy lifestyle that rarely show concern about the consequences of sexual promiscuity. The language varieties that appear in Bongo Flava include *Lugha ya Mitaani* (Street Swahili), appropriated forms of African American English (AAE) and various types of blending with English including codeswitching, often referred to by Tanzanians themselves as Swahinglish or Swanglish. Elements of Jamaican Creole also sometimes appear in Bongo Flava lyrics, alongside musical influences from reggae and dancehall.

Initially, monolectal forms of English infused with American themes characterized Tanzanian hip hop, as seen in Kwanza Unit's song 'Inahouse', first released in 1992. Kwanza Unit ('first unit') is considered Tanzania's first hip hop group (cited in Perullo & Fenn, 2003: 26):

> Ladies in lingerie, passion, menage a trois ...
> I'm sipping older sex Mafioso ...
> I'm in my silk robe, puffing a cigar, laying on my waterbed
> I'm about to be fed by this Puerto Rican love child. ('Inahouse', Kwanza Unit, 2002 [1992])

In the past decade, though, more than a few rappers have begun offering advice for how to live sexually responsible lifestyles. At the same time, the ways rappers use varieties of English and Swahinglish in their lyrics has changed. To explore this shift further, I look at examples of re-entextualizations of several English-derived words that relate to sexual behaviors that reference Tanzanian women.

One of these words, *sista*, is actually *bivalent* (Woolard, 1998) since it can be heard as both Tanzanian English for 'nun', and as a way to refer to a young woman in both Tanzanian English and Swahili. *Sista* is a re-entextualized form of the English word 'sister', (borrowed originally to refer to nuns within the domain of Christian missions), but it has more recently acquired the re-entextualizations of AAE 'sistah', and it can also be interpreted as a calque of Swahili *dada* ('sister'), a common vocative for young women in East Africa. The word has acquired its most recent re-entextualization in hip hop lyrics. If it comes along with *du*, (an interjection particle meaning 'oh!') it becomes Street Swahili *sista du*, meaning 'hottie' or 'beautiful towngirl' (Reuster-Jahn & Kießling, 2006). The phrase *masista du* (here with plural marker *ma-*) is very similar to another English-derived word for young women, *demu*, (< 'dame'). *Demu* is used in less respectful ways than *sista* or *sista du* and is typically a reference for a woman who is not present or out of earshot. Young men often use the word to refer to their girlfriends or to point out someone else's embarrassing lack of having a girlfriend. Significantly, the word *demu* also gets used in gossip-oriented newspapers involving scandalous stories about sexually loose women.

Whether these words are Swahili or English is difficult to say. In interviews with young adults in Dar es Salaam, most people identified *sista* as historically English while they preferred to label *demu* as 'street language', sometimes calling it *Kiswahili cha Mitaani* ('Street Swahili'). While it could be argued that Swahili phonology is apparent through the r-lessness of 'sister' and through the occurrence of *-u* on *demu*, these are also features of localized Tanzanian Englishes. Rather than trying to sort out which language these terms belong to, though, my purpose here is to see how these terms *mean* in their hip hop contexts.

Rapping about living it up

A great deal of Bongo Flava has used the terms *sista*, *masista du* and *mademu* (with variations in spelling on album covers) to sing about a certain kind of modern young woman whose (always urban) lifestyle is marked by spending a great deal of leisure time in nightclubs and expensive bars, seeking the company of well-to-do men, dressing in tight, western clothing and being sexually liberated. The phrase *sista du* was first made popular by well-known Tanzanian rapper Professor Jay who sang '*Masista du wa Bongo wanazidi kupanda chati*' ('The hotties of Dar es Salaam are climbing the charts') in his 2002 song 'Bongo Dar es Salaam'. Ngwair's 2005 song 'She Gotta Gwan' makes use of *masista du* in the same way, for it exalts the beauty of a young woman who stands out in the crowd at a dance club. Here, *masista du* refers to a woman who is prized mostly for her sexuality, as she is described as having been with many men and because she is a woman who, at the end of the song, is willing to go home with a man from the disco.

Tukianzia uzuri tu she gotta gwan	If we start with the best, she got it goin on
Tabia, heshima ndio duh she gotta gwan	Personality, respect, yes, she got it goin on
*Mpaka kwa **masista du** yeeh nabaki tu kusema* uuh she gotta gwan	Of all the **sisters**, yeah, I still say, uhh she got it goin on
Sitojali ashatembea na wangapi	I won't care that she's been with many
Kuwa nawe maishani naona bahati ...	Being with you in life is lucky
Nionyeshe zaidi ya nguo zako ulizovaa	Show me more than the clothes you wear
Nionyeshe zaidi ya ngozi yako ya kung'aa	Show me your skin that glistens
Nioneshe kile ambacho kitanipa raha	Show me everything that gives me pleasure
Hey hey hey hey	Hey hey hey hey
('She Gotta Gwan', Ngwair, 2005)	

Similarly, in Dully Sykes's song 'Ladies Free', *mademu* and *masista du* are characterized as sexually aggressive women who enjoy their leisure time in Dar es Salaam's nightclubs and who take advantage of men with means, such as Sykes himself. Here, the *mademu* and the *masista du* are part of a hip urban scene in which rappers (Kebi, Jerry and Mr II) and modern living intermingle. Sykes's song makes heavy use of Swahinglish and Street Swahili, two language varieties that strongly convey a cosmopolitan indexicality.

Ladies free, *wala sijakosa* Friday *hii*	Ladies free, and I haven't missed a Friday
Tena kulikucha wiki hii	Again it's coming this week

Hey yo **mademu** wanajazana kila kona	Hey yo **dames** are packed in every corner
Bilicana na Mambo Club	Club Bilicanas and Mambo Club
Hey! hey oh! natoka kaunta ya chini	Hey! Hey oh! I leave the lower counter
nakwenda ya juu	And head upstairs
Nawaona Kebi na Jerry wapo na Mr.II	I see Kebi and Jerry who are with Mr II
Kwenye makochi meusi wapo **masista du**	On the black couches are some **sisters**, oh!
Mmoja ananibomu nimnunulie redbull	One of them aks me to buy her a redbull
Nikaona safi tu ah! mbona poa tu	I thought it was best, so just do it
Nikajiminya mwanaume nikatoa blue	I stopped complaining, and pulled out a blue
Nikamwambia keep change oh baby	I told her keep the change oh baby.

('Ladies Free', Dully Sykes, 2004)

Here, the club scene, the linguistic choices, and references to urban commodities like Redbull entextualize *mademu* and *masista* in a particular kind of context. This urban and freewheeling setting is established through the expression 'Ladies Free', through the surrounding thematic content of being in the club, and through the juxtaposition of *mademu* and *masista du* with other Street Swahili expressions such as *ananibom* ('she keeps asking me') and *blue* (a 10,000 Shilling note, blue in color) whose meanings are not at all transparent from the English components alone. It is also significant that Sykes can tell the young woman who keeps 'bombing' him for a drink to keep the change on a 10,000 shilling note (approximately $9 USD), as this helps to construct Sykes's carefree attitude towards money and living it up, enjoying a life of leisure. Even in the expensive club, she would have kept at least half of the money as the change, a substantial amount for most Tanzanians.

The song 'T-shirt na Jeans' ('T-shirt and Jeans') by University Corner also illustrates the use of Swahinglish to describe *masista du* and their male counterparts as urban hipsters dressed in western clothing at a disco.

Waone **masista duu** au wacheki machizi	Look at the **sisters** oh, check out the guys
Mtazame kidume kisha wacheki matozi	Look at the guys, then check out the braggarts

Wamevaa t-shirt *na* jeans	They wear t-shirts and jeans
Wamenoga kichizi	They're so attractive
Hata idadi ya mitumba mingi	Even many of the used clothes
ni t-shirt *na* jeans	are t-shirts and jeans
Kutia jeans *za buku kwa wale wenzangu*	For 1000 shillings they sell jeans to my friends
na mimi	and me

('T-shirt na Jeans', University Corner, 2004)

Here we see Swahili street language such as *matozi* 'braggarts' (*tozi* < Beetles; according to Reuster-Jahn & Kießling, 2006, this may be a reference to VW Beetle vehicles which produce more noise than speed) as well as *buku*, the 1000 shilling note (< 'book').

In these three songs, we see that the party scene depicted in the lyrics (and the videos) provides the words *mademu* and *masista du* with particular contexts in which they obtain meaning. Interviews with residents of Dar es Salaam confirmed that these words would be used in a positive way if the singers were singing about love, lust and pretty girls. When asked to consider the use of the words that reference women, one young man in secondary school said the following:

Mimi nikisema ni 'demu wangu' kwa sisi vijana inamaanisha kwamba fulani ni mpenzi wangu. Halafu tukiongelea 'masista', sijui, sababu masista ni wale wa kanisani au ni masista duu ambao ni wasichana wale wa club ambao ni wasichana wa kujirusha. Kwa wasichana hawa, wanasema kuna 'ki-loose'.

For me, if I say 'my *demu*', for us young people it means something, it means my girlfriend. And if we're saying *masista*, then I don't know, *masista* are those people of church, or there are *masista duu* who are the women who go to clubs and dance. To refer to these girls, we say they are loose.

In asking for explanations for the difference between *sista, sista du,* and *demu,* I received generally unified accounts of these terms for women. *Sista* was usually seen as a respectable reference for any young woman, and it was considered to be a word used by everyone. Several young women did not see a difference between *sista* and *sista du* and *demu*. However, most male interviewees described *sista* as a respectful term, in contrast to *sista du* and *demu* references for girls who attach themselves to men at clubs and were described as *wahuni* ('hooligans') and *machangudoa* ('prostitutes'). Interestingly, *sista* and *sista du* were usually interpreted as coming from English while *demu* was most often understood as Street Swahili.

When I asked about the meanings behind these songs, one 25-year-old woman remarked that they did not seem to be very relevant to the current context of Tanzania, given the threat of HIV/AIDS:

> *Nyimbo zao hazilengi jamii yetu ya sasa hivi, kwa mfano hiyo ya Ngwair ya 'She Gotta Gwan'. Kama hapo anaposema kuwa yeye hajali huyo msichana ametembea na wanaume wangapi. Hiyo sidhani kama inatufundisha katika jamii yetu, hasa kwa sasa hivi kuna hili janga la UKIMWI na magonjwa mengi tu ya zinaa.*

> These songs don't target our society of today, for example, Ngwair's song 'She Gotta Gwan'. Like here when he says that he doesn't care that the girl has been with however many men. I don't think that this teaches our society anything, especially now that there is the calamity of AIDS and lots of sexually transmitted diseases.

The fact of HIV/AIDS in Tanzania has indeed shifted the social context of Bongo Flava, and this has had an impact on the way that some artists sing about women and sexual relationships. In the next section, I examine the impact of these shifting contexts.

Re-entextualization due to shifting contexts

Party songs focusing on enjoying the good life are still big hits in Bongo Flava, but this entextualization of *masista du* and *mademu* now competes with another entextualization which uses these words within a context of critique. This more recent re-entextualization is likely driven by the macro-context of increasing HIV rates in Tanzania and calls from the government and public health sector for hip hop artists to do what they can to battle the disease. Public discourses about HIV/AIDS have become much more possible in Tanzania since 1999, when the Tanzanian government declared AIDS a national crisis. It is not surprising that the first popular song to focus on HIV/AIDS in Tanzania, 'Sister sister' by King Crazy GK, was released in 2000. Other macro-contextual changes during this time promoted public discussions of the disease, including the formation of a governmental organization called the Tanzanian Commission on AIDS (TACAIDS), that would implement a multisectoral campaign to fight the transmission of HIV. Additional discourses that have been circulating in Dar es Salaam since 1999 include prevention messages from non-governmental organizations which reach young people through hip hop and other edu-tainment methods, and which have saturated the city with t-shirts, posters, billboards, and advertisements about HIV/AIDS. As Chapter 6 shows, these public health advertisements make use of street-conscious language as a means of getting the attention of their target audience, that is, youth aged 18–24. Additionally, the example of neighboring Uganda and its very public discussion of sexual behaviors and behavior change has created an impetus in Tanzania to be more frank about sexuality and promiscuity.

In the next section, we see how the discursive construction of street-conscious identities for young women becomes re-territorialized in a context of critique. This is achieved through re-entextualization that retains the meanings of the previous contexts involving the celebration of sexual liberation; the new indexicalities are created through using these terms to critique, rather than to celebrate women's sexual behaviors.

Masista and Mademu re-entextualized as behaviors for critique

In contrast to songs that focus on leisure time and nightlife are songs by artists such as King Crazy GK, whose song titled 'Sister sister'[2] characterizes *masista* as the target of criticism instead of symbols of desire. In the first part of the song, we see the words 'sister sister' to describe a 'nice girl who got lost' and a 'dear who became disabled', expressions that depict the 'sister' as wayward while also entextualizing the standard Swahili references for 'nice girl' (*msichana mzuri*) and 'dear' (*mpenzi*) as preferred ways of being. The actions of the sista of turning her back on her parents are described as *akasacrifice*, a Swahinglish word that shows judgement on the part of the lyricist.

Maisha umeyachezea sasa	You've played around with your life
mpenzi unalia	now you cry
Sister sister!	**Sister sister!**
Eeh yo! *Nakamata* microphone rap	Eeh yo! I grab the microphone (to) rap
Na safari hii Crazy GK	This is the journey of Crazy GK
Siyo kama naimba bali nalia	It's not that I'm singing, I'm crying out
Namlilia **msichana mzuri** *aliyepotea*	I cry for a **nice girl** who got became lost
Akaitoa shule sadaka sababu ya starehe za muda mfupi	She left school for the offer of good times
*Halafu aka*sacrifice *wazazi wake*	And then she sacrificed her parents
ili awafuate mabwana	to follow men

Bwana akamkimbia	Her man left her
Mpenzi akawa kiguru na njia	The dear became disabled on the way (w/o a man)
('Sister sister', King Crazy GK, 2000)	

The song continues, and the outcome of 'sister' cutting ties with her parents follows. As a result of quitting school and leaving home, she gets pregnant again and again, actions which are described in Swahinglish as '*ame*punch *mpenzi, machine akatega tena*' ('She "punched" her lover and the machine worked again'). The grim consequences of AIDS follow and 'sister' becomes entextualized with a negative set of behaviors as King Crazy GK laments 'Oh, sister sister'.

Wazazi nyumbani akawasusia	She stopped visiting her parents
Akajiona amepunch mpenzi	She punched (had sex) with her lover and the
machine akatega tena	machine got her (she became pregnant again)
Ni watoto watano sasa anao	She's got five children now
UKIMWI juu ameambulia	and AIDS too
Ohh **sister sister**	Oh **sister sister**

King Crazy GK then explains that 'sister' died because '*aka*change lifestyle', a Swahinglish expression that does not translate directly to 'she changed her lifestyle', but rather 'to adopt a sordid lifestyle' of having sex with sugar daddies, expressed in the slang Swahili '*kuchuna mabuzi*' ('extort wealthy men with sex') so that she could feed her children.

Sister *mwili akaweka rehani,*	This **sister's** body was put in heaven
*ikabidi aka*change lifestyle *akaisha*	She had to change her lifestyle,
maisha ya kuchuna mabuzi	having sex with sugar daddies
ili mradi fedha apate watoto cha	in order to get money to
kuwalisha	feed her children

In the final part of the song, King Crazy GK uses the Swahili term *dada* (Swahili 'sister') and *wapenzi* (Swahili 'dears') to implore Tanzanian girls to listen to the story of this sister and learn from her mistakes. The Swahili vocative indexes young women who have not (yet) experienced the events of 'sister's' story. They are young women who can still make choices about the directions their lives will take.

Kwenu wapendwa **dada** *zangu*	In your situation, my **sisters**
Na huu ni wakala wangu kwenu	I am your agent
Wapenzi *ninawaomba muupokee*	**My dears** I beg you to heed this message
Chini muukalie na yale machache nitakayoyasema	Sit down and hear what I have said
Basi maanani muyatilie msiyazembee	Don't take what I say lightly
Ili msije kulia machozi ya damu	so that you don't cry tears of blood
Kwani gonjwa hili ni mwana haramu,	Because this disease is a danger
Na halina nidhamu	And it doesn't care who you are
Na chanzo chake kikubwa tamaa ya starehe na fedha	Its main source is desire for pleasure and money
Ebu sikiliza vizuri stori ya **sister**	now listen carefully to the story of **sister**.

In interviews with several young adults in Dar es Salaam, I asked what difference it would make in this final verse to use *dada* over *sista*. Even though some interviewees claimed that there was no difference between the two words in general, many did see meaning in the choice of *dada* here. One male interviewee explained that if a person were to call someone *sista* instead of *dada*, it would be an act of '*kihuni fulani*' ('some kind of hooliganism'), and he said that while *sista* can be enunciated to produce various meanings, *dada* can never be heard as any kind of *kihuni*. Another male interviewee agreed, and stated that the word *dada* could not possibly refer to a romantic relationship; *dada* clearly invokes the meaning of a respectful relationship with a young woman. Finally, a female interviewee explained that *dada* expresses a closer relationship than *sista*.

Another popular rapper, Noorah also critiqued the actions of young, urban women who enjoy the high life in his song '*Ukurasa wa Pili*' ('Page Two'). The lyrics relate to the female groupies who fawn over him because of his success. A fellow emcee chimes in as well, offering comments on Noorah's tale at the end of most verses.

Attention please
This is another public announcement
from MJ Records

Yo *ndani ya gari navinjari*	Yo in the car I'm hangin
na Prince Dully Sykes	with Prince Dully Sykes
Namuona du! White, *simjui*	I see her, hey! Light-skinned, I don't know her

Amevaa glasses	She's wearing shades
'Eti mambo!' Safi. 'Samahani,	'What's up?' Nothin.
naomba lifti'	'Excuse me, can I get a lift?'
Unataka lifti? 'Eeh'. Kapande	You want a lift? 'Yes'.
kitega uchumi	Then take an elevator
'Ah kaka mbona unanijibu majibu	'Oh fella why do you talk
ya kihuni'	to me like a hooligan?'
Hebu toka hapa mtakufa na UKIMWI	From this you will die from
nyie **mabinti**	AIDS, you **daughters**
MC: *Jamani*	MC: C'mon, people
('Ukurasa wa Pili', Noorah, 2006)	

Here we see the use of AAE 'yo' mixed with Street Swahili such as *navinjari* ('I'm hangin') alongside Swahinglish such as *'amevaa* glasses' ('wearing (sun)glasses'). The *demu* in this case uses Swahinglish *'naomba lifti'* herself to ask for a 'lift', an expression which is quite common in Dar es Salaam. Here and throughout the song, Noorah depicts himself as smarter than these girls, using language that is either over their heads because of its streetwise quality, or through simply making fun of them. Like King Crazy GK, Noorah gives advice at the end of the verse to all young women, using the respectful Swahili word, *mabinti* ('daughters'), to warn them about the threat of HIV/AIDS.

The song continues with explicit critique of *demu*. Like the young woman asking for a lift, these are women who pester Noorah with their interest in him, which he depicts as disingenuous since they only call him when he's just been on tour (and likely to have money). He jokes around with one woman who calls him on the phone, responding to the question *'Mbona siku hizi huonekani?'* ('Why don't I see you these days?') in a playful manner ('Have I gotten too dark (skinned)?'), and also by pretending that his female caller has confused him with his fellow rapper Ngwair, implying that the woman has relationships with many rappers who she cannot keep straight. Again, the *mademu* here are characterized in part by their use of Swahinglish, as in *'Noorah umekuwa* handsome' ('Noorah you've become handsome', pronounced [hændsamu]).

Halafu kuna **demu** *huwa anapenda*	Then there's another **dame**
sana kunizingua	who really likes to bug me
Huwa hanitafuti mpaka asikike	She doesn't look for me until
nimetoka tour	she hears I'm off tour
(Rings) *Hallo! 'Mbona siku hizi*	(rings) Hello? 'Why don't
huonekani?'	I see you these days?'
Nimekuwa mweusi? 'Ah we acha utani'.	Have I gotten too dark?

The Polyphony of East African Hip Hop

Hivi unajua kwanza unaongea na nani?	'Ah, stop joking'. Do you know who you called?
'Si Noorah?' Ni Ngwair. 'Basi samahani'.	'Not Noorah?' This is Ngwair. 'Excuse me'.
Halafu kuna mwingine huwa anapita bila hata salamu	Then there's another who used to go by without greeting
Nashangaa siku hizi eti 'Noorah umekuwa handsome'.	I'm surprised, these days, it's 'Noorah, you're handsome'.
MC: *Anajipendekeza*	**MC:** She's ingratiating herself

Next, Noorah catches another *demu* who tries to make him responsible for a presumably fake pregnancy. In response to her letter asking for help with the child, he tells her he can help her pick out a name. The refrain of the song expresses Noorah's frustration with women like this and entextualizes the term *mademu* with these behaviors quite clearly.

Mwingine nilienda Tanga ku-perform	Another, I went to Tanga to perform
Nakumbuka vizuri sana kuwa nilitumia condom	I remember well that I used a condom
Wiki mbili baadaye si akaniandikia barua	Two weeks later she wrote me a letter
Kuwa ana mimba miezi ya tisa, anataka kujifungua	Saying she was 9 months pregnant, ready to give birth
MC: *Anataka pesa*	**MC:** She wants money
Kama ni kuhusu fedha, mama cha kukusaidia sina	If it's about money, I can't help you mama
Labda nikusaidie tu kumchagulia jina	Maybe what I can do is help to choose the name
MC: *ha ha eh bwana*	**MC:** ha ha, that's right my friend
Chorus	
Ohh! *Hawa* **mademu** *sijui ni vipi*	Oh these **dames** I don't know what
Ohh! *wananighasi ghasi ghasi*	Oh they get on my nerves

At the end of the song, Noorah returns explicitly to the link between *mademu* behaviors and HIV/AIDS by ridiculing *mademu* for their actions. He shows his exasperation in his lyrics, stating '*Kama ana ngoma unamuongezea gitaa na keyboard na kila kitu*' ('If she has AIDS, you can give her a guitar, a keyboard, everything'). Here, *ngoma* literally means 'drum', but it also is a Street Swahili euphemism for sex and also HIV/AIDS. Noorah exploits this double meaning to mock *mademu* who get infected with HIV by singing about how he'll give them musical instruments to go along with their *ngoma*.

Another example of the re-entextualization of *sista* and *mademu* towards advice and critique is in Ferooz's song '*Starehe*' ('recreation/leisure'). The song is a narrative about a man who is sick with AIDS, talking about his past mistakes from his bed. This song is the only one I have found which has a male protaganist who suffers as a result of sexual promiscuity. However, it contains many references to *mademu* and *masista* as well.

Hapa nilipo mimi niko kitandani	Here I am in bed
Starehe zimeniweka matatani	Recreation put me in trouble
Kupona tena mimi haiwezekani	I can't get better
Masela wangu ndugu zangu buriani	My homies in the graves
Kwaherini (×3)	Good bye (×3)
Saa saba juu ya alama saa nikiitazama	It's one o'clock, I'm looking at my watch
Nimeshaachana na Jackie sasa namfuata	I've parted with Jackie, now I'm looking for
Salama	Salama
Saa kumi na mbili nna appointment *na **mademu** wawili*	At six o'clock I have an appointment with two **dames**
Achana na lile ambaye tutakutana saa mbili	Aside from the one (it) I'll see again at eight
Jane wa Mikocheni ambaye sasa hayuko duniani	Jane in Mikocheni who has already died
Aliyekuwa akinisubiria pale Vatican Kijiweni	She used to wait for me at the Vatican club in Kijiweni
('Starehe', Ferooz, 2005)	

Again, here we see *sista* and *mademu* used in conjunction with English and Swahili mixing, as in '*Saa kumi na mbili nna (nina)* appointment *na mademu wawili*' ('At 6 o'clock I've got a date with two dames'). The Swahinglish '*nna* appointment' ('I've got a date') is a euphemism for a date of a sexually-oriented nature that involves a semantic shift from English. The use of *lile* for 'the one' to refer to one of the women is also significant since, in Swahili, *lile* as opposed to *yule* is used for inanimate objects or for living things that one wishes to denigrate by dehumanizing them grammatically.

Ferooz's narrative is clearly a moral tale, as he explains how his actions took him on a path to hell, listing his interactions with women of three different kinds along the way.

Amina na Semeni nakutana kwa Macheni	Amina and Semeni I meet at Macheni (club)
Na kila siku nabadilisha tena kwa foleni	And every day I slept with a long line of them
Huo ndio ulikuwa mwenendo wa maisha yangu	That was my daily routine of my life
Mimi viwanja kujivinjari na machangu oh	I was hanging out with whores, oh
Niliona fahahari hii eee	I felt proud, eeh
Starehe mimi nilizifanyia papara	I carelessly loved the 'high' life
*Nilibadili **mademu** kama vidaladala*	I changed **dames** like commuter busses
Nkenda nimepanda hili nikirudi lile	I went and boarded this then climbed aboard that
Nilitamani starehe zote nizitawale	I wished I could rule all the night life
Hata kumkumbuka Mola wangu ilikuwa ndoto	Even to try and remember my God was just a dream
Nilitekwa na ulimwengu kumbe naukimbilia moto	I was captured by the world, I didn't know I was running toward hell
Tabia ya kubadili wasichana mimi nilikubuhu	For changing girls I was a fool
*Nilitembea na **watoto wa gate**, **machangu** na **masister du***	I slept with **sheltered girls**, **whores** and **loose women**

He describes sleeping with many women, including *watoto wa gate* ('children of gates', that is, young women of an upper class background who live in gated homes), *machangu* (prostitutes) and *mademu* and *masister du*, women of a third category who are not explicitly prostitutes but whose actions fall into a similar realm of behavior. The song continues using a frame in which Ferooz visits a doctor, who is played by Professor Jay, a well-known Tanzanian rapper, and discovers that he is HIV positive. It is quite unusual that a male character suffers the consequences of sexual promiscuity in a rap song. That a male rapper portrayed a male character infected with HIV did not go unnoticed in Tanzania. In fact, after the song became popular, *feroozi* entered the lexicon of Street Swahili as yet another euphemism for AIDS. In the final verse, Ferooz's character becomes overwhelmed with despair and says he will end his life. The doctor tries to encourage him to have hope:

Kipimo kinaonyehsa ni kweli umehathirika	The test shows that you are infected
I'm very sorry kupoteza nguvu ya taifa	I'm very sorry to lose our nation's manpower
Ni vema kufanya ibada na kumrudia Muumba wako	It's better to do prayers and repent to your God
Kula vizuri fanya mazoezi pumzisha mwili wako	Eat well, do exercise and get enough rest for your body
Ukizingitia hayo utaishi kwa matumaini	Take note of this and you will live in hope
By the way unayo nafasi hebu jiamini	By the way, you still have a chance, be confident
(Professor Jay)	

In the doctor's lines, we see a different type of English and Swahili codeswitching altogether, a sociolect associated with educated and affluent Tanzanians such as doctors and university professors (Blommaert, 1992). This way of speaking is more or less the juxtaposition of monolingual forms of English and Swahili rather than a hybrid Swahinglish variety that exhibits semantic shift or new meanings based on the blend of two languages, such as *demu*. The doctor tells him that he is indeed HIV positive prefaced with 'I'm very sorry', rather than using other very common expressions of sympathy in Swahili. The doctor's use of 'By the way' on the final line of the excerpt is pragmatically awkward and probably would not appear in the speech of Tanzanian doctors; its use here is likely due to the fact that Professor Jay and Ferooz have penned the lyrics. As Blommaert (2005b) notes, the sociolects are indicative of divisions among the social classes that are the byproduct of different access to education and different needs for English in daily life. For rappers, English is a language that can be used to produce new meanings when blended with Swahili. For others such as medical doctors, English codeswitches serve a different function, namely more instrumental purposes which require monolingual capabilities in both languages.

It is important to reiterate that the words I have chosen to look at here are still entextualized in at least two ways in urban Tanzania. However, it seems to me that the second entextualization is becoming increasingly dominant among hip hop artists and in popular culture since HIV/AIDS has become such a strong discourse. This trend would fit well with the many themes in Tanzanian hip hop which have served to critique societal corruption, disarray and change for the worse which development and modernization seem to have brought about. At the same time, and perhaps because hip hop is dominated by men, there is a prevalence of discourses in these socially responsible lyrics that puts the burden of sexual morality and sexual health on women's shoulders. With more artists like Ferooz and more female artists voicing their opinions, Bongo Flava may experience another contextual shift that will provide the framework for new entextualizations of gender relations.

Thus far, the discussion of lyrics has focused on how language can develop new indexicalities because of changes in the macrocontext of a society. Next, I examine how the meanings of hip hop can be altered when hip hop lyrics are appropriated by individuals in another domain of social life, namely, Kenyan politics. The re-entextualization of the lyrics in the sphere of politics had lasting effects on the meaning of the song and permanently altered the relationship between hip hop and politics in Kenya.

Re-entextualizing Beyond the Music Scene

In 2002, Kenyan rappers Gidi Gidi Maji Maji released 'Who Can Bwogo Me?', and the song quickly became the number one song on Kenya's radio charts. The song came to be known as 'Unbwogable', a Sheng word that is comprised of the Dholuo word *bwogo* ('to be shaken') inside an English frame, thus meaning 'un-scare-able'. The song was written as Gidi Gidi Maji Maji's 'come back' effort after the commercial failure of their first album due to corrupt music industry producers (Nyairo & Ogude, 2005). The first verse of the song voices the rappers' frustration with the music industry, but the lyrics seemed to voice the feelings of many Kenyans who faced daily encounters with bureaucracy, corruption and a decayed economy. In the verse, Maji Maji, one of the singers of the group, asserts his ethnic identity as Luo, and this characteristic is presented as an aspect of perseverance in the lyrics.

What the hell is you looking for
Can a young Luo make money any more
Shake your feet baby girl *enango* ('what is it?')
Majimaji *nyakwar ondijo* ('Maji Maji grandchild of Ondinjo, I am Luo')
Am a Luo but who are you?
What are you?
Who the hell do you think you are?
Do you know me?
Do I know you?
Get the hell out of ma face because hey I am un*bwog*able
I am unbeatable
I am unsueable
So if you like ma song sing it for me I say

Chorus
Who can *bwogo* me (3×)
I am un*bwog*able
('Who Can *Bwogo* Me?' Gidi Gidi Maji Maji, 2002)

The third verse of the song provides Gidi Gidi, the other member of the group, with the chance to advertise his own determination in the face of challenging obstacles. He declares himself to be well known and his music to be lucrative, like a 'hot pepper' (in Swahili). Then, he turns to Dholuo to pronounce his greatness, stating that no one in Kanyamwar or Homabay (Luo-populated districts of Kenya) compare to him.

Listen, nobody can *bwogo* me
Neither nobody can *bwogo* this
Gidigidi big name, am saleable
Kama pilipili, yes am terrible ('Like hot peppers')
Kanyamwa homabay *ng'ama chalo koda* ('in Kanyamwar, Homabay, who is like me?')
Do you know Gidigidi is un*bwog*able

While this self-praise could be identified as a form of conceit often found in west-based hip hop and ultimately derived from African American storytelling traditions (Maultsby, 1995), Nyairo and Ogude (2005: 237) explain that the Luo group is performing the Dhuluo practice of *pakruok* ('self praise'), the act of 'inject[ing] one's social credentials and authority' into a musical performance in order to receive the attention one deserves from the audience. This is a case of what Osumare (2007) claims about the Africanist aesthetic of hip hop, and what Pennycook and Mitchell

(2009 : 30) describe as the indigeneity of hip hop when they write, 'It is not so much the case that hip hop merely takes on local characteristics, but rather that *it has always been local*'. In the case of 'Unbwogable', it becomes impossible to know to what degree the acts of self-aggrandizement are influenced by west-based hip hop, or how much they represent the indigenous cultural practices of the Luo people. The point to be made is that these lyrics of self-praise echo both local and global cultural practices at the same time, thereby producing multivocality.

This multivocality is what precisely what seems to have allowed the song to become an anthem for the first political party to challenge the ruling party in 2002, the year that Kenya's first democratic elections were held since independence in 1963. Mwai Kibaki, the leader of the opposition parties known as the National Rainbow Coalition (NARC), led a campaign that garnered great optimism as it promised real reforms in a country that had experienced a high degree of false promises and corruption under the ruling party, the Kenyan African National Union (KANU). In a pre-election rally, Kibaki shouted to the audience 'We are unbwogable!', and in the months that followed, *Unbwogable* became the slogan for Kibaki's campaign. In an analysis of why a song that promoted the Luo so clearly was politically successful in a nation that has endured decades of tribal politics, Nyairo and Ogude (2005: 239) explain 'This fusing of tongues – English and Luo – is a testament to a new Kenya, one that breaks with the earlier constructed Kenyan past in the sense of separate ethnic identities, and instead attests to the multiple and fluid identities that are increasingly defining post-colonial, particularly urban, Kenya'.

After the song became associated with Kibaki's campaign, the government-regulated radio station (which was overseen by KANU officials) stopped playing the popular song. It lost its original entextualization of being a 'come back' song for Gidi Gidi Maji Maji and became a 'we will overcome' song for the NARC Coalition. Though they initially did not admit it, Gidi Gidi Maji Maji signed a licensing deal with NARC and the multivocality of *unbwogable* continued to gain new voices. They produced remixes of the song that rewrote KANU's history, pointing out the corruption of the ruling party during the pre-election months (Nyairo & Ogude, 2005). The band also marketed t-shirts and other paraphernalia with the slogan *unbwogable* on it, and these became a very popular way of expressing support for the opposition to the ruling party.

While the word was identified as Sheng and as Luo in its earlier incarnations, the word became classified as a form of English due to its circulation (and value) in political spheres of life. By December of 2002, Daniel Arap Moi, the nation's longstanding leader, was replaced by Kibaki. After being sworn in as Kenya's president, Kibaki continued to use the term to praise the 'unbwogable' character of the Kenyan people in political speeches. Once the new government was in power, *unbwogable* found its way into parliamentary proceedings, and when the word was questioned by the Speaker as 'unparliamentary language', Vice-President Michael Wamalwa defended its use, arguing that the 'English language is a growing language ... Unbwogable captures the mood and soon it will be acceptable' (*East African Standard*, 20 February 2003, cited in Nyairo & Ogude, 2005: 244).

Conclusion

The three facets of hip hop language in East Africa examined here provide illustrations of how the meanings of texts change as they travel across the boundaries of social life. These texts pick up new meanings through dialogue with new sets of discourses, and sometimes, they bring these discourses back to the original context, ultimately changing its meaning there. The examples examined here show that meaning does not always inhere in a text, but is made and remade as the text moves through a set of overlapping 'scapes', the spatialities that result from global cultural flows (Appadurai, 1990). The scapes themselves change shape in the process as they stretch the boundaries of their linguistic registers. As we have seen, the register of hip hop lyrics in Tanzania has added words like *sista du* to celebrate a certain lifestyle, and then has critiqued that very lifestyle due to the overlapping scape of public health, thereby altering the scape once more. Conversely, the world of public health has adjusted its cultural and linguistic landscape by including hip hop as a legitimate avenue for educating East Africans. Similarly, the scape of politics has changed in Kenya after making hip hop synonymous with political change, and without necessarily agreeing to it, hip hop in turn has become a site for national politics.[3]

In comparison with the two previous chapters, these examples of hip hop demonstrate the greatest degree of hybridity and multivocality. A focus on popular culture texts has allowed for an exploration of the ways multilingualism involving English can continually yield new meanings that play off of old ones, and how linguistic hybridity can simultaneously index local and global references. Rather than viewing East African hip hop as a form of mimicry of the west, the examples of naming practices, re-entextualizations of English-derived words referencing women, and the re-territorialization of 'unbwogable' reveal the African origins of these verbal performances. The data examined here also indicate that the language of hip hop seems to be increasingly relevant for a number of multilingual spaces, including AIDS education and politics. It appears that the flows of language and cultural references from hip hop are entering into other domains and reshaping them, which in turn re-invents hip hop. In the next chapter, we see how popular culture interacts with advertising, another realm of social life that embraces multivocality and reaps its benefits.

Notes

1. Cassidy and LePage (1967) cite *gwan* as a meaning 'go on'. Jamaican forms of music such as reggae and dancehall have had a strong influence on hip hop, not only in the United States, but in many other contexts. Jamaican music acts as a major sphere of influence for African popular music in particular (Forman, 2002; Potter, 1995; Richardson, 2006).
2. In August, 1998, the United States embassies in Nairobi and Dar es Salaam were the targets of terrorist attacks that killed over 200 and wounded many more. The majority of the deaths were in Nairobi. The attack has been linked to Osama bin Laden and the al Qaeda network.
3. The title of the song is spelled as it would be in English on the cassettes and CD inserts. However, the pronunciation in the song itself is r-less.
4. The MTV campaign 'vote or die' offers a parallel example of the overlapping scapes of politics and popular music in the United States.

Chapter 6
Selling Fasta Fasta in the East African Marketplace

> People's involvement in politics is less and less as citizens and more and more as consumers; and their bases of participation are less and less the real communities they belong to, and more and more the political equivalents of consumption communities.
> Fairclough, 1989: 211

As Fairclough (1989) points out, a strong characteristic of modern societies is the decreasing relevance of national, regional and ethnic identifications and the growing importance of consumer identities. In the fields of applied linguistics and sociolinguistics, recent scholarship on multilingual[1] advertising demonstrates how this realm of life has become a significant site of language contact with English (Kelly-Holmes, 2005; Piller, 2003), and researchers have found advertising to be a fascinating site for identity construction in a number of countries, including Germany (Piller, 2001), France (Martin, 2006), India (Bhatia, 2000), New Zealand (Bell, 1999), Japan (Backhaus, 2007) and Korea (Lee, 2006a). Multilingual advertising illustrates how local consumer identities are made using the resource of English in its global and local forms. Of course, these consumer identities should be read as constructs created for the domain of the market since much of this advertising exhibits 'fake multilingualism' that fetishizes languages for their idealized symbolic values, and which fails to represent how speakers actually use languages in their sociolinguistic contexts (Kelly-Holmes, 2005). At the same time, while market-driven language is often fabricated to serve business interests, it often intersects with language use in other domains, and hence, can contribute to new forms of multivocality in other multilingual spaces (*cf.* Haarman, 1989; Tranter, 2008).

In spite of many struggles with various aspects of economic development, there is no doubt about the importance of consumerism in East Africa, particularly for those living in urban areas. In fact, compared to many 'developed' nations, advertising in Kenya and Tanzania appears to be relatively unhampered by government regulations. While Swahili has an important role in articulating consumer identities in advertising in these nations, these identities are increasingly being constructed by and for local consumers through the global resource of English and hybrid languages such as Sheng, Swahinglish and Street Swahili. Advertising is occasionally in monolingual forms of English in Kenya and Tanzania, but more often than not, consumers are constructed as multilingual through the use of more than one language in advertisements. Of course, this phenomenon is not limited to East Africa since English has become a global discursive practice that is often used to symbolize modernity, sophistication and worldliness.

Multilingual advertising involving English is symbolic of a new world order that is taking shape at both economic and linguistic levels, a new form of 'modern living' that challenges binary concepts of the global and the local. Just as individuals' consumer identities are no longer strictly local ones, manufactured only in local languages, there are no longer limited avenues for experiencing global aspects of consumerism. Instead, transcultural consumer identities constructed through multilingualism involving English are increasingly found worldwide. These transcultural consumer identities relate well to what Giddens (1990) calls the 'disembedding' of social relations and social practices (such as advertising) from particular places and contexts and their generalization across temporal and spatial boundaries. Transcultural discursive resources such as English are hence disembedded from their colonial pasts and re-embedded through processes of appropriation, thereby creating a sense of the local. The local is a very hybrid construction, however, as 'it is a global-local dialectic wherein disembedded language practices increasingly flow across linguistic and cultural boundaries, but are assembled in distinctive hybridisations which contribute to the reconstitution of separate identities of place' (Chouliaraki & Fairclough, 1999: 83).

The presence of English in advertising across a variety of both post-colonial and currently globalizing locations is reflective of our increasingly globally interconnected lifeworlds (Cope & Kalantzis, 2000) in which globalized communications provide a new and very contemporary world order. From a more critical perspective though, such advertising involving English indicates how populations around the world experience the marketization of social life, a key characteristic of the current period of *late modernity* (Chouliaraki & Fairclough, 1999). What we buy defines us more significantly than ever before, more so than our ethnicity, social class or religious affiliation. In this new global order, nation-based economies have, to some degree, lost their relevance; in a parallel manner, English no longer has an immediate connection to specific nations, particularly Great Britain and the United States. Just as the flow of trade has accelerated due to increasingly permeable borders, English has also infused other languages and cultures and has become part of the local linguistic landscape. The result seems to be a new sociolinguistic world order in the form of Englishization. While aspects of linguistic and economic imperialism are surely part of this new sociolinguistic world order, what seems increasingly clear is that strong forces of localization are also present. Here, divisions between the local and the global fall apart, and English and the languages it comes into contact with are altered through processes of hybridization, appropriation and localization.

In this chapter, I analyze how English helps to construct both a new world order and a sense of the local by investigating how it is used as a commodity and as a source of creativity in Tanzania and Kenya. The simultaneously consumerist and creative elements of advertising fit well with Bakhtin's concept of dialogism, as does the potential duality of meaning that emerges in multilingual advertising texts. While these concepts have not been applied to the linguistic analysis of advertising in any depth (except Piller, 2001), his view of language as dialogue is very relevant for making sense of identity construction. Multilingual advertisements offer consumers the opportunity to layer monolingual and bilingual readings of the texts simultaneously, resulting in dialogic readings. Because they offer multiple strata of readings to consumers, they provide many opportunities for *transgredience*, Bakhtin's (1981) concept of how the self can become saturated with otherness through dialogue. Transgredience takes place when the self interacts with others, and meanings of utterances change due to the 'surplus' of what others see. Transgredience explains how language change happens over time, and it also explains how words and phrases might develop multiple readings. In advertising, dialogic readings and transgredience take place through readers' interactions with texts, rather than face-to-face encounters. Transgredience is not restricted to the context of texts though, since texts are in constant dialogue with other texts and with other utterances from daily life. Holquist describes this dialogic relationship between texts and other utterances as

> a site of constant struggle between the chaos of events and the ordering ability of language. The effect of order which language achieves is produced by reducing the possible catalogue of happenings, which at any moment is potentially endless, to a restricted number that

perception can then process as occurring in understandable relations. What happens in an utterance, no matter how commonplace, is always more ordered than what happens outside an utterance. (Holquist, 2002: 84)

The intertextual relationships between advertising texts and utterances from daily life will be examined at more length in the discussion below.

Dialogism in advertising offers the chance to see how English has become a language of identity construction in East Africa. Though English is often still treated as a largely utilitarian language, useful only for the domains of education, international politics and international business exchange, advertising involving English shows a high degree of creativity and playfulness. Many of these advertisements use the global capital of English for local commercial purposes, and in the process, they create cosmopolitan yet highly localized subject positions for multilingual, multiliterate consumers. For advertisements circulated primarily in Kenya, English dominates, with rather small amounts of Swahili use and sometimes, Sheng. These advertisements produce heteroglossia through dual sets of tensions, which include commodity and creativity, local and global identifications, and Swahili and English (and Swahinglish) literacies.

The 'multilanguagedness' of the domain of advertising reveals some loyalty to standardized varieties of language since many 'hi-tech' products such as computers and business products are advertised solely in very standardized varieties of English (see Figure 6.1). However, the purposeful use of multilingual advertising and advertising involving non-standardized varieties seems to challenge the *cultural capital* of monologic forms of English or Swahili. The creative hybrid language practices

Figure 6.1 Advertisement for computers in Dar es Salaam

found in this domain are often more powerful forms of communication for East Africans. In a consumerist world, then, prescriptive attitudes towards purity in language and the maintenance of boundaries between languages are no longer relevant. The radically different perspectives in language ideologies towards hybrid languages across domains of life, including in education, will be discussed further in Chapter 7.

Beyond understanding how English functions symbolically in particular societies, multilingual advertising involving English raises many questions regarding the types of literacies consumers are expected to have in order to appreciate these advertisements. Furthermore, an exploration of these literacies allows us to evaluate to what degree the language in such advertising is fabricated, or is part of speakers' sociolinguistic repertoires. Thus far, most studies of multilingual advertising have largely focused on indexical meanings of English such as sophistication, internationalism and technological superiority (e.g. Bhatia, 2000; Lee, 2006a; Martin, 2006; Piller, 2001). While some attention has been paid to the ways in which hybrid forms of English establish new meanings for consumers, there has been little discussion about the relationship between advertising and the new literacies (New London Group, 1996; Street, 1995) that may be developing as a result of English-dominant multilingualism. Moreover, little is known about how the interpretation of hybrid advertisements may vary depending on the linguistic repertoires of consumers. In this chapter, I examine the range of language use in advertising texts, and following some of the methods used in Chapter 4, I address the issue of interpretation by including interview data.

Studies of Multilingual Advertising

Among researchers who have categorized multilingualism in advertising, Reh (2004) offers the most comprehensive framework in her analysis of multilingual public writing – which includes advertising – in Lira Town in the northern part of Uganda. She describes four types of writing that involves more than one language. First, *duplicating* writing presents the exact same information in more than one language; second, information may be *fragmentary*, in that an advertisement provides all information in one language with selected elements in an additional language or languages. Third, *overlapping* writing is found when only part of the information is repeated in more than one language, while other parts of the text are presented in only one language. As Reh (2004: 12) explains, 'This type of multilingual language use informs monolingual readers sufficiently and at the same time neither bores bilingual readers through exact repetition as

> **RADIO UGANDA AGENT**
>
> *Cwal kwena iwel ayot*

Figure 6.2 Advertisement for commercial advertising in Uganda. *Note*: The Lwo text means 'Send your messages at a low price'.

in the case of duplicating [or fragmentary] multilingualism.' Finally, *complementary* writing presents different parts of a text in different languages in a manner that requires readers to have literacy in all the languages. Reh (2004: 14) gives the example of an advertisement for a radio agent as an illustration of complementary writing. In this case, readers would need to understand both the English and the Lwo to interpret the sign as an advertisement for private and commercial radio advertising (see Figure 6.2).

Reh explains that the linguistic repertoires of residents of Lira Town involve a range of languages including Lwo, a language comprised of Lango, Acholi and Kumam, plus some English for those with some degree of formal schooling. Luganda appears in some advertisements for mobile phones, while Swahili words are often used as the names of restaurants, bars and stores. The public domain of multilingual texts and advertisements reveals that forms of Lwo are rarely used monolingually, however; much more frequently, Lwo appears in combination with English in the form of complementary and overlapping multilingualism, thereby indicating requisite literacy levels for the target consumers of these texts.

While Reh's study reveals that many Ugandans in Lira Town are required to have complementary literacies in Lwo and English in order to make sense of the multilingual texts and advertisements in their vicinity, her research does not necessarily provide examples in which these two languages work in tandem to produce new or creative meanings as a result of their juxtapositioning. Usually, Lwo provides an advertising hook through culturally meaningful messages while English is typically relegated to neutral information, as illustrated by the advertisement in Figure 6.3 (Reh, 2004: 27).

In contrast to what Reh reports for the Ugandan context, other studies of multilingual advertising do provide data in which the combination of

> ANENO LYEC ENTERPRISES
>
> Spairs And Chemicals

Figure 6.3 An advertisement for car service. *Note*: The first line in Lwo means 'I-see-an-elephant Enterprises'. Spairs [sic] refers to spare tires

two or more languages provides new meanings that are not simply the product of two monolingual capacities combined. These texts are a kind of complementary multilingual writing, but they tend to involve a greater degree of linguistic blending at the lexical and even morphosyntactic levels of language as well. Such texts not only demand literacy among consumers in both languages, but they demand hybrid literacies to interpret the dialogic relationship that the use of two or more languages produces.

Several studies on multilingual advertising have examined how local and global identities are constructed in multilingual advertisements. Bhatia (2000) uses the term *glocalization* to refer to the hybridity in advertisements in rural India, by which he means the integration of at least two linguistic systems. In his work, glocalization is paraphrased as 'think and act both global and local at the same time' (Bhatia, 2000: 161). In contrast, globalization is 'thinking and acting globally' (i.e. advertising in English), while localization is 'thinking locally and acting locally' (i.e. advertising in the local regional language). An advertisement for Brooke Bond tea provides an illustration of Bhatia's concept of glocalization (underlined words appear on the sign in Hindi and in Devanagari script) (Bhatia, 2000: 161):

Brooke Bond A1 ... <u>kaRak</u>   <u>chaap caay</u>
                    KaRak (thunder)   brand tea
'Brooke Bond A1 ... the KaRak brand tea'

For Bhatia, then, multilingual advertisements are 'glocal' by virtue of being multilingual.

Piller (2001) examines advertisements that assert new meanings as a result of their multilingual nature. Drawing on Bakhtin's notion of dialogism, she provides examples in the German context that heteroglossia in the form of English and German. One example comes from Arcor Mannesmann, a now defunct telecommunications company which produced an advertisement whose headline was *'Pfennigfuchsing'* ('penny pinching'), a combination of the German noun *Pfennigfuchser* ('penny pincher') with the English affix -ing. According to Piller, the linguistic hybridity in this new bilingual word maintains the concept of a fiscally savvy company while adding the quality of being modern and cool, as well as globally minded. Here, the 'voice' of fiscal conservatism comes in German while the 'voice' of global sophistication comes through English. Piller demonstrates how the voices of English and German are not static by examining how German non-profit agencies use English rather differently to provide Germans with anticonsumerist identities. The example of a nonprofit which lobbies for the interests of bicyclists and for environmental issues shows how English can be appropriated. It reads 'Rush hour = *Rasch aua*' ('quick ouch'), which associates English with a German homophone relating to the stress of driving in heavy traffic. Unlike commercial advertising that presents German consumers with German-English bilingualism as a toolkit for identity construction, nonprofit advertisements tend to use English to subvert consumerist identities such as those illustrated by Arcor Mannesmann.

Also within the European context, Martin (2006) explores how local and global identities are formulated through multilingual advertisements in France. Martin focuses on the ways that global marketing campaigns are adapted to the French market and how French advertisers use English and foreign products in localized manners. To illustrate how global campaigns are adapted for French consumers, she provides a print advertisement for the Ford Mondeo, a vehicle sold by a US-based automaker whose safety features are highlighted for the French market. The advertisement is a close-up of the driver's seat, and two tape measures that are marked with centimeters rather than inches are arranged across the seat to mimic a seat belt. The tape measures symbolize the idea of measuring the driver's body measurements in order to electronically adjust the airbag in the event of a collision. The advertisement is further localized through the use of a larger font for the French slogan '*Protection sur mesure?*' ('tailored protection') which is the most prominent text in the advertisement, followed by smaller text which reads 'IPS: Intelligent Protection System' (Martin, 2006: 151).

Beyond complementary bilingual advertisements are advertisements for French companies and products that make use of English in their efforts to appeal to French consumers. Bilingual creativity that demands the ability to decipher the double voices in 'Youth Frenglish' often appears in advertisements targeted at young consumers, as in '*Relooker ton mobile*' ('change the look of your mobile phone'), where the English verb 'look' is turned into French through the addition of affixes *re-* ('again') and *-er* (a verbal ending) (Martin, 2006: 183). Similarly, on a poster in a Paris subway, the slogan '*Je dunkerai for you*' ('I will [land a slam] dunk for you') uses the English 'dunk' within French grammar (Martin, 2006: 187). A print advertisement for Givenchy also makes use of English, but to provide an echo of a French word. The slogan *'L'autre façon de porter HOT Couture'* ('the other way to wear HOT Couture', translation Martin) calls up the French *haute* within the phrase *haute couture* ('high fashion') and grabs attention through a language contrast and the use of capital letters (Martin, 2006: 198). All of these examples demonstrate how consumers might need to potentially draw on knowledge of French and English in order to interpret the ads, but as Martin (2006: 45–46) states, 'audience interpretations of code-mixed advertising text, visuals and jingles (particularly in terms of their cultural specificity) remain a largely untapped area for empirical research'.

Bilingual advertising in South Korea also provides examples of hybrid language use that cannot be classified as merely complementary. Lee (2006a) gives the example of a cellular phone provider that uses Korean alongside English to refer to the practice of sharing leftover phone minutes with friends. The advertisement reads *'Let's KT. Bigi KTF'* (KTF = Korea Telecommunications Freetel). Here, KT is used as a verb, and the Korean verb *bigita* ('to end in a tie' or 'come out even') is truncated and used as a promotion for the company. In this example, Lee explains that the use of roman letters for the Korean phrase *Bigi KTF* produces parity with the English text *Let's KT*, thereby constructing a very urban and youth-oriented identity for consumers.

These examples from South Korea, France and Germany are better understood as making use of *dialogic multilingualism* since they ask readers to tap into more than their knowledge of both English and another language. These advertisements rely on consumers' abilities to decipher third codes (as in the case of *relooker*), and to interpret the 'voice' of English in these multilingual advertisements as the voice of global and local modernity.

Advertisements in East Africa

I now look at advertisements from a variety of contexts in Tanzania and Kenya that illustrate how various forms of multilingualism are used to construct consumer identities. The advertisements have primarily been collected through my own photography, though some advertisements come from newspapers, magazines and other products I have collected in East Africa since 2001. First, I discuss advertisements that require monolingual language abilities, some of which relate to Reh's classifications of duplicating and complementary multilingualism. Then, I turn to examples which require hybrid language literacies and which have multiple potential readings.

Advertisements that require monolingual language abilities

Many advertisements in Tanzania and Kenya are either monolingual or use both Swahili and English to duplicate the information presented to consumers. Both types establish the target consumer audience as comprised of monolinguals in one language or the other, rather than both. Consequently, many advertisements rely on monolingual varieties of English and Swahili to market products. Figures 6.4 and 6.5 provide examples of two monolingual advertisements that were found in several regions of Tanzania in 2007. Figure 6.4 has a somewhat different message for Swahili readers than the English version, as *Maisha msisimko na Coca Cola* translates directly as 'Life – thrill and Coca Cola'.

Monolingual advertisements also appeared in signs that were used to promote locally owned businesses. Figures 6.6 and 6.7 illustrate advertisements for the same English language and computer training school, and each one is entirely in English or Swahili. The content of the signs is nearly identical, but it is likely that the English-medium sign was a bigger investment for the college since it is a signboard rather than a banner. Compared

Figure 6.4   Swahili Coca Cola ad in Zanzibar

Figure 6.5 English Coca Cola ad in Zanzibar

Figure 6.6 English-medium sign for English Fountain College, Dar es Salaam

Selling Fasta Fasta in the East African Marketplace

Figure 6.7 Swahili-medium sign for English Fountain College, Dar es Salaam

to the signboard, the hand-painted banner maintains the English name of the institution but with the word 'college' missing; it contains slightly more information regarding the college's location as well. It reads *'TUPO: K/NONDONI MUSLIM KARIBU NA TX MARKET'* ('We are at: Kinondoni Muslim near TX market'). The English-medium sign proclaims its courses to be of 'quality', whereas no similar claims are made in the Swahili-medium banner.

Figure 6.8 provides another example of two signs that appear in one language each while demonstrating that geographic location does not necessarily dictate the language of the advertisements. On the left side of

Figure 6.8 Monolingual advertisements side by side in Dar es Salaam

the photograph are English words and phrases advertising services on the doors of a music and film editing store such as *Video shooting, Still Picture* and *Music VCD Library*. To the right of the store is an entirely Swahili-medium banner that advertises a weekly newspaper. It reads '*Soma Gazeti Zeze kila Alhamisi*' ('Read Zeze newspaper every Thursday').

Figure 6.9 depicts a storefront for a pharmacy in Iringa Town, a small city in the western central part of Tanzania. The advertising on the storefront is an example of both overlapping and duplicating bilingualism. At the top of the photograph is an English-medium sign that reads 'Iringa Highlands Pharmacy' that provides the contact information for the store. Below this is another sign that reads PHARMACY – *DUKA LA MADAWA* (literally, 'store of medicine'). Another storefront in Iringa Town (Figure 6.10) reveals overlapping multilingualism on a sign for a store that sells paper, notebooks and school supplies. Like the pharmacy, this storefront has an official sign at the top entirely in English, followed by hand-painted Swahili-medium text. The information provided in both signs is identical and the English sign provides the additional information of 'book sales, furniture and cleaning material'.

Both duplicating and complementary multilingualism were much more common in the Iringa region compared to the Dar es Salaam area, where

Figure 6.9   Duplicating sign in Iringa town

Selling Fasta Fasta in the East African Marketplace

Figure 6.10 Overlapping multilingualism near Iringa Town

monolingual signs or hybrid signs were more often found. Figure 6.11 illustrates English-only advertising on a store that sells stationary supplies and which also offers Internet services. Based on my observations, stores selling such products and services were likely to advertise exclusively in English in the urban centers of Tanzania and Kenya, Dar es Salaam and Nairobi. Quite often, the advertisements in Nairobi that use complementary multilingualism are those that use Swahili for slogans and English for the remainder of the advertising copy. For example, Kenya Power and Lighting Company's current slogan is '*Umeme Pamoja*' ('Electricity together/ for all'), but in magazine advertisements for the company, the slogan and its subheading '*Njia rahisi ya kupata stima*' ('An easy way to get electricity') is all that appears in Swahili while the rest of the text is in English.

Localized English in advertisements

Advertisements that contain reappropriations of English have become a significant part of the East African linguistic landscape. This type of advertisements demonstrates processes of localization and appropriation

130   English as a Local Language

Figure 6.11   Monolingual signs for secretarial services in Dar es Salaam

through adaptations in the linguistic structure of English. In Kenya, examples of localized English taken mostly from non-advertising contexts have been documented in Angogo and Hancock (1980), Zuengler (1982) and Buregeya (2006). These include Kenyan phrasal verbs ('to be picked by a car' and 'fill a form'), formations of analogous compounds ('overlisten', meaning to eavesdrop), the use of adjectives as nouns ('first born', 'primary', 'secretarial') and the expansion of politeness strategies (e.g. 'thank you' as a reply to 'good bye'). This research is rather descriptive, and as Skandera (1999) and Buregeya (2006) point out, much of it is anecdotal and based on the (sometimes Kenyan) researchers' views of Kenyan varieties, rather than actual usage.

In Tanzania, local varieties of English have received less attention in general, though appropriations of the language have been discussed by Blommaert (1999a, 2005b), whose main interest is in the use of what he calls *Public English*, his term for the use of largely 'inaccurate' and often semantically ambiguous forms of English that are frequently used for commercial purposes (see Table 6.1). These forms are similar to what has been well-documented in Japan as forms of Japanized English, Japlish and Engrish, including examples like shampoo bottles that are unabashedly labeled *Shampoo for extra damage* (Seaton, 2001: 233). As Blommaert points out, it is crucial to understand the value of these forms within their local context. In Tanzania, English is valued among a Tanzanian

Selling Fasta Fasta in the East African Marketplace 131

Table 6.1 Public English in Tanzania (from Blommaert, 2005b: 403)

(a)	*Fund rising dinner party*	on a banner in central Dar es Salaam
(b)	*Disabled Kiosk*	the name of a 'kiosk' – a converted container that serves as a small shop operated by a disabled man
(c)	*Shekilango Nescafé*	the name of a café on Shekilango road in Dar es Salaam
(d)	*Approxi Mately*	written on a bus

customer base, and a wider variety of English counts as cultural capital in this context.

Aside from the many cases of Public English which appear to miss the 'target' of Standard (presumably British) English, some locally produced advertisements assert a high degree of creativity quite straightforwardly. For example, Figure 6.12 illustrates a business in Dar es Salaam called *Za Car Wash* using a spelling that acknowledges the localized pronunciation of voiced English 'th' sounds among most Tanzanians. At the same location is a business called *Za Cafe Food & Soft Drinks* as well. Figure 6.13 demonstrates a type of localized English that is the result of semantic shift in Tanzania. While the term *grocery* is used in North America as a synonym for supermarket, in Tanzania, the word is used to refer to a small

Figure 6.12 Sign for a garage and restaurant in Dar es Salaam

Figure 6.13 Sign for a bar in Dar es Salaam

and informal bar where beers are served, typically in the afternoon and evening. Another similar example of localized English includes the very Tanzanian use of *Saloon*[2] (< salon) to refer to a beauty parlor for women.

Sheng and localized Swahili

Many advertisements for mobile phone companies make use of trends, including trendy language. Since early in 2007, Safaricom, Kenya's largest provider, has used the Sheng word *bamba* ('grab, take') in their *Bamba 50* campaign to sell very low-cost vouchers (50 Kenyan shillings is worth roughly USD $0.75). On billboards in 2007, *Bamba 50* appeared above a fist that gripped the 50 shilling scratch cards, followed by *Ibambe sasa!* ('Grab it now'). In 2007, the company also used Sheng to name their *Bonga* ('chat') package to subscribers, a campaign which requires consumers to register and keep track of bonus points in order to earn rewards and to qualify for prize giveaways.

In Tanzania, these companies use the language most equivalent to Sheng, *Lugha ya mitaani* ('Street Swahili') frequently in advertising campaigns, thereby constructing their consumers as knowledgeable about this linguistic form. In 2005, Buzz Cellular heavily promoted the expansion of its network in most Tanzanian newspapers. One advertisement that referred to the improved network in Zanzibar read:

> *Ongea kwa muda unaotaka ukiwa baharini kwani Buzz ingekupa huduma **kibao** kwa gharama ya chini. Kuwa mjanja pata Buzz.* ('Talk for as long as

you want when you are on the islands because Buzz gives you **a ton** of service for a low price. Be smart and get Buzz'.)

Here, the use of *kibao* is Street Swahili meaning something like 'a lot', but is interpreted as slang by most Tanzanians and is better translated as 'a ton', or perhaps more accurately as 'mad service', as it carries the same sort of street consciousness found in the African American English adverb 'mad'.

The same campaign regularly uses the alliterative slogan *Buzz ni **bomba*** ('Buzz is **awesome**') in advertisements that are otherwise monolingual in either Swahili or English (see Figure 6.14). Here, the phone company makes use of the Street Swahili form *bomba* (originally borrowed from Portuguese 'pipe, pump'). This word has shifted to mean 'cool' in most Street Swahili, and there appears to be influence from African American English's 'da bomb' ('the ultimate, the best') as well (Higgins, 2009). In this way, global hip hop culture is a source for transgredience in providing new meanings of Street Swahili.

Non-governmental organizations that promote condom use through condom marketing also make use of *bomba*, as seen in Figure 6.15, a billboard for condoms that contains this Street Swahili in its brand name as well as complementary multilingualism involving standard forms of Swahili and English.

Additional examples of advertisements about condoms include the *Ishi* ('live') campaign sponsored by USAID. Since 2004, the slogan of this campaign has used the Street Swahili expression *Usione soo!* ('don't be shy') to encourage young people to discuss condom use before becoming sexually active with their partners. According to Reuster-Jahn and Kießling (2006),

Figure 6.14   Billboard in Dar es Salaam for Buzz Cellular

Figure 6.15   Billboard for condoms in Dar es Salaam

Street Swahili *soo* may originate from either the truncation of another Street Swahili word *songombingo* ('chaos'), or else Standard Swahili *soni* ('shyness'). According to the non-governmental organization that implements the Ishi campaign in Tanzania, the campaign seeks to increase perception among youths aged 15–24 about personal risk for HIV through behavior change communication efforts (fhi.org). Through using youth language, the condom advertisement simultaneously constructs the consumers as young people who speak Street Swahili and who are conscientious about sexual health.[3]

Hybrid Advertisements

Other advertisements use English alongside new varieties of Swahili to create specific new meanings. On billboards, in newspaper advertisements and in radio and television commercials, varieties of English and Swahili are often placed together in ways that forge new meanings from the juxtaposition of the two languages, thereby demanding new kinds of multilingual knowledge in the form of new hybrid literacies. Sometimes, these hybrid advertisements require consumers to have dialogic literacies that allow them to see the monologic and multiply-layered dialogic meanings present. Other hybrid advertisements depend on consumers' abilities to know a third code, a code perhaps best represented by names such as Swahinglish. Contrary to the knowledge required by complementary bilingualism, full appreciation of the meanings of these advertisements cannot be attained from knowledge of English and Swahili as two separate languages. Consequentially, these advertisements raise questions such as whether and to what degree Tanzanians from varying walks of life are literate in these hybrid codes, and what meanings they glean from these advertisements.

To investigate this issue, I explore how varieties of Swahili and English are layered in advertising, and I illustrate two types of meanings that result when Swahili and English are juxtaposed creatively. First, the two languages are used in a complementary manner that requires knowledge of both Swahili and English to fully appreciate the meaning of the hybrid advertisement. Secondly, the two languages are used in ways that create new, third meanings, unconnected to the monolectal meanings of either Swahili or English. These two types of meanings represent a continuum more than a binary set of options, however, due to the various literacies that consumers possess. Drawing on interviews with Tanzanians, I show how some consumers read the advertisements as monolingual, not recognizing the presence of English at all. Others read these advertisements as texts that contain language mixing, but they do not necessarily find extra meaning in them due to the presence of two languages. And, others read the advertisements as bilingual texts that do have new meanings due to the juxtaposition of Swahili and English. These three possible readings relate well to Auer's (1999) framework for three types of bilingual speech that form a cline from pragmatics to grammaticalization, discussed in Chapter 2.

Dialogic multilingualism

My examination of Swahili-English hybrid advertisements will focus on mobile phone companies, as they provide several very interesting examples of hybrid codes. My data are advertisements in Tanzania and interviews carried out with consumers living in two different parts of the country, Dar es Salaam and Iringa. The Tanzanian government deregulated its telecommunications in the mid-1990s, and following this move, the number of mobile providers grew and the number of mobile subscribers has skyrocketed. A high degree of competition among the providers followed, providing a benefit to consumers in terms of lower prices. Consequently, advertising for low rates and special promotions dominates billboards, taxiboards, newspapers and business walls. Subscribers to each mobile company receive advertising in the form of text messages as well, an effective advertising strategy that can overcome geographic barriers such as lack of roads and intermittent electricity.[4]

Advertisements requiring dialogic literacies

An advertisement by Vodacom that circulated in 2007 provides an illustrative example of dialogic hybridity. To promote the lower rate for calls made late at night and on the weekends, Vodacom used the promotion 'Chombeza time' ('chat time'), an expression that uses a Street Swahili word. Chombeza can be translated as 'chat', but this word has many additional connotations associated with 'sweet-talking' someone, particularly someone of the opposite sex. When asked to translate this expression, Tanzanians replied with 'conversation among lovers', 'time for young people to talk to their girl/boyfriends' and 'seducing one another'. Vodacom's use of chombeza to refer to lower rates for late-night phone calls fits the context of sweet-talking rather well. The advertisement also cleverly combines a Street Swahili word with English 'time' in a way that mirrors the well-known expression of 'Kili Time' in Tanzania, another advertising phrase used by Kilimanjaro Breweries to refer to a period of time after work to enjoy a beer with friends. 'Kili Time' is presumably based on the phrase 'Miller Time' used to advertise a brand of beer produced in the United States.

In regard to 'Chombeza time', it seems that the juxtaposition of chombeza with 'time' does not necessarily create a meaningful codeswitch in itself, but its parallel and intertextually designed structure with 'Kili Time' creates meaning that could not be made relevant in one language. In interviews with 12 residents of Dar es Salaam and Iringa, everyone interviewed identified Chombeza Time as a bilingual advertisement and recognized chombeza as Street Swahili. When asked to translate the phrase into English and into Swahili, most of the interviewees commented on Kilimanjaro Breweries' campaign as well as a way to express their understanding of the English part of the advertisement, that is, as a time of the day that was set aside for a particular activity.

Additional advertisements provide more complex forms of hybridity. One advertisement for Tigo Cellular (formerly Buzz) that circulated in Tanzania in 2007 (Figure 6.16) illustrates this very well. The large text in the center of the billboard reads 'X-TRA LONGA' and refers to the low rates of three shillings per minute during the week and one shilling per minute on nights and weekends. One reading of 'X-TRA LONGA' is 'extra chat' since longa can translate as 'chat' in Street Swahili. This reading makes sense in the realm of mobile phone use as it refers to the idea that consumers receive many minutes on their plans for a low price. At the same time, longa can also be heard as English pronounced in typical Tanzanian r-less fashion. This reading is made even more possible by the

Selling Fasta Fasta in the East African Marketplace 137

Figure 6.16 Tigo advertisement, Dar es Salaam

syntax of the phrase, which follows English structure of adverb + adjective, rather than Swahili's typical structure of adjective + adverb.

To appreciate all of the possible and doubled meanings in *'X-TRA LONGA'*, a consumer would have to have multiple and hybrid literacies in several languages and several language varieties. First, one must recognize that *'X-TRA'* indexes the English word 'extra'. Secondly, one must know some Street Swahili to decipher *longa*. Consumers who do not have recourse to Street Swahili might use their knowledge of English to interpret *longa* as 'longer' since the phrase can also be interpreted that way. For the consumer who is multiliterate in all of these languages and varieties, the meaning of the phrase is doubled and the creativity of the phrase is more fully appreciated. For readers with multiple literacies, the result is that *'X-TRA LONGA'* does not necessarily mean *either* 'extra longer' *or* 'extra chat'; it means both at the same time, and its cleverness is derived from this simultaneity.

In interviews with residents of Dar es Salaam, a variety of readings were shown to exist for the Tigo advertisement. Table 6.2 summarizes the interpretations of the phrase *X-TRA LONGA*. I asked a selection of men and women of varying ages who were living in Dar es Salaam to identify the languages in the advertisement and to explain what each word meant. Most of them gave the meanings in Swahili. Then, I asked them to translate the whole phrase into 'pure' English and 'pure' Swahili. The results are summarized in Table 6.2.

All of the participants were able to translate *'X-TRA LONGA'* into 'pure' English except for the watchman, who only had a primary school

Table 6.2 Dar es Salaam residents' interpretations of *X-TRA LONGA*

Gender	Age	Occupation	X-TRA is what language?	Meaning of X-TRA	LONGA is what language?	Meaning of LONGA	'Pure English'	'Pure Swahili'
F	54	Retired primary teacher	English	*Zaidi* 'more'	Street Swahili	*Ongea* 'talk'	Talk more for less cost	*Ongea zaidi kwa gharamu nafuu*
M	48	Driver	English	*Zaidi* 'more'	Street Swahili	*Ongea* 'talk'	Talk more for less	*Ongea zaidi kwa bei rahisi*
M	31	Watchman	English	*Bora* 'better'	Swahili	*Tongoza* 'seduce'	—	*Kutongozana kwa bei rahisi*
F	26	Sales clerk for mobile company	English	*Zaidi* 'more'	Street Swahili, slang	*Ongea* 'talk'	More talk less cost	*Ongea zaidi kwa gharama chache*
M	22	AIDS educator, volunteer	English	*Zaidi* 'more'	Kilugulu, borrowed Swahili	*Ongea* 'talk'	To talk more	*Ongea zaidi*

education. The participants' translations of *'X-TRA LONGA'* into 'pure' Swahili are equivalent to their English translations. The watchman's translation into 'pure Swahili' means 'to seduce one another at a cheap price'. Throughout his interview, the watchman expressed a lot of doubt about his ability to interpret the English. It appears that his interpretation of *longa* relates to the idea of 'sweet talk' rather than simply 'talk', as mentioned by the other three participants.

Residents outside of Dar es Salaam were also asked the same questions in order to evaluate the degree to which multiliteracy in hybrid codes are related to urban living. I asked four young people living near Iringa town similar questions about *'X-TRA LONGA'*. The results of these interviews are summarized in Table 6.3. Of interest is that all participants felt *X-TRA* was English and that *LONGA* was some form of Swahili in spite of its possible reading as an entirely English phrase.

In a very similar manner, a widespread 2004 advertisement for Vodacom in Tanzania offered several potential multiple readings for multiliterate consumers. The advertisement read *'Kamata jero chapchap'* ('Grab 500 shillings quickly'). The translation is rather intricate due to the use of Street Swahili *jero* and a double meaning for *chapchap*. *Jero* is in fact a clipping of 'Pajero', a sport utility vehicle manufactured by Mitsubishi of Japan. The word has been borrowed into Swahili through processes of transgredience and now means 500 shillings; it is a well-known form of Street Swahili. *Chapchap* is ambiguous as it can be read as Swahili (the adverbial form of the verb *kuchapuka*, 'to put force into, to speed up'), or as a localized version of 'chop-chop' ('make haste'), a word that, according to the Oxford English Dictionary, originated as Pidgin English in Hong Kong.[5] In the Vodacom advertisement, the spelling has changed but the meaning remains the same.

Interviews with residents of Dar es Salaam and Iringa Town revealed no ambiguity regarding *chapchap*, suggesting that previously multiple meanings of this word may have faded into the obscurity of dictionary etymologies. Nearly everyone I interviewed labeled *chapchap* as Swahili, in contrast to the word *jero*, which everyone labeled as Street Swahili and as a word that was 'invented by young people'.[6] A watchman labeled both *jero* and *chapchap* as Street Swahili. The two Dar es Salaam residents who were near 50 years old knew that *jero* refers to 500 shillings, which indicates that this Street Swahili word is not a word only known among young people. Again, the participant with the least amount of education had the most difficulty with interpreting the advertisement. When asked, he explained that it meant that Vodacom's network had spread to all corners of the country.

Through seeing how Tanzanians think about the English and Swahili words in hybrid advertisements, it is possible to establish a grounded

Table 6.3 Iringa town residents' interpretations of *X-TRA LONGA*

Gender	Age	Occupation	X-TRA is what language?	Meaning of X-TRA	LONGA is what language?	Meaning of LONGA	'Pure English'	'Pure Swahili'
M	21	Student	English	*Zaidi* 'more'	Swahili	*Ongea* 'talk'	Talk more using Tigo	*Ongea zaidi kwa kutumia Tigo*
F	22	Student	English	*Zaidi* 'more'	Street Swahili	*Ongea* 'talk'	More time to talk	*Muda wa ziada*
M	23	Student	Advertising language	*Zaidi* 'more'	Street Swahili	*Ongea* 'talk'	More talking time	*Muda wa maongezi ya ziada*
M	28	Driver	English	Extra	Street Swahili	*Ongea* 'talk'	Extra talk	*Muda wa ziada kwa kuongea*

understanding of whether borrowings have become opaque to them and to see how much literacy they have in reading playfully double-voiced advertisements. For *'X-TRA LONGA'*, it is clear that *x-tra* is still seen as English by the participants I interviewed, and that *longa* is only Swahili for them, though most of them categorize it more specifically as Street Swahili. For the example of *'Kamata jero chapchap'*, it seems that *jero* is widely understood as a form of well-known Street Swahili, and *chapchap* is read as Swahili for most people. In the next section, I consider another mobile phone advertisement that seems to be more ambiguous for consumers. This advertisement illustrates how languages are used in ways that create new, third meanings, unconnected to the monolectal meanings of either Swahili or English. It also demonstrates how consumers appropriate the discourse of consumerism for different purposes in popular discourse, illustrating the process by which domain-based languages move beyond their domain boundaries.

Since 2004, Vodacom seems to have updated the English in its advertisements. The word *chapchap* is no longer used, but beginning in 2006, the word *fasta* started to appear everywhere as the *'Voda Fasta'* campaign (Figure 6.17). Here, *Voda* is a clipped version of Vodacom, and *Fasta* clearly comes from the English 'faster', though it has been localized for Tanzanian r-less pronunciation. *'Voda Fasta'* refers to a sales incentive the company offers its vendors that earns retailers a 3% sales bonus if they sell 20,000 shillings or more of airtime directly to customers in one day. The incentive is a sort of pyramid plan since it allows wholesalers to qualify for a 2% bonus for each of their vendors who sell the 20,000 shillings worth of airtime. Given this understanding, the use of *fasta* relates to the idea that the

Figure 6.17 Voda Fasta advertisement, Dar es Salaam

bulk sales will lead to sales commissions for vendors (vodacom.co.tz). Hence, from the corporate perspective, *fasta* does not simply mean 'faster'. Instead, it has developed a new meaning that is neither equivalent to English 'faster' nor the Swahili word for *fast* (haraka).

Compared to *chapchap, fasta* has more varied readings among secondary school students living in Iringa. A 21-year-old man in Iringa town felt that *fasta* could be translated to Swahili *haraka* 'faster' and that it was indeed English 'faster'. One 22-year-old woman's comments about the word evoke the double voice that the word carries. In Swahili, she explained that *fasta* 'came from the street and is a word that has been eaten from English. People have placed it into Swahili'. Two others recognized it as language of the streets without specifying it as either English or Swahili. When asked why they thought mobile phone companies used such advertisements, one person said, 'Many mobile phone users are young people who speak street language. They have to target young people'. Another explained that the language was used for attracting customers. She said, 'Young people use this language and even some of the older people use it too' (translated from Swahili).

In Dar es Salaam, *fasta* was read variously as English and as Swahili, as summarized in Table 6.4. All respondents translated it as *haraka*, which is a literal translation for 'fast'. One interviewee, a male journalist, initially declared *fasta* to be English, but his explanation of the word revealed a double meaning. He said, '*Fasta* is a word that totally resembles the English word, so *fasta* is a Swahili word that has a meaning which is very similar to the English one' (translated from Swahili). In his comments, he made it clear to me that the Swahili *fasta* is a separate word from the English version, even though they have shared meanings.

Table 6.4   Dar es Salaam residents' interpretations of *'VODA FASTA'*

Gender	Age	Occupation	Meaning of FASTA	FASTA is what language?
F	54	Retired primary teacher	*Haraka* 'fast'	Swahili
M	48	Driver	*Haraka* 'fast'	Swahili
M	35	Journalist	*Haraka* 'fast'	English
M	31	Watchman	*Haraka* 'fast'	Swahili
F	26	Sales clerk for mobile company	*Haraka* 'fast'	Swahili
M	22	AIDS educator, volunteer	*Haraka* 'fast'	English

The expression *fasta* has developed a range of uses in Tanzania, some of which are a result of the Vodacom campaign. Some people use *fastafasta* to tell someone to hurry up (*fanya fastafasta!* 'do it faster!'), much like *chap-chap* or even *haraka*. *Fasta* is also used in marketing retail services to mean 'fast service'. In Dar es Salaam, the phrase '*Huduma fasta*' ('fast service') is painted on storefronts such as 'express' laundries and three-minute passport photo shops. Separate from the world of consumerism, however, is an interesting development in the realm of education and the training of teachers. The phrase '*walimu wa Voda fasta*' ('Voda fasta teachers') sprang up in 2007 as a way to refer to teachers who receive a teaching license after a four-week licensing program in order to fill the tremendous demand for teachers in government-sponsored schools. The Tanzanian government made the four-week licensing programs even more attractive by offering teachers who completed it the opportunity to resume their tertiary studies after they had completed two years of teaching in government schools and to continue receiving their salaries while they study.

The *walimu wa Voda fasta* have been critiqued in the press as lacking the necessary knowledge for teaching, lacking the knowledge to carry out administrative duties, and having overly informal teaching styles with their students (who are typically of roughly the same age). *Walimu fastafasta* are further specified as teachers who have returned to their studies and continue to receive their salaries. According to the Tanzanian press, some of these teachers had fulfilled the two-year commitment required by the government, but others had not. In September of 2007, it appeared that many teachers had taken the opportunity to continue with their studies, thus creating a shortage of teachers in many schools. As a result, the Ministry of Education decided not to continue paying the salaries of any teachers who had not fulfilled the two-year requirement in an effort to solve the problem. The word *fasta* in *walimu wa Voda fasta* is used to refer to the brevity of the training and to the efforts of the Tanzanian government to recruit many teachers while investing relatively little in their training. The use of *fastafasta* seems to imply cleverness on the part of the teachers (akin to 'pulling a fast one').

In September of 2007 on a discussion board on Darhotwire.com, commentators showed their interpretations of the problematic system. One contributor said '*Kwa jinsi hii ya walimu fastafasta tutatoa wanafunzi fastafasta*' ('The same way we get *fastafasta* teachers, we will produce *fastafasta* students'). Another commentator blamed the Ministry of Education for the problems rather than directing criticism at the *Voda Fasta* teachers for seeking further education. This contributor wrote, '*Watawala wakumbuke* GARBAGE IN, GARBAGE OUT' ('Leaders, remember GARBAGE IN,

GARBAGE OUT'). The use of *fastafasta* to refer to poorly trained teachers and poorly trained students shows a clear semantic shift from the original meaning of *Voda Fasta* and produces a meaning that is not connected to the monolectal meanings of English 'faster' or Swahili *'haraka'*. While its (re)use here can be interpreted as evidence of the power of consumerism in everyday people's lives, this example also reveals the creative forces at work as people reappropriate English for nonconsumerist domains of social life.

Conclusion

In this chapter, I have focused on the ways in which English and Swahili and hybrid languages are used in advertising in bilingual and multivocal ways. The range of language use in these advertisements is similar in scope to the range found in the newspaper office in Chapter 3, as much of the language of advertising depends on monolingual abilities in Swahili and English. However, mobile phone advertisements provide the type of multivocal multilingualism also observed in much of the language in the hip hop domain, described in Chapter 5. Interviews with consumers revealed that the linguistic hybridity in older mobile phone advertisements were widely interpreted as Swahili, in spite of the potential for multiple readings; interviews also demonstrated that the hybridity in more recent advertisements was still interpreted as multilingual, and that some consumers were able to appreciate the word play that capitalized on their knowledge of multiple languages. This suggests that hybrid languages may lose their double-voices over time, and that they eventually get relocated into one of the dominant languages in the sociolinguistic context.

At the socio-political level, my analysis of mobile phone advertisements indicates that 'illegitimate' hybridized forms of language earn new value as a result of their use in the domain of marketing. It seems that similar processes are at work for other illegitimated languages, including African American English in the United States, which has developed an enhanced status due to the popularity (and economic success) of hip hop music. In both Kenya and Tanzania, nonstandardized and hybrid languages like Sheng, Street Swahili, and hybrid Swahili-English have earned their own linguistic markets, first through hip hop, and now, in the field of advertising. A similar shifting of domains was also seen in Chapter 5 in the discussion of Gidi Gidi Maji Maji's song 'Unbwogable' ('un-scareable'). First earning respect in the hip hop market among Nairobi youth, this Sheng expression entered the political market in 2002, when presidential candidate Mwai Kibaki used it as a campaign slogan to mean 'We Kenyans are unbeatable!'

The domain-dependent status of these languages relates well to Blommaert's (2005b) discussion of language and inequality. Echoing Bakhtin's (1986) discussion of speech genres, he writes, 'Inequality has to do with *modes of language use*, not with languages, and if we intend to do something about it, we need to develop an awareness that it is not necessarily the language you speak, but *how* you speak it, *when* you can speak it, and *to whom* that matters. It is a matter of *voice*, not of language' (Bakhtin, 2005b: 411). In the mode of advertising, Street Swahili and hybrid Swahili-English phrases are spoken with the voice of the mass market, that is, a population of consumers who speak these languages. The mode of advertising puts the consumer in a position of power; the consumer has the

Figure 6.18 Cartoon featured in *Kingo*, 1999. Reproduced with permission of Gaba Ltd

ability to choose between Tigo, Vodacom and several other companies, and hence, the language used to appeal to these consumers is the language of the streets and the language of everyday life. In other modes such as education where power brokers are the ones who make the decisions, it is not surprising that the language used often does not represent the voice of the masses.

At the same time, though, there are many valid concerns over the spread of capitalism in East Africa, including serious questions about who benefits when markets are 'free', the increasing divide between the haves and the have-nots, and the role of international agencies such as the IMF and the World Bank in delivering policies that will benefit developing nations, rather than further demoralizing them with heavy debts or unhelpful trade restrictions. A cartoon by the satirical comic book *Kingo* (Figure 6.18) summarizes many aspects of the reality of a capitalist world as experienced by (many) poor Tanzanians.

At the linguistic level, anyhow, capitalism does seem to have brought about more equality for varieties of language at the local level. It seems that Bourdieu's (1991) economic metaphor for the value of language could not be more appropriate for describing the use of these linguistic forms, given the tight relation between their value and their marketability. In the next chapter, I examine the competing domains of language planning and language in education wherein varieties of languages remain stifled. These domains of social life differ completely from the domains of popular culture and advertising in regard to the value of nonstandardized languages.

Notes

1. I use the term multilingual here to include bilingualism in advertisements. In fact, the term 'multilingual' is more accurate since many 'bilingual' advertisements use varieties of languages to market their products.
2. The use of *saloon* to refer to a beauty parlor is found in other parts of Africa as well (Tope Ominiyi, personal communication).
3. The Ishi campaign's slogan *Usione soo* became a heated matter for public debate because the slogan was part of a television commercial that showed young people kissing and hugging one another. Letters to the editor in many newspapers showed disdain for the advertisement and many disliked the advertisement for its failure to promote 'African' values. The Tanzanian parliament discussed the issue at length in 2004, and several members advocated that the name be changed to *Uone soo* ('be shy') to prevent the idea of encouraging sexual activity (http://parliament.go.tz).
4. Despite lack of electrical power grids in rural areas, enterprising entrepreneurs have acquired solar panels to generate electricity in even the remotest areas of Tanzania and Kenya. One can charge one's mobile phone for approximately 30 cents.

5. The word chop-chop is cited in the OED as the formation of Pidgin English through borrowing the Cantonese *k'wâi-k'wâi* ('chop-chop', referring to chopping food faster).
6. Linguist Deo Ngonyani (personal communication) believes the etymology of *chapchap* to be English since the word makes more sense if understood as a reduplicated ideophone rather than as an adverbial from a Swahili root.

Chapter 7
New Wor(l)d Order

Throughout the chapters of this book, heteroglossia in the form of multivoiced multilingualism has been shown to be a source of creativity, playfulness, strategy and most of all, identification. I have argued that East Africans exploit the heteroglossia of language to perform modern identities through localizing global linguistic and cultural resources while generally maintaining the multiple layers of meaning from both the global and the local. I have looked closely at language as it is used in society as a means of theorizing how post-colonial multilinguals exercise multivocality in their domains of social life, and how these domains in turn influence the kinds of language that are deemed appropriate. It has become clear that some domains have allowed for the inclusion of more hybridity than others, but each domain examined has shown some evidence of tolerance for heteroglossia. Rather than merely appropriating English for the African context, I have shown that Kenyans and Tanzanians use English alongside Swahili and hybrid languages to operate in the interstices of globalization and localization, and to double-identify as local and global actors. In addition, the previous chapters have shown how speakers relocate linguistic forms associated with particular sociolinguistic contexts into new spheres of language use in an effort to capitalize on the original domain's indexicalities. Examples included the movement of linguistic hybridity in hip hop into the domains of advertising and politics. I argued that the relocation of these hybrid languages transformed the linguistic landscapes of the new domains, and their former meanings were also altered in the process.

In this chapter, I compare the East African context with other regions of the world to discuss how the simultaneity of reference points, anchored in both the global and the local, establishes the basis of a new world order. I call it a new wor(l)d order to intentionally play on the double meanings that can be found in any societal multilingualism involving English. This new wor(l)d order describes what is happening in East Africa, and in all parts of the world where English has traveled. In exploring how the use of English in multilingual East Africa relates to other geographic contexts, I come face to face with a final domain of social life that has typically been rather impervious to multivocality – formal education. In comparing the possibilities for heteroglossia in education to other domains of social life, my aim is to probe what I see as a reluctance to legitimize the hybridity that English generates in many societies, and to look for any promising signs of change.

Legitimating Language

Canagarajah (2005: xxiii) writes that 'A general fluidity and mixing in languages, cultures, and identifies is becoming a fact of life ... Transnational life makes borders porous as ideas, goods, and people flow with greater mobility.' In the current period of late modernity, the intersection of global and local cultural flows continually alters linguistic landscapes. These flows are relatively unimpeded in expressions of popular culture and in everyday conversations, though speech genres still exist which distinguish 'hip hop language' from 'advertising language'. As linguistic and cultural flows come together, however, processes of reterritorialization take place; what counts as legitimate language is always contingent, rather than permanently codified, and speech genres are increasingly difficult to separate. In the case of advertising in the previous chapter, hybrid languages involving English seem to have become the most legitimate forms of language for selling goods and services, but more importantly, for selling consumer identities. Similarly, examples of hybrid English in popular culture in the form of localized hip hop create new forms of cultural capital that speak to increasingly transcultural and audiences. As we saw in Chapter 5, this cultural capital is occasionally borrowed for use in new contexts such as politics, and reterritorialization happens once more.

In spite of increasingly narrow language policies around the world that focus on the utility of standard English as the language of globalization, it is fascinating that language users in East Africa and all corners of the globe continue to create new forms of social life through reterritorializing and localizing English. Though the centripetal forces of a unified standard English appear insurmountable in the field of English language teaching, they are challenged by such cases as Koreanized English (Konglish) being used to market mobile phone companies, or to sell millions of K-pop records. There seems to be little recognition of varieties like Konglish, however, which is probably the result of South Korea's notorious English fever and its annual 10.5 billion US dollar industry (Roh, 2007) that valorizes the MUSE variety of American English (Lippi-Green, 1997). Even though most Korean teachers of English admit using Konglish in their daily lives, they generally do not recognize the examples in Lee (2006a, 2006b) as any sort of valid English for the context of teaching (Flattery, 2007). Similarly, in India, the kind of English found in Hindi pop, in thousands of Bollywood films, and in daily conversations is frequently part of a mixed language rather than the sort of English one needs to receive high grades in school.

Even in Japan, where foreign languages are typically treated as ideologically and linguistically separate from Japanese, English appears with tremendous frequency in the form of Japlish, Engrish and Japanese-English mixing. At the same time, however, Japanese teachers and learners of English as a foreign language in Japan do not recognize the English that decorates thousands of neon billboards and street signs as the same language they spend hours studying behind classroom walls. Backhaus (2006, 2007) shows how differences in language use on official and nonofficial signs in Tokyo reflect these two different stances towards English very clearly. Taking the surrounding environments of the Yamanote subway line as his fieldwork site, Backhaus analyzed official and unofficial signs. Of the official signs that contained other languages, Backhaus found that Japanese always appeared as the most prominent language, usually in larger text. Approximately 98% of them were Japanese and English, and the small remainder contained Japanese and Chinese, Korean and Latin. Official signs always used duplicating or overlapping multilingualism, forms of language use which conceive of readers as coming from separate social spheres, rather than sharing multiple languages. On the other hand, most nonofficial multilingual signs exhibited complementary multilingualism, presupposing a multilingual readership rather than consumers who do not know one another's language. Backhaus interprets the linguistic elements of official signs as evidence of monolingual ideology and a display of power on the part of governmental agencies to assert linguistic hierarchy. The nonofficial signs allow for more intermingling of languages; nearly 40% of them placed Japanese in a secondary position. In making sense of the different treatment of other languages on nonofficial signs, Backhaus explains that

> English on these signs can be interpreted as a symbolic expression by Japanese sign writers to join the English language community and to associate with the values that are typically attached to it (American/ Western culture, internationalisation, etc.) ... Use of Korean as the most frequent foreign language next after English on the nonofficial

signs of the sample communicates a different kind of solidarity ... Unlike in the case of English shop signs, the relationship between sign writer and language on a sign is real rather than merely desired. (Backhaus, 2006: 63).

Clearly, these forms of trans-scape multilingual language use do not align very well with purist language ideologies. However, consumerism and artistic creativity seem to legitimate hybrid language practices without regard for national language policy or prescriptivist notions of language segregation. The result seems to be the development of two separate worlds where heterogeny and homogeny each govern language without acknowledging the presence of the other world. While some aspects of popular culture are more fluid than others, it seems clear that the deepest lines are drawn between the domain of education and the spheres of life inhabited by mediated popular culture, consumerism and creative expression. Education continues to be a place where the interconnected nature of language in multilingual societies is 'uncoupled' (Makoni, 2003), and where the invention of languages remains the least challenged. The compartmentalization of language in education is problematic, however, since, as the previous chapters have shown, linguistic hybridity is the norm for communication in many people's daily lives, across a number of domains. Describing the South African context, Makoni notes the prevalence of multilingual hybridity on the radio, on television, and in popular magazines, and he suggests that 'these linguae francae may resolve the educational problems which standard African languages are now causing in South African schools. Not only does this urban, hybridized speech reflect the sociolinguistic practices of students; local teachers are also expert in this lingua franca' (Makoni, 2003: 149).

The Landscape of Language-in-Education

In contrast to the heteroglossic walls of Japan's subway system, the multivocality in Hindi movies or the hybrid linguistic structures in Tanzanian and Kenyan advertisements, the context of formal education seems to mostly perpetuate monoglossia. In the post-colonial world, multivocality in the classroom has a long history of being rejected in the classroom and punished. From personal experience, Ngugi wa Thiong'o writes about his own education in Kenya during the 1950s:

> One of the most humiliating experiences was to be caught speaking Gikuyu in the vicinity of the school. The culprit was given corporal punishment – three to five strokes of the cane on bare buttocks – or

was made to carry a metal plate around the neck with inscriptions such as I AM STUPID or I AM A DONKEY. Sometimes the culprits were fined with money they could hardly afford (Ngugi wa Thiong'o, 1986: 11).

Disturbing stories about the punishments given to students who use languages other than English in the classroom are not hard to find in other contexts as well. Canagarajah (1999: 125) provides examples of one teacher's responses to student's language mixing, who explains, 'I could never bring myself to fine them. Instead, I've used a plastic hammer (the kind you buy in toy shops) which makes a noise when you hammer it – to lightly "hit" students who lapse into speaking L1. None of my students seem to have been particularly offended by this "punishment"'. Similarly, Ncoko et al. (2000) describe a case in South Africa where a young boy who had been asked to hand out worksheets to his classmates was punished for asking some of them whether they had the worksheets or not in languages other than English.

For several decades now, sociolinguists have studied codeswitching in classrooms to see how it functions as a resource for managing classroom activity. Many studies have examined the role of first and other languages in classroom communication alongside English (e.g. Bunyi, 2005; Canagarajah, 1999; Heller, 1988, 1999; Lin, 1999, 2006; Martin, 2005; Martin-Jones, 1995; Merritt, 1992). Much of this research describes how codeswitching is used as a means by which teachers create order, provide scaffolding for learning new concepts, mitigate low proficiency in the medium of instruction, and encourage student participation. Bunyi (2005), Brock-Utne (2005) and Rubagumya (2003) have explored the functions of language switching in Kenya and Tanzania. Their research focuses largely on switches among teachers, and it shows that switches are used to check understanding, to translate difficult vocabulary and to keep students on task. While this research tends to describe language practices in classrooms, rather than advocating for educational policies, some have used codeswitching as evidence for poor English skills in the classroom to promote a return to mother tongue-medium instruction (Brock-Utne, 2005; Roy-Campbell & Qorro, 1997). In EFL contexts, where English is taught for a handful of hours per week by local teachers, codeswitching is often described as due to a lack of language proficiency and is described as a source of embarrassment by teachers (Butler, 2004; Liu et al., 2004).

Researchers have only recently ventured into exploring how educators can more explicitly incorporate hybrid linguistic and cultural practices as the content and form of education. Beyond advocating for codeswitching as a teaching tool for clarifying material or for carrying out administrative tasks with students, various forms of language mixing and more generally, the status of English in society, can also be examined as the topic of learning. Fabrício and Santos (2006) discuss their pedagogical research in Brazilian college classrooms where they made the role of English in Brazilian society the focus of learning. They asked students to examine media texts and clothing the students were wearing to analyze the kinds of English they found, and to reflect on the ways that English might represent both global and local dimensions. They write, 'What all of these texts have in common is that they represented English-in-the-new-global-order in ways particularly relevant to that local community of particular teachers and learners' (Fabrício & Santos, 2006: 75).

Similarly, in her study of an anti-racism camp in Toronto for immigrant ESL students, Taylor (2006) explores how awareness-raising activities helped participants to identify discourses of race, racism and language ability that they encountered on a daily basis. The goals of the camp included challenging the positionality of ESL students as somehow 'less Canadian', challenging culture and race-based essentialisms, and exploring the possibilities of identifying as in-between or transcultural individuals, rather than as immigrants in a foreign land.

Focusing more on cultural forms, Pennycook (2007) surveys educational research that describes how hip hop as a cultural practice has recently been brought into the domain of education. Some of the uses of hip hop in schooling are straightforwardly strategies to encourage 'reluctant learners' to engage in formal schooling, but Pennycook explains that bringing hip hop into classrooms can mean much more. He writes, 'Rather than viewing hiphop as a hook to motivate students or as a cultural achieve to be included in the curriculum, they look outward into the larger world of which classrooms are a part. As they do so, they shift a sense of what school knowledge is and of how it relates to the larger context' (Pennycook, 2007: 148).

These few examples show how increasingly fluid relations have become among language, race, cultural identity, nationality and a sense of belonging in the world, and they illustrate the possibilities for greater degrees of multivocality in the domain of education. Next, I examine whether such examples are surfacing in the context of education in East Africa.

Increased Multivocality in the Scape of Education?

Language use in popular culture/consumer domains stands in great contrast with that of governmental policy, as represented by official bodies such as Tanzania's Ministry of Education and the National Swahili Council

(BAKITA), a government-sponsored organization that regulates Swahili by developing standards for written publication, promoting Swahili use in all domains of social life, developing new words in Swahili (typically needed because of technological developments or language contact), and regulating the use of Swahili textbooks used in schools. The Ministry of Education and BAKITA act as providers of standards, and these standards include monolingual forms of English and Swahili. In Kenya, no regulating body for Swahili exists, but standards provided by the Ministry of Education also assume monolingual English as the medium of instruction.

Educational policies towards language in schools promote monolingual forms of instruction, whether this is mother tongue instruction in Kenya's primary schools, Swahili in Tanzania's primary schools, or English in both nation's secondary schools. In spite of the policies, language mixing among teachers and students can be heard in most classrooms (Brock-Utne, 2005; Kadeghe, 2000; Roy-Campbell, 2001). In a way, codeswitching in classrooms in spite of English or Swahili-only policy is a subversive legitimation of multivocality, as it gains legitimacy from being the forum in which knowledge is produced among teachers and students. In fact, many times, classrooms where codeswitching is allowed are more participatory than those in which teachers impose English-only policies, as students feel less constrained by the medium of expression (Bunyi, 2005; Kadeghe, 2000). However, codeswitching has not been granted any official level of legitimation in the realm of education, and it is often described as 'destroying Swahili' as well as 'killing English' by teachers, students and parents alike.

Michael Kadeghe, a lecturer in the Department of Linguistics and Foreign Languages at the University of Dar es Salaam, is a strong advocate for codeswitching as a medium of instruction in Tanzania. He recommends that preservice teachers receive instruction about codeswitching so they can capitalize on its utility in teaching, and that codeswitching on national exams be tolerated as well. He writes, 'The language policy implementers should make use of the synergy that has been created by the two languages in the classrooms rather than treating them as separate hostile entities so that their combined effect becomes greater than the sum of their individual effects' (Kadeghe, 2000: 241). Advocates for Sheng in Kenya do not support its use in classrooms, though this may change in the future if the literary codification of Sheng continues. It is relevant that there is now a Sheng dictionary available and the Kenya Publishers Association recently announced that they would begin to publish books in Sheng, given the demands of the market.

While there do seem to be small indicators of support for including hybrid language practices in classrooms, educators in East Africa remain resistant to using materials that involve Sheng, Swahinglish or Street Swahili since they are also resistant to including forms of popular or consumer culture in the curriculum. Generally, popular culture is seen as a non-serious distraction by teachers, and therefore, cultural forms like hip hop are not explored as an avenue for learning. A 2007 edition of the cartoon *Besela* summarizes the firm boundaries that separate popular culture and formal schooling. The three-frame cartoon depicts a middle-aged male teacher who is teaching a Swahili lesson on proverbs, a form of 'culture' teaching that is dominant in Tanzanian schools. In the second frame, the teacher asks one of the students, Besela, to finish a proverb that begins with *Mficha uchi* ('One who hides their nakedness'). This is one of the best-known Swahili proverbs, and every Tanzanian and Kenyan would know that it finishes with *hazai* ('doesn't have children'), meaning that people should disclose their secrets or shameful news in order to get help from others. The proverb has been incorporated into a Bongo Flava song by Mchizi Mox, where it has been re-entextualized with a strongly sexual nature. In the final frame of the cartoon, Besela stands up and sings a verse of Mchizi Mox's song, leading the teacher to drop his Swahili book, clap his hand to his forehead, and say *'Toba yarabi Bongo Flava kha! Mox, umeniharibia kazi. Aisee kamusi zote zimeekspiya sasa'* ('Good grief this Bongo Flava! Mox, you've destroyed my work. Now, all of the dictionaries have expired'). In the domain of popular culture, the *Besela* cartoon engages with the sphere of education and the idea that language can *ekspiya* 'expire' because of the influence of other domains of life. However, from the perspective of educators, policy-makers and students themselves, this cartoon exists at the level of imagination only, achieving its humor by poking fun at education for its reluctance to engage with life outside of classroom walls.

For many years, researchers in education and applied linguistics have advocated for the inclusion of more relevant materials in classrooms, that is, materials that engage with young people's senses of who they are in the world and how they make sense of their own contemporary experiences (e.g. Delpit, 2002; Heath, 1983; Norton & Vanderheyden, 2004; Rampton, 2006; Willis, 2003). As Pennycook (2007: 158) writes, 'Students are in the flow; pedagogy needs to go with the flow'. While it appears doubtful that the domain of education in East Africa (or many other contexts where education is highly centralized) will open up to the flow any time soon, it does seem the case in East Africa that other domains have opened up to education. HIV/AIDS prevention efforts targeting youth in Kenya and Tanzania have made use of hip hop to educate young people about safe sex, and many hip hop artists are on the payrolls of non-governmental organizations. As Chapter 5 shows, hip hop artists have entered the arena of public health education by singing about sexual responsibility and the grim consequences of HIV/AIDS. Chapter 6 illustrates how some advertisements take on educational purposes as well, particularly those sponsored by non-government organizations that work in the area of public health and social services. The result is that the boundaries between these areas of social life are indeed becoming blurred.

Though specific suggestions for the inclusion of hybrid languages in education would need to be the subject of another writing project (though see contributions in Makoni & Pennycook, 2005), my purpose in engaging with the domain of education in this chapter is to draw attention to the need for educators and policy-makers to consider the sociolinguistic realities of their own communities, and, following Makoni's (2003) suggestions, to do more to disinvent the language ideologies and language policies that prevent linguistic hybridity from entering into the domain of education. While it is unlikely that hybrid languages will ever become the approved medium of instruction, they can at the very least serve as valuable resources in the teaching of more 'standard' varieties, but only if they are acknowledged as part of students' linguistic repertoires. Perhaps more feasibly, they can become resources for engaging with young people's senses of who they are in the world and how they use language to make sense of their experiences.

These suggestions are not limited to East Africa, of course, as the discussion of English in this chapter illustrates that hybrid languages involving English are found across the globe, in post-colonial nations and also in countries which are generally (and wrongly) perceived as monolingual, such as Korea and Japan. It is hoped that greater engagements with the sociolinguistic realities in various domains of use in these contexts will help to disinvent, and reinvent, the concept of English as a global language.

Appendix

Transcription Conventions

[	simultaneous talk overlapping with another speaker
=	contiguous utterance
(1.0)	one second pause
(.)	micropause
-	abrupt cut-off
te<u>x</u>t	Emphasis (underlining)
.hh	inbreath
hh..	outbreath
te:xt	sound stretch (colons)
((text))	nonverbal behavior
(text)	uncertain transcription
xxx	utterance unclear
?	rising intonation
.	falling intonation
,	continuing intonation
↑	sudden rise in pitch

Abbreviations

cns	consecutive marker
dem	demonstrative
hab	habitual
loc	locative
neg	negation particle
obj	object particle
pfc	perfective

pl   plural
prs   present tense
pst   past tense
psv   passive
sjb   subjunctive

References

Abdulaziz, M. and Osinde, K. (1997) Sheng and Engsh in Nairobi. *International Journal of the Sociology of Language* 125 (1), 1–21.
Achebe, C. (1966) The English language and the African writer. *Insight* 20, 19–20.
Adejunmobi, M. (2004a) *Vernacular Palaver. Imaginations of the Local and Non-Native Languages in West Africa*. Clevedon: Multilingual Matters.
Adejunmobi, M. (2004b) Polyglots, vernaculars, and global markets: Variable trends in West Africa. *Language and Intercultural Communication* 4 (3), 159–174.
Alim, H.S. (2004) Hip hop nation language. In E. Finegan and J.R. Rickford (eds) *Language in the USA: Themes for the Twenty-first Century* (pp. 387–409). Cambridge: Cambridge University Press.
Alim, H.S., Ibrahim, A. and Pennycook, A. (eds) (2009) *Global Linguistic Flows: Hip Hop Cultures, Youth Identities, and the Politics of Language*. Mahwah, NJ: Erlbaum.
Angogo, R. and Hancock, I.F. (1980) English in Africa: Emerging standards or diverging regionalisms? *English World-Wide* 1 (1), 67–96.
Appadurai, A. (1990) Disjuncture and difference in the global cultural economy. *Theory, Culture and Society* 7 (2), 295–310.
Appiah, K.A. (1992) *In My Father's House: Africa in the Philosophy of Culture*. Oxford: Oxford University Press.
Armory, D.P. (1998) *Mashoga, mabasha*, and *magai*: 'Homosexuality' on the East African coast. In S. Murray and W. Roscoe (eds) *Boy-wives and Female Husbands: Studies in African Homosexualities* (pp. 67–87). New York: St Martin's Press.
Ashcroft, B., Griffiths, G. and Tiffin, H. (1989) *The Empire Writes Back: Theory and Practice in Post-colonial Literatures*. London: Routledge.
Askew, K. (2002) *Performing the Nation: Swahili Music and Cultural Politics in Tanzania*. Chicago: University of Chicago Press.
Atkinson, J. and Heritage, J.M. (1984) Jefferson's transcript notation. In J.M. Atkinson and J. Heritage (eds) *Structures of Social Action: Studies in Conversation Analysis*. Cambridge: Cambridge University Press.
Auer, P. (1998) Bilingual conversation revisited. In P. Auer (ed.) *Codeswitching in Conversation: Language, Interaction, and Identity* (pp. 1–24). New York: Routledge.
Auer, P. (1999) From codeswitching via language mixing to fused lects: Toward a dynamic typology of bilingual speech. *The International Journal of Bilingualism* 3 (4), 309–332.
Backhaus, P. (2006) Multilingualism in Tokyo: A look into the linguistic landscape. *International Journal of Multilingualism* 3 (1), 52–66.
Backhaus, P. (2007) *Linguistic Landscapes*. Clevedon: Multilingual Matters.

Bakhtin, M. (1968) *Rabelais and His World* (H. Iswolsky, trans.). Cambridge, MA: MIT Press.
Bakhtin, M. (1981) *The Dialogic Imagination* (M. Holquist, ed. and C. Emerson and M. Holquist, transl.). Austin: University of Texas Press.
Bakhtin, M. (1984) *Problems of Dostoevsky's Poetics* (C. Emerson, ed. and trans.). Minneapolis: University of Minnesota Press.
Bakhtin, M. (1986) *Speech Genres & Other Essays* (C. Emerson and M. Holquist, eds., V. McGee, trans.). Austin: University of Texas Press.
Bamgbose, A., Banjo, A. and Thomas, A. (eds) (1995) *New Englishes: A West African Perspective*. Ibadan: Mosuro Publishers for the British Council.
Barber, K. (1995) African-language literature and postcolonial criticism. *Research in African Literatures* 26 (4), 3–30.
Batibo, H. (1995) The growth of Kiswahili as language of education and administration in Tanzania. In M. Pütz (ed.) *Discrimination Through Language in Africa?: Perspectives on the Namibian Experience* (pp. 57–82). Berlin: Mouton de Gruyter.
Batibo, H. (2000) The linguistic situation of Tanzania. In K. Kahigi and M. Mous (eds) *Lugha za Tanzania – Languages of Tanzania* (pp. 5–18). Leiden: CNWS Publications.
Batibo, H. (2005) *Language Decline and Death in Africa: Causes, Consequences and Challenges*. Clevedon: Multilingual Matters.
Bauman, R. and Briggs, C. (1990) Poetics and performance as critical perspectives on language and social life. *Annual Review of Anthropology* 19, 59–88.
Baxter, L. (2004) Relationships as dialogues. *Personal Relationships* 11, 1–22.
Bell, A. (1999) Styling the other to define the self: A study in New Zealand identity making. *Journal of Sociolinguistics* 3 (4), 523–541.
Bhabha, H. (1994) *The Location of Culture*. London and New York: Routledge.
Bhatia, T. (2000) *Advertising in Rural India*. Tokyo: Toyko University of Foreign Studies.
Billings, S. (2006) Speaking beauties: Language use and linguistic ideologies in Tanzanian beauty pageants. Unpublished doctoral dissertation, University of Chicago.
Blom, J.P. and Gumperz, J.J. (1972) Social meaning in linguistic structures: Codeswitching in Norway. In J.J. Gumperz and D. Hymes (eds) *Directions in Sociolinguistics* (pp. 407–435). New York: Holt, Rinehart and Winston.
Blommaert, J. (1992) Codeswitching and the exclusivity of social identities: Some data from Campus Kiswahili. *Journal of Multilingual and Multicultural Development* 13 (1–2), 57–70.
Blommaert, J. (1999a) *State Ideology and Language in Tanzania*. Köln: Koppe.
Blommaert, J. (1999b) The debate is open. In J. Blommaert (ed.) *Language Ideological Debates* (pp. 1–38). Berlin: Mouton de Gruyter.
Blommaert, J. (2005a) *Discourse*. Cambridge: Cambridge University Press.
Blommaert, J. (2005b) Situating language rights: English and Swahili in Tanzania revisited. *Journal of Sociolinguistics* 9 (3), 390–417.
Blommaert, J., Collins, J. and Slembrouck, S. (2005) Spaces of multilingualism. *Language & Communication* 25 (3), 197–216.
Bourdieu, P. (1991) *Language and Symbolic Power*. Oxford: Polity Press.
Brock-Utne, B. (2002) *Language, Democracy and Education in Africa*. Uppsala: Nordic Africa Institute.
Brock-Utne, B. (2005) Language-in-education policies and practices in Africa with a special focus on Tanzania and South Africa – Insights from research in progress.

References

In A. Lin and P. Martin (eds) *Decolonisation, Globalisation: Language-in-Education Policy and Practice* (pp. 173–193). Clevedon: Multilingual Matters.

Bunyi, G. (2005) Language practices in Kenya. In A. Lin and P. Martin (eds) *Decolonisation, Globalisation: Language-in-Education Policy and Practice* (pp. 31–152). Clevedon: Multilingual Matters.

Buregeya, A. (2006) Grammatical features of Kenyan English and the extent of their acceptability. *English World-Wide* 27 (2), 199–216.

Butler, Y.G. (2004) What level of English proficiency do elementary school teachers need to attain in order to teach EFL? Case studies from Korea, Taiwan, and Japan. *TESOL Quarterly* 38 (2), 245–278.

Cameron, D. (1995) *Verbal Hygiene*. London and New York: Routledge.

Canagarajah, S. (1999) *Resisting Linguistic Imperialism in English Language Teaching*. Oxford: Oxford University Press.

Canagarajah, S. (2005) Introduction. In S. Canagarajah (ed.) *Reclaiming the Local in Language Policy and Practice* (pp. xiii–xxx). Mahwah, NJ: Erlbaum.

Canagarajah, S. (2006) Negotiating the local in English as a Lingua Franca. *Annual Review of Applied Linguistics* 26, 197–218.

Cassidy, F.G. and LePage, R. (eds) (1967) *Dictionary of Jamaican English*. Cambridge: Cambridge University Press.

Chouliaraki, L. and Fairclough, N. (1999) *Discourse in Late Modernity: Rethinking Critical Discourse Analysis*. Edinburgh: Edinburgh University Press.

Cope, B. and Kalantzis, M. (2000) Designs for social futures. In B. Cope and M. Kalantzis (eds) *Multiliteracies: Literacy Learning and the Design of Social Futures* (pp. 203–224). London: Routledge.

Dakubu, M.E.K. (1997) *Korle Meets the Sea: A Sociolinguistic History of Accra*. New York, Oxford: Oxford University Press.

de Beauvoir, S. (1953) *The Second Sex*. New York: Pantheon Books.

Delpit, L. (2002) No kinda sense. In L. Delpit and J. Dowdy (eds) *The Skin that We Speak: Thoughts on Language and Culture in the Classroom* (pp. 49–61). New York: The New Press.

Erickson, F. and Schultz, J.J. (1982) *The Counselor as Gatekeeper*. New York: Academic Press.

Fabrício, B. and Santos, D. (2006) The (re-)framing process as a collaborative locus for change. In J. Edge (ed.) *(Re)locating TESOL in an Age of Empire* (pp. 65–83). London and New York: Palgrave.

Fanon, F. (1961) *The Wretched of the Earth* (C. Farrington, trans.). New York: Grove.

Fanon, F. (1967) *Black Skin, White Masks* (C.L. Markmann, trans.). New York: Grove Press.

Fairclough, N. (1989) *Language and Power*. London: Longman.

Fairclough, N. (1995) *Critical Discourse Analysis*. London: Longman.

Fairclough, N. (2001) *Language and Power* (2nd edn). London: Longman.

Finlayson, R. and Slabbert, S. (1997) 'We just mix': Codeswitching in a South African township. *International Journal of the Sociology of Language* 125, 65–98.

Flattery, B. (2007) Language, culture, and pedagogy: An overview of English in South Korea. On WWW at http://www.chass.toronto.edu/~cpercy/courses/eng6365-flattery.htm. Accessed 20.11.07.

Forman, M. (2002) *The 'Hood Comes First: Race, Space, and Place in Rap and Hip-Hop*. Middletown, CT: Wesleyan University Press.

Friedan, B. (1963) *The Feminine Mystique*. New York: Dell Books.
Gee, J.P. (2003) *What Video Games Have to Teach Us about Learning and Literacy*. New York: Palgrave/Macmillian.
Giddens, A. (1990) *The Consequences of Modernity*. Cambridge: Polity Press.
Githinji, P. (2006) Sheng and variation: The construction and negotiation of multiple identities. Unpublished doctoral dissertation, Michigan State University.
Githiora, C. (2002) Sheng: Peer language, Swahili dialect, or emerging Creole? *Journal of African Cultural Studies* 15 (2), 159–181.
Gorman, T.P. (1974) The development of language policy in Kenya with particular reference to the educational system. In W.H. Whiteley (ed.) *Language in Kenya* (pp. 397–455). Nairobi: Oxford University Press.
Goyvaerts, D. (1992) Codeswitching in Bukavu. *Journal of Multilingual and Multicultural Development* 13 (1/2), 71–82.
Goyvaerts, D. (1996) Kibalele: Form and function of a secret language in Bukavu (Zaïre). *Journal of Pragmatics* 25 (1), 123–143.
Gumperz, J.J. (1982) *Discourse Strategies*. Cambridge: Cambridge University Press.
Haarman, H. (1989) *Symbolic Values of Foreign Language Use, from the Japanese Case to a General Sociolinguistic Perspective*. Berlin & New York: Mouton de Gruyter.
Hall, K. (2005) Intertextual sexuality: Parodies of class, identity, and desire in liminal Delhi. *Journal of Linguistic Anthropology* 15, 125–144.
Hall, S. (ed.) (1997) *Representation: Cultural Representations and Signifying Practices*. London: Sage.
Heath, S.B. (1983) *Ways with Words: Language, Life and Work in Communities and Classrooms*. Cambridge: Cambridge University Press.
Heller, M. (ed.) (1988) *Codeswitching: Anthropological and Sociolinguistic Perspectives*. Berlin: Mouton de Gruyter.
Heller, M. (1999) *Linguistic Minorities and Modernity: A Sociolinguistic Ethnography*. London: Longman.
Higgins, C. (2003) 'Ownership' in the outer circle: An alternative to the NS-NNS dichotomy. *TESOL Quarterly* 37 (4), 615–644.
Higgins, C. (2004) Swahili-English bilingual conversation: A vehicle for the study of language ideology. Unpublished doctoral dissertation, University of Wisconsin-Madison.
Higgins, C. (2007) Shifting tactics of intersubjectivity to align indexicalities: A case of joking around in Swahinglish. *Language in Society* 36 (1), 1–38.
Higgins, C. (2009) From da bomb to bomba: Global hip hop nation language in Tanzania. In A. Ibrahim, S. Alim and A. Pennycook (eds) *Global Linguistic Flows: Hip Hop Cultures, Youth Identities, and the Politics of Language* (pp. 95–112). Mahwah, NJ: Erlbaum.
Hill, J. (1999) Syncretism. *Journal of Linguistic Anthropology* 9 (1–2), 244–246.
Hill, J. and Hill, K.C. (1986) *Speaking Mexicano: Dynamics of Syncretic Language in Central Mexico*. Tucson: University of Arizona Press.
Hodgson, D. (2001) *Once Intrepid Warriors: Gender, Ethnicity and the Cultural Politics of Maasai Development*. Bloomington, IN: Indiana University Press.
Holquist, M. (2002) *Dialogism* (2nd edn). New York: Routledge.
Ivaska, A. (2002) Anti-mini militants meet modern misses: 'Urban style,' gender, and the politics of national culture in 1960s Dar es Salaam, Tanzania. *Gender and History* 14, 584–607.
Kachru, B.B. (1965) The Indianness in Indian English. *Word* 21, 391–410.

Kachru, B.B. (1986) *The Alchemy of English*. Urbana, IL: University of Illinois Press.
Kachru, B.B. (ed.) (1992a) *The Other Tongue* (2nd edn). Urbana, IL: University of Illinois Press.
Kachru, B.B. (1992b) Models for non-native Englishes. In B.B. Kachru (ed.) *The Other Tongue* (pp. 48–74). Urbana: University of Illinois Press.
Kadeghe, M. (2000) The implications of bilingualism in learning and teaching: The case of Tanzania secondary schools. Unpublished doctoral dissertation, University of Dar es Salaam.
Kelly-Holmes, H. (2005) *Advertising as Multilingual Communication*. Basingstoke, Hants and New York: Palgrave-Macmillan.
Kihore, Y. (1976) Tanzania's language policy and Kiswahili's historical background. *Kiswahili* 46, 47–69.
Kumaravadivelu, B. (2006) Dangerous liaison: Globalization, empire and TESOL. In J. Edge (ed.) *(Re)locating TESOL in an Age of Empire* (pp. 1–26). New York: Palgrave.
Lee, J.S. (2006a) Linguistic constructions of modernity: English mixing in Korean television commercials. *Language in Society* 35 (1), 59–91.
Lee, J.S. (2006b) Crossing and crossers in East Asian pop music: Korea and Japan. *World Englishes* 25 (2), 235–250.
Lemarchand, R. (1996) *Burundi: Ethnic Conflict and Genocide*. Cambridge: Cambridge University Press.
Lewinson, A. (2003) Imagining the metropolis, globalizing the nation: Dar es Salaam and national culture in Tanzanian cartoons. *City and Society* 15, 9–30.
Lin, A. (1999) Doing-English-lessons in the reproduction or transformation of social worlds *TESOL Quarterly* 33 (3), 393–412.
Lin, A. (2006) Beyond linguistic purism in language-in-education policy and practice: Exploring bilingual pedagogies in a Hong Kong science classroom. *Language and Education* 20, 287–305.
Lippi-Green, R. (1997) *English with an Accent: Language Ideology and Discrimination in the United States*. New York: Routledge.
Liu, D., Ahn, G., Baek, K. and Han, N. (2004) South Korean high school English teachers' code switching: Questions and challenges in the drive for maximal use of English in teaching. *TESOL Quarterly* 38 (4), 605–638.
Makoni, S. (1998) "In the beginning was the missionaries' word": The European invention of African languages. In K. Prah (ed.) *Between Distinction and Extinction*. Cape Town: Center for advanced Studies of African Society.
Makoni, S. (2003) From misinvention to disinvention of language: Multilingualism and the South African Constitution. In S. Makoni, G. Smitherman, A.F. Ball and A.K. Spears (eds) *Black Linguistics: Language, Society, and Politics in Africa and the Americas* (pp. 132–152). London and New York: Routledge.
Makoni, S. and Pennycook, A. (eds) (2005) *Disinventing and Reconstituting Languages*. Clevedon: Multilingual Matters.
Makoni, S., Brutt-Griffler, J. and Mashiri, P. (2007) The use of "indigenous" and urban vernaculars in Zimbabwe. *Language in Society* 36 (1), 25–49.
Martin, E. (2006) *Marketing Identities through Language: English and Global Imagery in French Advertising*. New York: Palgrave.
Martin, P. (2005) 'Safe' language practices in two rural schools in Malaysia: Tensions between policy and practice. In A. Lin and P. Martin (eds) *Decolonisation, Globalisation: Language-in-Education Policy and Practice* (pp. 74–97). Clevedon: Multilingual Matters.

Martin-Jones, M. (1995) Code-switching in the classroom: Two decades of research. In L. Milroy and P. Muysken (eds) *One Speaker, Two Languages, Cross-disciplinary Perspectives on Code-switching* (pp. 90–111). Cambridge: Cambridge University Press.
Maultsby, P. (1995) Music in African-American culture. In V. Berry and G. Manning-Miller (eds) *Mediated Messages and African American Culture: Contemporary Issues* (pp. 241–262). Thousand Oaks, CA: Sage.
Mazrui, A.A. (1975) *The Political Sociology of the English Language: An African Perspective.* The Hague: Mouton.
Mazrui, A.A. (1996) Perspective: The muse of modernity and the quest for development. In P.G. Albach and S.M. Hassan (eds) *The Muse of Modernity* (pp. 5–19). Trenton, NJ: Africa World Press.
Mazrui, A.M. (1995) Slang and codeswitching: The case of Sheng in Kenya. *Afrikanistische Arbeitspapiere* 42, 168–179.
Mazrui, A.M. (2004) *English in Africa after the Cold War.* Clevedon: Multilingual Matters.
Mazrui, A.A. and Mazrui, A.M. (1995) *Swahili, State and Society: The Political Economy of an African Language.* Nairobi: East African Educational Publishers.
Mazrui, A.A. and Mazrui, A.M. (1998) *The Power of Babel: Language & Governance in the African Experience.* London: James Currey.
Mazrui, A.A. and Mazrui, A.M. (1999) *Political Culture of Language: Swahili, Society and the State.* Albany: Binghamton University Institute of Global Cultural Studies.
Mbaabu, I. and Nzuga, K. (2003) *Sheng-English Dictionary: Deciphering East Africa's Underworld Language.* Dar es Salaam: TUKI.
Meeuwis, M. and Blommaert, J. (1998) A monolectal view of code-switching: Layered code-switching among Zairians in Belgium. In P. Auer (ed.) *Codeswitching in Conversation: Language, Interaction, and Identity* (pp. 76–98). New York: Routledge.
Merritt, M. (1992) Socialising multilingualism: Determinants of codeswitching in Kenyan primary classrooms. *Journal of Multilingual and Multicultural Development* 13 (1 & 2), 103–121.
Mesthrie, R. (1992) *English in Language Shift: The History, Structure, and Sociolinguistics of South African Indian English.* Cambridge: Cambridge University Press.
Michieka, M.M. (2005) English in Kenya: a sociolinguistic profile. *World Englishes* 24, 173–186.
Mitchell, T. (2003) Doin' damage in my native language: The use of 'resistance vernaculars' in hip hop in France, Italy, and Aotearoa/New Zealand. In H.M. Berger and M.T. Caroll (eds) *Global Pop, Local Language* (pp. 3–17). Jackson, MS: University Press of Mississippi.
Mkangi, K.G.C. (1985) The political economy of Kiswahili: A Kenya-Tanzania comparison. In J. Maw and D. Parkin (eds) *Swahili Language and Society* (pp. 331–348). Vienna: Beitrage zur Afrikanistik.
Morson, G.S. and Emerson, C. (1990) *Mikhail Bakhtin: Creation of a Prosaics.* Stanford: Stanford University Press.
Mudimbe, V.Y. (1988) *The Invention of Africa: Gnosis, Philosophy, and the Order of Knowledge.* Bloomington: Indiana University Press.
Muthwii, M. (2004) Language of instruction: A qualitative analysis of the perceptions of parents, pupils and teachers among the Kalenjin in Kenya. *Language, Culture and Curriculum* 17 (1), 15–32.

Muthwii, M. and Kioko, A. (eds) (2004) *New Language Bearings in Africa: A Fresh Quest*. Clevedon: Multilingual Matters.
Mwangi, E. (2007) Sex, music, and the city in a globalized East Africa. *PMLA* 122 (4), 321–324.
Myers-Scotton, C. (1983) The negotiation of identities in conversation: A theory of markedness and code choice. *International Journal of the Sociology of Language* 44, 115–136.
Myers-Scotton, C. (1992) Comparing codeswitching and borrowing. *Journal of Multilingual and Multicultural Development* 13 (1–2), 19–39.
Myers-Scotton, C. (1993a) *Social Motivations of Code-switching: Evidence from Africa*. Oxford: Clarendon Press.
Myers-Scotton, C. (1993b) Elite closure as a powerful language strategy: The African case. *International Journal of the Sociology of Language* 103, 149–163.
Ncoko, S.O.S., Osman, R. and Cockroft, K. (2000) Codeswitching among multilingual learners in primary schools in South Africa: An exploratory study. *International Journal of Bilingual Education and Bilingualism* 3 (4), 225–241.
Neke, S.M. (2003) English in Tanzania: An anatomy of hegemony. Unpublished doctoral dissertation, University of Ghent, Belgium.
New London Group (1996) A pedagogy of multiliteracies: Designing social futures. *Harvard Educational Review* 66 (1), 60–92.
Ngugi wa Thiong'o (1986) *Decolonising the African Mind: The Politics of Language in African Literature*. London: James Currey Ltd.
Ngugi wa Thiong'o (2000) Europhonism, universities, and the magic fountain: The future of African literature and scholarship. *Research in African Literatures* 31 (1), 1–11.
Norton, B. (1997) Language, identity, and the ownership of English. *TESOL Quarterly* 31 (3), 409–429.
Norton, B. and Vanderheyden, K. (2004) Comic book culture and second language learners. In B. Norton and K. Toohey (eds) *Critical Pedagogies and Language Learning* (pp. 201–221). Cambridge: Cambridge University Press.
Nurse, D. and Spear, T. (1985) *The Swahili: Reconstructing the History and Language of an African Society*, (pp. 800–1500). Philadelphia: University of Pennsylvania Press.
Nyairo, J. and Ogude, J. (2005) Popular music, popular politics: Unbwogable and the idioms of freedom in Kenyan popular music. *African Affairs* 104 (415), 225–249.
Nyerere, J. (1967) *Education for Self-reliance*. Dar es Salaam: Government Printer.
Omoniyi, T. (2004) *The Sociolinguistics of Borderlands: Two Nations, One Community*. Trenton, New Jersey and Asmara, Eritrea: Africa World Press.
Omoniyi, T. (2006) Hip-hop through the world Englishes lens: A response to globalization. *World Englishes* 25 (2), 195–208.
Oyewumi, O. (1997) *The Invention of Women: Making an African Sense of Western Gender Discourses*. Minneapolis: University of Minnesota Press.
Osumare, H. (2007) *The Africanist Aesthetic in Global Hip-Hop: Power Moves*. New York: Palgrave.
Pakir, A. (1991) The range and depth of English-knowing bilinguals in Singapore. *World Englishes* 10 (2), 167–179.
Peirce, B.N. (1995) Social identity, investment, and language learning. *TESOL Quarterly* 29 (1), 9–32.
Pennycook, A. (1998) *English and the Discourses of Colonialism*. London: Routledge.

Pennycook, A. (2001) *Critical Applied Linguistics: A Critical Introduction*. Mawhah, NJ: Erlbaum.
Pennycook, A. (2003a) Global Englishes, Rip Slyme, and performativity. *Journal of Sociolinguistics* 7 (4), 513–533.
Pennycook, A. (2003b) Beyond homogeny and heterogeny: English as a global and worldly language. In C. Mair (ed.) *The Politics of English as a World Language* (pp. 3–17). Amsterdam: Rodopi.
Pennycook, A. (2007) *Global Englishes and Transcultural Flows*. London and New York: Routledge.
Pennycook, A. and Mitchell, T. (2009) Hip hop as dusty foot philosophy: Engaging locality. In H.S. Alim, A. Ibrahim and A. Pennycook (eds) *Global Linguistic Flows: Hip Hop Cultures, Youth Identities, and the Politics of Language* (pp. 25–42). Mahwah, NJ: Erlbaum.
Perullo, A. and Fenn, J. (2003) Language ideologies, choices and practices in Eastern African hip hop. In H. Berger and M. Carroll (eds) *Global Pop, Local Language* (pp. 19–51). Jackson, MS: University of Mississippi Press.
Phillipson, R. (1992) *Linguistic Imperialism*. Oxford: Oxford University Press.
Piller, I. (2001) Identity constructions in multilingual advertising. *Language and Society* 30 (2), 153–186.
Piller, I. (2003) Advertising as a site of language contact. *Annual Review of Applied Linguistics* 23, 170–187.
Pomerantz, A., Fehr, B.J. and Ende, J. (1997) When supervising physicians see patients: Strategies used in difficult situations. *Human Communication Research* 23 (4), 589–615.
Potter, R. (1995) *Spectacular Vernaculars: Hip-Hop and the Politics of Postmodernism*. Albany: SUNY Press.
Ramanathan, V. (2004) *The English-Vernacular Divide*. Clevedon: Multilingual Matters.
Ramanathan, V. (2006) The vernacularization of English: Crossing global currents to re-dress West-based TESOL. *Critical Inquiry in Language Studies* 3 (2–3), 131–146.
Rampton, B. (1995) *Crossing: Language and Ethnicity among Adolescents*. New York: Longman.
Rampton, B. (2006) *Language in Late Modernity: Interaction in an Urban School*. Cambridge: Cambridge University Press.
Ranger, T. (1992) The invention of tradition in colonial Africa. In E. Hobsbawm and T. Ranger (eds) *The Invention of Tradition* (pp. 211–262). Cambridge: Cambridge University Press.
Reh, M. (2004) Multilingual writing: A reader-oriented typology – with examples from Lira Municipality (Uganda). *International Journal of the Sociology of Language* 170 (1), 1–41.
Reuster-Jahn, U. and Kießling, R. (2006) *Lugha ya mitaani* in Tanzania: The poetics and sociology of a young urban style of speaking with a dictionary comprising 1100 words and phrases. *Swahili Forum* 13, 1–200.
Richardson, E. (2006) *Hiphop Literacies*. Clevedon: Multilingual Matters.
Roh, M.H. (2007) Presidential speech at opening ceremony of EBS English. On WWW at http://www.yonhapnews.co.kr. Accessed 21.9.07.
Roy-Campbell, Z. (2001) *Empowerment through Language: The African Experience – Tanzania and Beyond*. Lawrenceville, NJ: Africa World Press.

References

Roy-Campbell, Z. and Qorro, M. (1997) *Language Crisis in Tanzania*. Dar es Salaam: Mkuki na Nyota Publishers.
Rubagumya, C. (1990) *Language in Education in Africa: A Tanzanian Perspective*. Clevedon: Multilingual Matters.
Rubagumya, C. (1994) Language values and bilingual classroom discourse in Tanzanian secondary schools. *Language, Culture and Curriculum* 7 (1), 41–53.
Rubagumya, C. (2003) English medium primary schools in Tanzania: A new 'linguistic market' in education. In B. Brock-Utne *et al.* (eds) *Language of Instruction in Tanzania and South Africa (LOITSA)* (pp. 149–169). Dar es Salaam: E & D Limited.
Said, E. (1978) *Orientalism*. London: Routledge and Kegan Paul.
Satyo, S. (2001) Kwaito-speak: A language variety created by the youth for the youth. In E. Ridge, S. Ridge and S. Makoni (eds) *Freedom and Discipline: Essays in Applied Linguistics from Southern Africa* (pp. 139–148). New Delhi: Bahri Publishers.
Scotton, C.M. (1982) The possibility of codeswitching: Motivation for maintaining multilingualism. *Anthropological Linguistics* 24 (4), 432–444.
Seaton, P. (2001) 'Shampoo for extra damage': Making sense of Japanized English. *Japan Forum* 13 (2), 233–247.
Sedgwick, P. (2002) Bakhtin. In A. Edgar and P. Sedgwick (eds) *Cultural Theory: The Key Thinkers* (pp. 15–16). London and New York: Routledge.
Silverstein, M. and Urban, G. (eds) (1996) *Natural Histories of Discourse*. Chicago: University of Chicago Press.
Skandera, P. (1999) What do we *really* know about Kenyan English? A pilot study in research methodology. *English World-Wide* 20 (2), 217–236.
Skutnabb-Kangas, T. (1988) Multilingualism and the education of minority children. In T. Skutnabb-Kangas and J. Cummins (eds) *Minority Education: From Shame to Struggle* (pp. 9–44). Clevedon: Multilingual Matters,
Smitherman, G. (1997) "The chain remain the same": Communicative practices in the Hip-Hop nation. *Journal of Black Studies* 28 (1), 3–25.
Spitulnik, D. (1998) The language of the city: Town Bemba as urban hybridity. *Journal of Linguistic Anthropology* 8 (1), 30–59.
Spivak, G. (1985) Three women's texts and a critique of imperialism. *Critical Inquiry* 18, 756–69.
Spivak, G. (1987) *In Other Worlds: Essays in Cultural Politics*. New York: Metheun.
Spivak, G. (1988) "Can the Subaltern Speak?" In C. Nelson and L. Grossberg (eds) *Marxism and the Interpretation of Culture*. (pp. 271–313). Chicago: University of Illinois Press.
Sridhar, K.K. and Sridhar, S.N. (1992) Bridging the paradigm gap: Second-language acquisition theory and indigenized varieties of English. In B.B. Kachru (ed.) *The Other Tongue* (2nd edn) (pp. 91–107). Urbana: University of Illinois Press.
Stambach, A. (1999) Curl up and dye: Civil society and the fashion-minded citizen. In J.L. Comaroff and J. Comaroff (eds) *Civil Society and the Political Imagination in Africa* (pp. 251–266). Chicago: University of Chicago Press.
Street, B. (1995) *Social Literacies: Critical Approaches to Literacy in Development, Ethnography and Education*. London: Longman.
Strevens, P. (1992) English as an international language: Directions in the 1990s. In B.B. Kachru (ed.) *The Other Tongue* (2nd edn) (pp. 27–47). Urbana: University of Illinois Press.

Suleri, S. (1992) Woman skin deep: Feminism and the postcolonial condition. *Critical Inquiry* 18, 756–769.
Sure, K. (1992) Falling standards in Kenya? *English Today* 32, 23–28.
Sure, K. and Webb, V. (2000) Languages in competition. In V. Webb and K. Sure (eds) *African Voices: An Introduction to the Languages and Linguistics of Africa* (pp. 109–132). Cape Town: Oxford University Press.
Tagama, H. (2003) Tanzania – a very African beauty contest: An alternative beauty pageant based on African values is taking Tanzania by storm and attracting both women and men in droves. *New African* 60, 16–17.
Taylor, L. (2006) Cultural translation and the double movement of difference in learning 'English as a second identity.' *Critical Inquiry in Language Studies* 3, 101–130.
Tranter, N. (2008) Nonconventional script choice in Japan. *International Journal of the Sociology of Language* 192, 133–151.
Tyler, A. (1995) The co-construction of miscommunication. *Studies in Second Language Acquisition* 17 (2), 129–152.
Van Leeuwen, T. (2005) *Introducing Social Semiotics*. London and New York: Routledge.
Vavrus, F. (2002) Postcoloniality and English: Exploring language policy and the politics of development in Tanzania. *TESOL Quarterly* 36, 373–397.
Weedon, C. (1987) *Feminist Practice and Poststructuralist Theory*. Malden, MA: Blackwell.
Willis, P. (2003) Foot soldiers of modernity: The dialectics of cultural consumption and the 21st century school. *Harvard Educational Review* 73 (3), 390–415.
Wolf, N. (1991) *The Beauty Myth*. New York: William Morrow & Co.
Wolfson, N. (1984) Pretty is as pretty does: A speech act view of sex roles. *Applied Linguistics* 5 (3), 236–244.
Wolfson, N. and Manes, J. (eds) (1985) *Language of Inequality*. Berlin: Mouton de Gruyter.
Whiteley, W. (1969) *Swahili: The Rise of a National Language*. London: Oxford University Press.
Widdowson, H. (1994) The ownership of English. *TESOL Quarterly* 28 (2), 377–388.
Woolard, K. (1988) Codeswitching and comedy in Catalonia. In M. Heller (ed.) *Codeswitching: Anthropological and Sociological Perspectives* (pp. 53–76). The Hague: Mouton de Gruyter.
Woolard, K. (1998) Simultaneity and bivalency as strategies in bilingualism. *Journal of Linguistic Anthropology* 8 (1), 3–29.
Yahya-Othman, S. (1995) Aren't you going to greet me? Impoliteness in Swahili greetings. *Text* 15 (2), 209–227.
Zuengler, J. (1982) Kenyan English. In B.B. Kachru (ed.) *The Other Tongue: English Across Cultures* (pp. 112–124). Urbana: University of Illinois Press.

Selected Discography

Ferooz (2005) *Safari*. Dar es Salaam: Bongo Records.
Gidigidi Majimaji (2000) *Ismarwa*. Nairobi: A'mish Records.
Kwanza Unit (2002) *Kwanzanians*. Dar es Salaam: Madunia/HH.
Ngwair (2005) *Bado Nimo a.k.a Mimi*. Dar es Salaam: Bongo Records.
Sykes, Dully (2004) *Handsome*. Dar es Salaam: Dhahabu Records.

Index

Abdulaziz, M. 3, 30, 159
Achebe, C. 11, 159
Adejunmobi, M. 12, 20, 159
aesthetics 66
– body image, female 66-67, 81, 88
– skin color 65-66, 71, 72, 73-74, 107
African American English 92, 97, 133, 144
African trickster 94
Alim, H.S. 93, 159, 162, 166
Angogo, R. 130, 159
Appadurai, A. 114, 159
Appiah , K.A. 80, 159
appropriation 5-6, 10, 11-15
Ashcroft, B. 11, 159
Askew, K. 91, 159
Auer, J. 7, 28-34, 135, 159, 164
authenticity 9, 13, 71, 74, 80-84, 87

Backhaus, P. 116, 150-151, 159
Bakhtin, M. 2-3, 6-8, 14-15, 37, 93, 118, 160
– assimilation 7
– carnivalesque humor 18, 66 83-85, 88-90
– dialogism 2, 118-119, 122-124
– double-voicing 7, 37-39, 122, 124, 141-144
– heteroglossia 6, 14-19, 44, 47, 53, 64, 83-84, 119, 148-149
– speech genres 3, 145, 149
Bamgbose, A. 5, 160
Banjo, A. 5, 160
Barber, K. 9-10, 160
Batibo, H. 3, 8, 24, 160
Bauman, R. 93, 160
Baxter, L. 7, 160
Bell, A. 116, 160
Bhabha, H. 9, 160
Bhatia, T. 116, 120, 122, 160
Billings, S. 69, 70, 79, 160
bivalency 7, 64, 94, 98
Blom, J.P. 38, 40, 160
Blommaert, J. 3, 4, 14-15, 20, 27, 32-34, 37-38, 42, 43, 44, 54, 68, 75, 110, 130-131, 145, 160, 164
Bourdieu, P. 9, 29, 55, 146, 160
Briggs, C. 93, 160

Brock-Utne, B. 3, 28, 152, 154, 160, 167
Bunyi, B. 27-28, 152, 154, 161
Buregeya, A. 130, 161

Calif Records 95
Cameron, D. 91, 161
Canagarajah, S. 4, 12, 16-17, 149, 152, 161
Cassidy, F. 115, 161
centrifugal forces 8, 11, 13-15, 64
centripetal forces 8, 13-15, 19, 149
Chouliaraki, L. 117, 161
codeswitching 4, 7, 18, 20, 29-32, 31, 34, 41, 44, 109, 110
– in classrooms 28, 152-154
– and humor 47-53
Cope, B. 15, 117, 161

Dakubu, M. 20, 161
de Beauvoir, S. 91, 161
Delpit, L. 155, 161
Dholuo 34, 38, 92, 111-112
dialogic literacies 134-144
domains 3-4, 11-12, 14-15, 32, 53, 79, 148-149
– in advertising 116, 119, 141, 144-146
– in education 151-156
– in female beauty 87-91
– in hip hop 93-94, 111, 115

education 19, 131, 143-146
– AIDS education 115, 155
– and hybrid language 151-156
– language policies in East Africa 25-28
– and social mobility 67-68
– and sociolects 33, 54, 61-62, 110
elite closure 39, 54, 63
English
– center varieties 2, 3, 11
– Kenyan English 130
– localization 5, 11, 13, 92, 129
– Tanzanian English 61, 98, 130
Erickson, F. 41, 161
E-sir 95
ethnic languages in East Africa 36, 38, 69, 74, 34, 38, 92, 111

169

Fabrício, B. 4, 153, 161
Fanon, F. 8-9, 80, 161
Fairclough, N. 67, 116-117, 161
Fenn, J. 97, 166
Ferooz 108-111, 168
Finlayson, R. 20, 161
Forman, M. 115, 161
Friedan, B. 91, 162
fused lect 40

Gee, J.P. 15, 57, 162
Giddens, A. 117, 162
Gidigidi Majimaji 92, 111-113, 144, 168
Githinji, P. 3, 29-30, 31, 162
Githiora, C. 29, 162
Gorman, T. 23, 25, 26, 27, 162
Goyvaerts, D. 20, 162
greetings 44-47
Griffiths, G. 11, 159
Gumperz, J.J. 38, 40-41, 160, 162

Haarman, H. 116, 162
Hall, K. 85, 162
Hall, S. 67, 162
Hancock, I. 130, 159
harambee 75, 78, 91
Heath, S.B. 155, 162
Heller M. 152, 162, 168
heterogeny 12, 151
Higgins, C. 11, 20, 39, 47, 68, 133, 174
Hip hop nation language 93
Hill, J. 7, 162
HIV/AIDS 102, 103, 106, 108, 110-111, 134, 155, 156
Hodgson, D. 79, 162
Holquist, M. 6, 20, 118-119, 162
homogeny 12, 151
hybridity 2-4, 8, 10, 13-14, 19, 20, 30, 38, 63-64, 66-67, 90, 114, 122-123, 136, 144, 148-149, 151, 156
– cultural hybridity 2, 4, 12, 66, 90, 113, 117
– hybrid literacies 15-16, 19, 119, 122, 135, 134-137

identification 2, 12, 29, 33, 116, 119, 148
– double identification 30, 39, 94-96
indexicality 15, 32, 72, 82, 95, 99, 103, 111, 120, 148
interpretive authority 15-17
invention/disinvention 5, 80, 91, 151
Ivaska, A. 69, 162

Jamaican Creole 92, 97, 115
Jua Cali 95

Kachru, B.B. 4, 5, 11, 162, 163
Kadeghe, M. 154, 163
Kalantzis, M. 15, 117, 161
Kelly-Holmes, H. 116, 163
Kibaki, Mwai 113-114, 145
Kießling, R. 34-35, 98, 101, 133, 166
Kihore, Y. 27, 163
King Crazy GK 94-95, 102, 103-105, 106
Kingo vii, 65, 66, 88, 89, 145-146
Kumaravadivelu, B. 5, 163
Kwanza Unit 97, 168

language mixing 2, 7, 28-33, 38, 41-42, 56, 64, 69, 90, 135, 152-154
Lee, J. 12, 116, 120, 124, 150, 163
Lemarchand, R. 91, 163
Lewinson, A. 79, 88, 163
linguistic imperialism 8, 12, 14-15
Lippi-Green, R. 2, 150, 163
Lugha ya mitaani 29, 34, 55, 97, 132

Maasai 23, 34, 69, 79-81, 93
Makoni, S. 2, 4-5, 12, 16, 20, 80-81, 151, 156, 163, 167
Martin, E. 116, 120, 123, 124, 163
Martin-Jones, M. 152, 164
Maultsby, P. 112, 164
Mazrui, A.A. 8, 10, 21, 22, 24-25, 26, 27, 68, 164
Mazrui, A.M. 8, 10, 21, 22, 24-25, 26, 27, 29, 68, 164
Mbaabu, I. 30, 164
Mchizi Mox 97, 155
Meeuwis, M. 44, 164
Merritt, M. 28, 152, 164
Mesthrie, R. 20, 164
Michieka, M. 21, 27, 68, 164
Mitchell, T. 93, 95, 112, 164, 166
Mkangi, K. 23, 24, 25, 26, 164
Morson, G. 84, 164
Mr. II 97
Mudimbe, V.Y. 5, 80, 164
multivocality 6-8, 13-15, 19, 21, 148-149
– in advertising 116
– in beauty 66-67, 89
– in conversation 39, 53
– in East Africa 28-36
– in education 151-156
– in hip hop 94-96, 113-115
Mutahi, Wahome 73-74, 83, 90, 91
Muthwii, M. 3, 21, 28, 164, 165
Mwana Falsafa 97
Mwangi, E. 95, 96, 165
Myers-Scotton, C. 3, 20, 31-32, 38-39, 54, 165

Index

naming 94-96
Necessary Noize 96
Neke, S. 27, 165
Ngugi wa Thiong'o 9-10, 11, 151-152, 165
Ngwair 92, 97, 99, 102, 106, 107, 168
Noorah 105-108
Norton, B. 11, 155, 165
Nurse, D. 22, 165
Nyairo, J. 111, 112, 113, 165
Nyerere, J. 27, 165
Nzuga, K. 30, 164

Ogude, J. 111, 112, 113, 165
Omoniyi, T. viii, 12, 20, 165
orientalism 9
Osinde, K. 3, 30, 159
Osumare, H. 93, 94, 112, 165
Oyewumi, O. 80, 91, 165

Pakir, A. 4, 165
Pennycook, A. 4, 5, 11-13, 15, 17, 37, 81, 84, 95, 112, 153, 155, 156, 159, 162, 163, 165, 166
Perullo , A. viii, 97, 166
Phillipson, R. 5, 8, 166
Piller, I. 116, 118, 120, 122-123, 166
polyphony 7, 83-84, 92, 93
Professor Jay 97, 99, 110
Public English 14, 130-131

Qorro, M. 152, 167

Ramanathan, V. 13-14, 16, 166
Rampton, B. 12, 37, 41, 155, 166
Ranger , T. 80, 166
re-entextualization 18-19, 32, 79, 93-94, 96-114, 155
Reh, M. 120-122, 125, 166
Reuster-Jahn, U. 34, 35, 98, 101, 133, 166
Richardson, E. 115, 166
Roy-Campbell, Z. 152, 154, 166, 167
Rubagumya, C. 3, 28, 152, 167

Said, E. 20-21, 65, 167
Santos, D. 4, 153, 161
Satyo, S. 20, 167

scapes 114-115, 151, 153
Schultz , J. 41, 161
self/other 9, 65, 67, 85
Shakur, Tupac 1
Sheng 1, 29-31
Silverstein, M. 93, 167
Skandera, P. 130, 167
Skutnabb-Kangas, T. 8, 167
Slabbert, S. 20, 161
Smitherman, G. 93, 163, 167
social class 34, 54, 55-56, 59, 110, 117
Spear, T. 22, 165
Spitulnik, D. 20, 167
Spivak, G. 8-9, 91, 167
Stambach, A. 65, 167
Steere, Bishop Edward 23
Street, B. 15, 167
Street Swahili 29, 34-35
Suleri, S. 91, 168
Sure, K. 30, 68, 168
Swahinglish 17, 18, 38-39, 41-44, 46, 49-50, 52, 53, 58, 93, 97-110, 117, 134, 155
Sykes, Dully 97, 99-100, 106

Thomas, A. 5, 60
Tiffin, H. 11, 159
transgredience 118, 133, 139

ujamaa 27, 75, 78, 91
University Corner 100-101

Vanderheyden, K. 155, 165
van Leeuwen, T. 67, 168
Vavrus , F. 27, 68, 168

Webb, V. 68, 168
Whiteley, W. 23, 162, 168
Willis, P. 155, 168
Wolf, N. 98, 168
Woolard, K. 7, 53, 64, 98, 168
World Englishes 11

Yahya-Othman, S. 44, 168

Zanzibar 22, 23, 24, 75, 125, 126, 132
Zuengler, J. 130, 168